1984

Building
Classroom
Discipline

Building
Classroom
Discipline

From Models to Practice

C. M. Charles
San Diego State University

Collaboration by
Karen Blaine

Longman
New York & London

BUILDING CLASSROOM DISCIPLINE
From Models to Practice

Longman Inc., 1560 Broadway, New York, N.Y. 10036
Associated companies, branches, and representatives
throughout the world.

Developmental Editor: Lane Akers
Editorial and Design Supervisor: Diane Perlmuth
Interior Design: Pencils Portfolio, Inc.
Manufacturing and Production Supervisor: Maria Chiarino
Composition: Alexander Typesetting Inc.
Printing and Binding: The Hunter Rose Company Ltd.

Library of Congress Cataloging in Publication Data
Charles, C. M.
    Building Classroom Discipline.
    Includes bibliographical references and index.
    1. School discipline. I. Blaine, Karen.
II. Title.
LB3012.C46   371.5   80-15109
ISBN 0-582-28146-6

Manufactured in Canada

9 8 7 6 5 4

Contents

371.5
C475

Building
Classroom
Discipline

The Sources of Discipline

Behavior, Misbehavior, Motives, and Controls
Discipline, Learning, Sanity, and Joy

Chapter 1

Behavior, Misbehavior, Motives, and Controls

The Concern about Discipline

Discipline is the number one topic in education. According to the 1979 Gallup Poll on attitudes toward education teachers, parents, students, and the public all place discipline at the top of their concerns. Teachers place it there because it affects learning, it affects their emotional lives, and it outweighs all other factors combined in determining teacher success. Parents place it there because they want their children to learn, behave properly in school, and relate well with others. Students place it there because they have a need for limits, for someone to urge them forward, and for a calm environment within which to learn. The public places it there because they fear that disrespect, hostility, and lack of self-control among youth pose dire threats to democracy, personal safety, and traditional freedoms.

In recent decades teachers have received little training in classroom discipline. The old standbys, intimidation and corporal punishment, fell out of favor as inhumane. They were abandoned, but nothing effective rose to take their place. Teachers hoped that kindness, concern, and good curriculum would maintain control, but the futility of that hope has become all too evident.

Recently, however, new light has appeared in the dark picture of classroom behavior. Positive systems for influencing behavior have grown out of reinforcement theory, social-learning theory, self-enhancement theory, and reality therapy. Psychologists have rediscovered individual needs for structure, limits, and security from threat. Public opinion is swinging strongly behind standards and enforcement. Teachers, knowing that classroom discipline makes the difference between professional (and sometimes physical) life and death, are beginning to insist on standards, controls, enforcement, and backing.

These emerging trends make the time ripe for a thorough examination of factors old and new that affect school discipline. Teachers need information about what is known in discipline, and about how to build their own effective systems. Such information is presented in the chapters that follow which are grouped into four parts, each providing essential information about and related to classroom control.

Part I deals with sources of discipline. It explores the concern about school discipline and examines human behavior, needs, motives, and controls. It shows that school learning without discipline is joyless, without direction, and senseless.

Part II presents seven models of classroom discipline. Those models show how respected authorities suggest that teachers forestall, confront, and correct student misbehavior.

Part III adds information and suggestions not stressed in the models that are known to make positive contributions to good discipline. These chapters explain the effects and classroom uses of seriousness, high expectations, good models, and support from parents.

Part IV shows teachers how to build systems of discipline that match the needs and personalities of students, and at the same time are compatible with their own needs. Recurring themes and strategies are isolated, suggestions are presented, and a list of practical steps shows how to build the kind of classroom discipline that promotes learning with enjoyment. That kind of discipline gives strong attention to the prevention of misbehavior, the support of student efforts to behave acceptably, and the correction of misbehavior when it does occur. This three-dimensional approach is called *total discipline*, and the material presented in this book all builds toward it.

Behavior and Misbehavior

Discipline is tied directly to misbehavior. It is intended to suppress, control, and redirect that sort of behavior. But what is misbehavior? What sets it apart from other behavior? How do we recognize it, in order that we might deal with it?

All teachers are perfectly sure they recognize misbehavior when they see it, but the term defies precise definition. It is akin to the definition of beauty that states it lies in the eye of the beholder. Still, there is considerable agreement about the term as we will see presently. One thing can be said with certainty: people use the term misbehavior to refer to behavior they do not like, approve of, or condone.

Teachers know that students sometimes behave in ways considered to be sweet, kind, gentle, considerate, helpful, and honest. They approve of those behaviors. They also know that students sometimes behave in ways considered hostile, abusive, and disinterested. They do not approve of those behaviors, which they call misbehavior.

For most teachers, then, misbehavior means student actions that disrupt, destroy, defy, hurt, or infringe on others' rights. It includes such specific categories of acts as cruelty, disrespect, boisterousness, cheating, fighting, name calling, sarcasm, defiance, and apathy. Such misbehavior reduces effectiveness and pleasure in teaching and learning and, therefore, needs to be suppressed or redirected. Teachers' attempts to prevent, suppress, control, and redirect those behaviors make up the essence of class control, or as it is commonly called, classroom discipline.

Motives

Often we can be more effective in dealing with behavior and misbehavior if we know something of their causes. When we speak of causes of behavior we must speak of *motives.* Motive is a term that refers to a drive or force that causes us to perform a given act.

Some motives are inborn, having a genetic basis. This is especially true for lower animals. Honey bees, for example, have in their genetic makeup all the behavior that they show during their entire lives. Little of their behavior, if any, results from learned motives. In humans, however, inborn motives are relatively few in number. They explain our attempts to meet basic physical needs, and they may account for some of our attitudinal and emotional predispositions. But the preponderance of motives that energize our behavior are learned.

Many renowned thinkers, philosophers, and theorists have proposed ideas that explain, each to a certain degree, why humans behave as they do. Among those great thinkers certain have received special attention in recent years. They include the behavioral psychologists with their notions of *deficit motivation.* They include Sigmund Freud, who gave us the concepts of *id, ego, superego, fixations,* and *defense mechanisms.* They include Erik Erikson, who wrote of *stages of man,* and Robert Havighurst, who wrote of *developmental tasks.* They include the humanistic psychologists, especially Abraham Maslow, who explained the *hierarchy of needs,* and Carl Rogers, who described the natural *growth of the self.* Jean Piaget has described stages of intellectual development, together with behaviors typical of those stages. Rudolf Dreikurs has identified *acceptance* as the prime goal of human behavior, and *mistaken goals* toward which people turn when unable to gain acceptance. We will examine very briefly some of the conclusions of these thinkers and see how they apply to behaviors that students show in the classroom.

Behaviorists' Deficit Motivation

The branch of psychology known as behaviorism holds that the only acceptable evidence for studying the natures of animals and humans consists of the behaviors they exhibit. This view is patterned after that of the natural sciences, where all evidence is obtained from observations made upon the natural environment. The behavioristic view of motivation holds that motives arise from deficits, from something needed but lacking in the organism. Food deficit is easy to manipulate and has been used for motivation in much experimentation with laboratory animals. This type of motivation, however, does not serve as an adequate basis for explaining higher-order human behavior, such as acts of altruism, a fact that will become more evident in the following sections.

Freud's Psychoanalysis

Sigmund Freud put forth the first great challenge to the behaviorists' view of motivation. He did not believe human behavior could be explained in terms of deficits. Naturally, he recognized that hungry people want food. But he saw that human activities were based far more on other factors than on the need for food and water. Even when well fed, people remained highly motivated to act.

Freud's work led him deep into some of the mysteries surrounding human motivation and behavior. He explained some of his views in terms of *stages of human development,* which he called the oral stage, the anal stage, and the phallic stage. Each of these stages provided opportunities for much pleasure and much frustration. What happened to the individual regarding that pleasure and frustration could produce fixations that affected behavior through later life.

Freud also developed the concepts of id, ego, and superego, which are, in order, our pleasure-seeking center, our neutral consciousness, and our conscience. Freud believed that these three entities reside within each person, and that much of human behavior can be explained as a continual interplay among them. He decided from his observations and deliberations that human beings will do almost anything to protect their fragile inner selves from harm. Sometimes events of the world become so frightening, so distasteful, so overpowering, that we take unconscious measures to protect our psychological selves. Freud called those measures *defense mechanisms.* He identified several such mechanisms, such as *rationalization* (making excuses and explanations for one's behavior), *projection* (assigning our own shortcomings to someone else), *displacement* (taking out our frustrations on people who do not threaten us in return), and *compensation* (building or showing off one aspect of ourself in order to mask a shortcoming).

Erikson's Stages of Man

The American psychologist Erik Erikson envisioned a large portion of human personality as resulting from the necessity to deal with crucial issues at various stages in life. Erikson identified eight such stages, each with its critical issue. Stages three, four, and five overlap the normal school years. They are *initiative vs. guilt*, age three to six years, *industry vs. inferiority*, age six to twelve years, and *identity vs. role confusion*, age twelve to eighteen years. Success in dealing with these issues builds initiative, industry, and personal identity. Lack of success builds guilt, a sense of inferiority, and difficulty in establishing role identity.

Havighurst's Developmental Tasks

In a vein similar to that followed by Erikson, Robert Havighurst identified key tasks—key problems—that are faced by all individuals at various stages in life. Havighurst saw the tasks as primary focal points toward which actions are directed, but he did not assign them great importance in personality development. Havighurst saw these tasks as occurring in stages that covered the entire span of normal life. Examples of the numerous tasks he identified are (1) learning sex differences and sexual modesty; (2) developing conscience, morality, and a scale of values; (3) achieving emotional independence from parents and other adults; and (4) acquiring a set of values and an ethical system as a guide to behavior.

Maslow's Hierarchy of Needs

Abraham Maslow gained prominence as one of the foremost humanistic psychologists. He gave attention to higher human qualities, those things that set humans apart from other animals. He believed that those qualities included interests, needs, aspirations, and the thrust for personal growth. His work produced his widely discussed hierarchy of needs.

In this scheme, Maslow indicates that lower-level needs must be met before higher-level needs come into play as prime motivators of behavior.

Maslow's hierarchy tells us much about what people are seeking; that is, about the basic dissatisfactions that serve as motives to behavior. Take students in the classroom, for example. They need to feel safe, to have a sense of belonging, to be receiving esteem from teacher and peers. When met, those needs release them to move toward self-actualization, which many consider one of the main goals of education.

Rogers' Growth of the Self

Along with Abraham Maslow, Carl Rogers has been a preeminent proponent of humanistic psychology. His writings have attracted worldwide attention, and he is in constant demand as a speaker. Rogers believes that human motivation can be viewed as an "inner striving toward maximum growth" that exists within each of us. We might think of Rogers' view as *growth motivation*, which holds that most of our daily activities, other than those routines necessary to maintain existence, can be traced to the desire to grow, to become more than we are.

Piaget and Intellectual Development

For more than fifty years Jean Piaget, one of the world's foremost developmental psychologists, has been looking into the nature of human intellectual development. In the course of his studies he has examined peoples' thinking at different periods in their lives that causes them to behave in certain ways. For example, teachers can expect the following behaviors in students enrolled in early primary grades:
1. They are poor at remembering rules.
2. They are prone to lie, but without intent to deceive.
3. They are almost totally accepting of adult authority.
4. They are lacking in adult feelings of guilt. (To be "bad" simply means to not please an adult.)
5. They are highly imitative: behavior is contagious.

Students in the middle elementary grades typically show the following characteristics:
1. They are highly argumentative with each other. Rarely will they argue with adults, though they no longer accept all adult acts as automatically correct.
2. They are easily hurt by sarcasm and name-calling.
3. Slowly they are becoming more reasonable, logical, and persuasive in their arguments.
4. They have a sense of honesty: if they lie, it is now with intent to deceive.
5. They can remember and follow rules.
6. They still accept adult authority, but question that authority behind adults' backs.

Students in junior and senior high school show the following behaviors:
1. They are highly susceptible to peer influence.
2. They pay great attention to social ideals and social justice.
3. They want rules to be just and applied equally.
4. Wrong-doing is seen as depending on intent and circumstance.

Dreikurs' Mistaken Goals

Rudolf Dreikurs believes that all students have a strong need to belong to a group, in the classroom, in the family, and so forth. When students are frustrated in this desire to belong, when they are thwarted, they have a tendency to turn toward mistaken goals. Almost always the behavior they exhibit in the pursuit of those mistaken goals turns out to be undesirable. In turn, that undesirable behavior causes them further difficulty in the classroom. The four mistaken goals and the order in which students seek them are (1) attention, (2) power, (3) revenge, and (4) seclusion.

Comfort/Stimulation

Taking into account the causes of behavior we can see that students live in perpetual vacillation between a desire for comfort and safety on the one hand, and stimulation, challenge, and variety on the other.

All of us seek stimulation. We look for interesting things to do, for variety, for challenge. We seek thrills to enliven our daily existence. At the same time, we have a great need to be able to retreat into comfort and security when the challenge and thrills become threatening or wearing. Thus, we vacillate. Both comfort and stimulation are essential to our existence—they complement each other. They are synergistic, in that they enliven each other and make our lives much more enjoyable than would either by itself.

When teachers recognize this dual necessity, and when they make allowances and accommodations for it, they provide a learning environment that is conducive to student growth. They provide comfort through continually showing students that they are accepted, that they belong, and that they can live without threat. They provide stimulation by allowing students to explore, by encouraging and pushing them, and by thrusting them into situations where errors are certain to occur.

Controls on Behavior

We have noted that the range of possible human behavior is almost limitless. Humans perform an incredible variety of acts, all considered human behavior. We have also seen that many different factors serve as motives or causes of those behaviors. In this section we will give attention to some of the forces that control behavior, that encourage, guide, and direct it. Chief among those forces are healthy growth of the self, models for imitation, reinforcement, role expectations, and group psychology. Two additional influences are teachers as controllers and students as controllers.

Healthy Growth of the Self

Earlier in this chapter the ideas of Carl Rogers and Abraham Maslow were mentioned. Those great humanistic psychologists believed that with proper levels of freedom, combined with sustenance and support from others, individuals grow in healthy directions. They unfold and fulfill themselves in positive ways that are considered to result in good behavior, while bad behavior results when individuals are unable to accomplish this natural unfolding.

If Rogers and Maslow are correct, this natural growth toward the healthy self must be seen as a major controlling influence in human behavior. As such, it should be encouraged. This growth depends on various factors: student initiative, freedom of choice, and an ever-present sense of responsibility for one's own acts. This responsibility involves full cognizance of the probable consequences of personal behavior, together with the willingness to abide by those consequences.

Models for Imitation

Albert Bandura, the Stanford psychologist, believes that most social learning occurs through a process he calls *modeling* or *imitation learning*. Imitation learning involves observing acts performed by others and then imitating those acts. The person or thing that presents the behavior to be imitated is called the *model*. Since socialization occurs through the process of imitation learning, models must be considered one of the most powerful controls on human behavior. They teach us proper and improper styles of behavior, fashions, etiquette, manners, and so forth. They shape much of the behavior that fills our daily lives.

Reinforcement

Reinforcement is a naturally occurring phenomenon that motivates and shapes a great deal of learned behavior in both humans and animals. The process occurs in this way: The individual, human or animal, performs a given act. If that act is followed by sufficient satisfaction or pleasure (reinforcement), the individual becomes more likely to repeat the act. For animals one of the best reinforcers is food. For humans other things such as praise, smiles, and pats on the back can be strongly reinforcing.

Role Expectations

Some years ago two researchers, Rosenthal and Jacobson, conducted a study in which they found that students tended to live up to the expectations held of them. When teachers believed their students were high achievers, even when they were not, those students tended to learn more. Rosenthal and Jacobson believed that the increased learning occurred because the teachers expected more from the students and the students tended to live up to the expectations. Their research was reported in a book entitled *Pygmalion in the Classroom*. They concluded that students, in general, are affected positively or negatively by what is expected of them, and they called this phenomenon the *self-fulfilling prophecy*. It holds that people tend to become what they believe they are. If students believe they are good they tend to become good. If they believe they are capable of much learning they tend to learn. These expectations, of course, must be genuine, and they must be communicated effectively to the students.

Group Psychology

In a way similar to that of role expectations, group psychology has an unusual and sometimes disquieting effect on human behavior. It is well documented that people in groups behave quite differently than when alone, expecially regarding conformity and *group mind*.

Conformity to peer standards is one of the most powerful controls on human behavior. This conformity, which helps people obtain security and a sense of belonging and status, reveals itself in numerous ways including matters of dress, speech, and interpersonal relations. Group mind is a phenomenon in which individuals submerge their identities into that of the group and perform acts, even atrocities, that they would never perform individually. Mob action sometimes results, in which a group scapegoats individuals or performs acts of destruction and tyranny.

Teachers as Controllers

Teachers exert powerful control over student behavior in numerous ways, including the following:
 1. Filling their assigned status role as director of the group.
 2. Trying their best to teach well, giving it their all, showing concern about students' learning and feelings.

3. Employing the self-fulfilling prophecy, truly expecting students to learn and behave as gentle human beings.
4. Attempting to build the student self, which grows from achievement, recognition, and the realization that someone (the teacher) prizes them as individuals.
5. Setting standards for learning and classroom demeanor, and enforcing those standards, the function we refer to as discipline.
6. Insisting on the best personal relations, continual modeling of desired behaviors, and the systematic reinforcement of desired behavior.

Students as Controllers

Students exert powerful controls on behavior both for themselves individually and for other students. If these controls are to have a positive effect, a sense of responsibility is required. Students acquire this sense of responsibility through being put into responsible situations. When they must be accountable for their actions, for keeping the classroom neat and orderly, for meeting assignments, for helping others, and so forth, they learn that they are responsible for their own acts. This sense of individual responsibility grows slowly, but its long-range effects are important.

Students also control their own behavior through their desire to learn. They channel that desire as they come to realize that their prime purpose in school is to learn. In order to learn they must pay attention, meet their responsibilities, and imitate the best examples they see.

Students control the behavior of other students through two main procedures. First, they present models of behavior that other students may imitate. Second, they exert pressures on other students toward group conformity. Some of these pressures are subtle and others are blatant.

Review

This chapter focused on the concern about school discipline, then progressed to a consideration of human behavior and misbehavior—its nature, causes, and controls. Its purpose was to set a foundation for the chapters to come, all of which build toward the concept of total discipline as comprised of prevention, support, and correction of misbehavior.

As you read ahead remember that discipline does not, in itself, provide school learning. It is, however, essential in providing a setting, an atmosphere, within which learning can occur efficiently and enjoyably.

References

Bandura, A. *Social Learning Theory*. New York: General Learning Corporation, 1971.

Dreikurs, R. *Psychology in the Classroom*. 2nd ed. New York: Harper and Row, 1968.

Erikson, E. *Childhood and Society*. New York: W. W. Norton, 1950.

Freud, S. *The Ego and Mechanisms of Defense*. London: Hogarth Press, 1937.

Havighurst, R. *Human Development and Education*. New York: David McKay, 1953.

Maslow, A. "A Theory of Human Motivation," *Psychological Review* 50:370–396, 1943.

Piaget, J. *The Psychology of Intelligence*. London: Routledge and Kegan Paul, 1950.

Rogers, C. *Freedom To Learn*. Columbus, Ohio: Charles E. Merrill, 1969.

Rosenthal, R., and Jacobson, L. *Pygmalion in the Classroom*. New York: Holt, Rinehart and Winston, 1968.

Skinner, B. F. *Science and Human Behavior*. New York: Macmillan, 1953.

Chapter 2

Discipline, Learning, Sanity, and Joy

Discipline, class control, classroom management—by whatever name you call it, keeping order in the classroom is a teacher's greatest concern. You may not like that fact; you may wish it weren't true. But it is. That's a given in the daily life of teachers. Discipline is so crucial, so basic to everything else in the classroom, that most educators agree: it is the one thing that makes or breaks teachers.

That doesn't mean discipline is the only important thing in teaching. Heaven knows the great teachers give their all in planning, organizing, motivating, presenting, counseling, evaluating, consoling, supporting, and urging. Their important functions are so numerous they would make a list of astonishing length. But without discipline a teacher's finest efforts go for naught. If students don't stay on task, they don't learn. At least they don't learn what they are supposed to. If they do whatever they want the best plans, activities, and materials don't mean a thing. It needn't be the whole class that misbehaves. Three or four students, even one, can so disrupt a class that learning becomes impossible for even the best behaved students.

Discipline's not everything; it's only a small part of teaching. But it's like the foundation of a house: nothing good can be built without it.

What is Discipline?

Discipline means somewhat different things to different people. To some it means cracking the whip, making students toe the mark. To some it means counseling the students, guiding and persuading them toward desired behavior. To some it means self-control with responsibility, and students who don't show it can simply leave the class. To some it means good manners and to some it means absolute quiet. To some it means purposeful activity that brings work-related noise in its wake. To virtually all it means that students do as they are asked, and do not defy the teacher.

When you find the common elements in these different views, you get at the heart of discipline. The common elements are that students should be (1) on task, (2) behaving responsibly, and (3) showing good human relations. Let's explore briefly the meanings of these three elements.

On Task

Students who are on task are working at activities assigned to them, or that they have selected with the consent of the teacher. They are paying attention, not daydreaming, doodling, wandering, or bothering others. They are engaged in an activity and are progressing at expected rates of speed.

The percentage of time spent on task partly determines how much students learn. That's important to teachers, of course. But equally important is the fact that on-task students don't misbehave. They don't waste time or disrupt learning for others, and they don't make teachers miserable.

Keeping students on task is the tricky part. That's where the teacher's planning, guile, and skills come into play. The assigned activities must be interesting and challenging, yet not too difficult. They must be paced, so that students remain alert. Unless the activity is especially interesting, it will need to have new inputs every twelve to fifteen minutes, about the length of time between commercials on television!

All activities can't be spellbinding. Some very important ones are rather dull and, therefore, teachers have to use techniques that help students stay on task. Entertainment, eye contact, reinforcement, pep talks, and personal attention all make contributions. The importance of on-task behavior in good discipline can hardly be overemphasized. Considerable attention with numerous specific suggestions is given to this topic in later chapters.

Responsible Behavior

Students who behave responsibly do what they know they are supposed to do, even when the teacher isn't looking. This behavior contributes, of course, to staying on task. It also reaches further, contributing to matters of self-control, respect for others' rights, nondisruption, and regard for the physical surroundings.

Self-control means being in conscious control of your own behavior. You keep a rein on your emotions, such as anger and exhiliration, that can produce disruptive boisterousness, hostility, aggression, and defiance of authority. You do not allow yourself to be easily influenced by others inclined toward misbehavior. You show a measure of composure and calm deliberation and refrain from doing silly things on the spur of the moment that can cause trouble for yourself and others.

Respect for others' rights means two things: (1) recognizing that every member of the class is entitled to peace, belongingness, freedom from threat, and the right to hold and voice their own opinions; and (2) unwillingness to interfere with the rights and privileges to which each individual is entitled. Thus, students who respect rights do not threaten, interfere, thwart, or suppress the acceptable activities of others, even when they do not agree with them.

Nondisruption means that students refrain from acts that disturb the learning of others in the class. They do not laugh and talk during quiet times, or pick at others, or act silly during serious times.

Regard for the physical surroundings means that students do not damage or deface facilities, equipment, and materials. Neither do they leave them in disarray when they have finished using them.

Good Human Relations

Good human relations means living by the golden rule, that is, treating others as you would like them to treat you. Most of us would like others to treat us in the following ways: to (1) be friendly, (2) show attention, (3) help and support, and (4) show appreciation. Friendly people smile. They greet you and talk nicely. They don't act cool or disinterested. They don't threaten you, and they don't harm you. Attention is a peculiar matter. We all want it; we all go out of our way to get it. But we want it in different forms, provided within a variety of circumstances. Most of us like to be noticed regularly, every day. We like to be greeted personally. Most, but not all of us, like to be remembered on birthdays and other times of personal significance. Some of us like to share experiences and receive attention in return. We all want to be noticed, but most of us don't want to be noticed too much. We all want to appear special, but we don't want to appear too different. Help and support are very important to all of us. Students and teachers surely need each other's help, and they need each other's support. To help means to give direct assistance with a task, to work, to facilitate. Support means to condone and to express approval publicly. Appreciation is needed in abundance, but it is usually given only sporadically. Appreciation is affirmation of worth — showing that you find value in a person or in what they have done. All of us want to be valued for ourselves and for our work. We want others to say we are fine, neat, super. We want them to laud our efforts, privately and publicly, through speech, writing, and awards.

These four golden-rule elements are things we all want. That means they are things we should all give to others. Many teachers strive hard to help students realize this fact, to teach students how to give attention, assistance, and recognition to each other. They consider that kind of behavior part of good discipline.

Why is Discipline Necessary?

To ask why we need discipline is almost like asking why we need laws and law enforcement. People rarely say anything good about the law. Many of us try to think of ways around it. We see it as blunting our freedoms, as thwarting our innocent intentions. However, we are sure it is necessary for everyone else, and we know we'd have utter chaos if it weren't enforced.

In many ways discipline is similar to law. The principal reasons why discipline is necessary are that it (1) is expected, (2) facilitates learning, (3) fosters socialization, (4) permits democracy, (5) is needed psychologically, and (6) brings joy. Some of these reasons may sound strange. Let's see why they are important.

Expected. Parents, teachers, administrators, students, and Jane Q. Public all agree: schools need discipline. It is the one thing besides learning that everyone expects and wants. Discipline helps many good things happen. But even if it didn't the fact is this—people want teachers to control their classes, and when they don't, those teachers are considered failures.

Facilitates learning. Humans have an incredible capacity for learning. They can learn under any circumstances, at any time. In fact, it is almost impossible to keep from learning. Nevertheless, many kinds of learning require close attention and uninterrupted work. This is especially true of the learning stressed in school which requires calm surroundings, purposeful direction, and time to think. These conditions cannot be maintained in classrooms without adequate discipline where disruptions are frequent, noise is at the threshold of pain, and students roam about as they please.

Socialization. Socialization is the process of acquiring the values, beliefs, and behaviors of the societal groups to which one belongs. It includes learning the best of human relations. Discussed previously, their key elements are friendliness, giving attention, helping and supporting, and showing appreciation. Human relations are codified to some degree in etiquette and manners. It may sound silly at first, but etiquette and manners are among the most important things we can teach people. They provide security in knowing approved ways of acting, and they help convey that important, good first impression. Without discipline, good human relations go by the board, and with them goes the finer part of socialization.

Democracy. Democracy is both a form of government and a way of life. It has allowed us to enjoy the greatest freedom and prosperity in the history of mankind. Democracy permits us to make important decisions about our own lives. It gives everyone equal status under the law and at the polls. In exchange for these benefits it requires that all opinions be heard, that everyone have equal opportunity, and that everyone live by the same code or law.

John Dewey, the great American philosopher, believed the schools had unique potential as training grounds for democracy. He thought they provided the best opportunity to practice equality, free exchange of ideas, initiative, responsibility, leadership, followership, and group endeavor. Many people have misunderstood Dewey's intentions: they thought he wanted students to do as they pleased. Nothing could be farther from the truth. Dewey asserted that individuals must abide by group rules. High expectations and strong discipline were needed.

All teachers know, too, that discipline is necessary for effective group work. Individualism is fine; it is to be prized. But it must not trample on the rights of others. Discipline is what allows individual excellence within group law—the hallmark of American democracy.

Psychological need. Psychologists and sociologists have discovered the interesting fact that people need discipline for their own personal sense of well-being. Most juvenile deviates and offenders agree that they sorely wanted someone who cared enough about them to lay down the law and make them stick to it. True, they wanted warmth, compassion, and understanding along with it, but the basic boundaries of right and wrong needed to be designated and enforced.

Discipline provides school students those boundaries by enforcing compliance with reasonable rules. It results in student security that comes with firm knowledge of standards, reduction of threat, and recognition that others expect the best from you. Thus, while all of us seek personal freedom and latitude of action, we at the same time need to know the lines beyond which we must not go. We need to know that someone cares enough about us to help us stay on the good side of the lines. Discipline provides that for students.

Joy. Perhaps it seems contradictory to say discipline brings joy. After all, you ask, how can we be happy when someone makes us do what we don't want to do? As with psychological need, here is another interesting fact of human nature. Many of us, much of the time, need someone to force us to do what we really wish we would do by ourselves. Sound paradoxical? Look at some examples:

1. Piano. Being able to play well brings great pleasure, and yet most people won't practice enough on their own to become really good. Somebody has to make them, and later, they are eternally grateful.

2. Language. Most of us keenly wish we could speak a foreign language fluently. We enroll in classes and excitedly do the first few lessons. Before long, we begin to lose enthusiasm, and we stop doing the lessons unless someone drives us. Later, if we are one of the very few who do acquire language fluency, we are joyfully proud of our ability.

3. Self-discipline. Most people yearn for greater self-direction, better organization, and increased work output, yet few have these traits naturally. They can be acquired, however. Someone has to urge us, to show us how to set our sights in accord with our abilities, to help us to organize, and to spur us on to work we are proud of. Once these habits are acquired, they bring the joy of self-control and productivity. These three examples illustrate how discipline brings joy. The paradoxes of joy through discipline are these:

   - Restricting freedom through discipline leads to greater freedom that comes from increased ability and self-direction.
   - Forcing us to behave as we should enables us better to behave in ways we most admire.
   - We sometimes have to be made to do what we truly want to do.
   - We have to be made into the people we truly want to be.

Why is Discipline Difficult?

Having considered all the fine effects of good discipline, and having recognized that everyone (including students) agrees that discipline has basic importance, you probably wonder, "Why in the world is discipline so difficult?" The answer has a lot to do with human nature. Some of our peculiarities show in the paradoxes just mentioned. Our personal angels and devils never stop feuding over us. Our secret hearts don't talk with our public minds.

Facts of Nature

Discipline is difficult because of four inescapable facts of human nature. They are:

1. We resist doing what others try to make us do. It doesn't matter how good the intentions, how laudable the goals, how big the ultimate payoff. Even when it's something we like to do, such as play golf, read, or walk the dog, our hackles rise just a bit when we are forced to do it. Discipline forces students to do certain things and behave in certain ways. Everyone knows it's important. But since it involves coercion, the built-in resistance rises against it.

2. It is fashionable to denigrate authority. People in positions of power get their names and fame thoroughly sullied. Think how we talk about the presidents of our country, at least while they are in office. Lincoln was reviled by great numbers of people during his tenure. Think how teachers talk about their administrators, how college students refer to their professors. Discipline and control interweave inextricably with authority. The disenchantment with authority figures adds to the burden of discipline.

3. Individuals have differing needs, values, interest and abilities. They come from backgrounds that reflect markedly different views of authority. These differences are highly significant. They make it impossible to implement any system of discipline that will even come close to suiting every student. Why not individualize discipline, you ask, just as one individualizes instruction? We can do that, but only to a limited degree. If there's anything students insist on, it's that teachers treat every student the same. They don't want to see anyone be the favorite, get too much special attention, or get away with breaking rules. They don't give a hoot about others' special needs. They want everybody to be treated alike, unless of course they themselves are getting the special treatment.

4. As students get older, they must undergo psychological weaning. Everybody knows that kids begin to act differently toward adults when they move into adolescence. You still see hero worship and passionate crushes. But even more you see love-hate attitudes begin to develop. This perfectly natural normal process distresses parents greatly and bothers teachers, too. All of us have to establish our psychological independence sooner or later. We can't be dependent on adults forever. But the transition is a rocky one, characterized by storm and strife. Students seem schizoid. They look up to adults, admire them, depend on them, love them, imitate them. But at the same time they reject them, disengage from their control, defy them, and often disappoint them greatly. This rejection of adults naturally affects discipline: adults impose discipline and students reject the two of them together. Some do it secretly in their heart of hearts. Others are blatantly up front about it. Most adolescent students still comply with rules and class control. Some do so willingly, others grudingly, and a few occasionally or not at all.

These four facts of human nature are what make discipline difficult. Don't be dismayed by them. They are simply phenomena with which we have to contend. They have that reasssuring silver lining, too: their machinations and manifestations to the contrary not withstanding, students as a group need and want order, security, and justice. That's another way of saying they need and want discipline.

What Experts Say

Much of what we know about human nature is common sense. That is, we see how individual people behave in different situations and from that we build an impression of how people in general think and act. In some cases, however, common sense lets us down. It doesn't fully explain many behaviors, especially of people who are young, culturally different from ourselves, or emotionally or behaviorally handicapped. Also, much of the basis of human nature lies hidden from the untrained eye.

That's why we must turn to experts, to recognized authorities whose life work has gone toward understanding human behavior. There we find great help from anthropologists, such as Margaret Mead, who explore the behaviors of different cultural groups; from psychoanalysts, such as Sigmund Freud, who delve into the subconscious levels of defense and motivation; from sociologists, such as Allison Davis, who look into the values and behaviors of different social classes; from behavioral psychologists, such as B. F. Skinner, who explore the effects of reward and punishment on human behavior; and from humanistic psychologists, such as Carl Rogers, who seek the elusive drive for personal growth that underlies so many human acts. Scholarly efforts in these areas have revealed quantities of information about human nature that common sense barely touched on.

In chapter 1, we examined some of the information that has come from those diverse fields. At this point, we would do well to review, once again, what Jean Piaget says about children's thinking and behavior. Then we will examine some of the findings about minority groups compiled by Miles Zintz.

Piaget

Jean Piaget, the great Swiss psychologist, explored the thinking of young children. From his findings he constructed his acclaimed theory of intellectual development. Along with intellectual development, Piaget clarified much about the nature of children—about their normal behaviors that often seem undesirable or incomprehensible to adults. For example, Piaget found that children just entering school have a world view quite different from adults. They can't reason as we do; therefore they don't behave "logically." They don't understand cause and effect, or means to ends. They may not understand other speakers accurately. They cannot remember more than three or four rules. They talk a great deal. They argue and call each other names. They are highly imitative. They fabricate: teachers worry about their lying, but their intentions are not to deceive maliciously. They accept adult authority without question, even though they may not like its consequences.

As children move into intermediate grades their intellectual processes change dramatically. They begin to think more like adults, although their abstract thought processes are poorly developed. They understand the logic of rules, and they can remember more of them. They become highly competitive, with a powerful desire to win. Conflict runs rampant on the playgrounds. Rarely can they complete a game without several verbal squabbles, which tend to become loud and abusive. They accept adult authority, but they expect it to be impartial, consistent, and absolutely fair.

By the time students enter junior high school they are able to think abstractly and logically. They get emotionally involved in thought and discussions about morality, politics, ecology, war, and fair treatment of individuals and groups. They see things with a purity of vision, a right-or-wrong perspective, without the adult constraints of social reality, tradition, and economic pressures. This causes them to be highly critical of many institutions and customs. They have also begun their love-hate relationships with adults. They usually accept adult authority but they test it frequently and rebel if they find it unjust or without logic.

Zintz

Miles V. Zintz, an American educator, has done considerable research and writing in the area of multicultural education. He has pointed out that different cultural groups have significantly different views of the world. They have different systems of values and beliefs, and they have different notions of the ways in which people should relate to each other.

Zintz noted that the views, values, beliefs, and relations that characterize minority-group students often clash with those of their teachers. The teachers, even those from minority groups themselves, reflect the basic views, beliefs, and values of middle-class Anglo society. These clashes influence discipline strongly. Behavior that might be considered good and right by a minority student might be considered bad and wrong by a teacher.

With that fact in mind, teachers should acquaint themselves as much as possible with the views, values, and so forth, of the students they teach. This acquaintance will alert teachers to behaviors they can expect from students. It will help them understand the reasons for the behavior, and it will help them know better how to deal with it.

Zintz has not outlined the value-belief-relationship systems of all minority groups. His work dealt with Indian and Hispanic groups of the Southwest. He did not explore those aspects of such groups as blacks, Asians, Puerto Ricans, or Cubans. Nevertheless, his observations suggest areas where conflict might occur. He outlines predominant Anglo value-belief-relationship patterns. That outline instructs teachers on the values they hold and it alerts them to areas where different views might present problems.

Examples of conflicting views held by Anglos and Southwestern Hispanics include the following:

1. *Time orientation.* Anglos value accomplishment, which causes them to be future oriented and punctual. Hispanics are more oriented toward the present, the here and now.
2. *Universalism vs. particularism.* Anglos work and save with an eye toward an overall (universal) better life. Hispanics take a particularistic view of work; they are concerned with the effects it produces on single parts of their immediate lives.
3. *Personalism.* Anglos have their sights set toward professional goals in life, toward what their work roles will be. Hispanics are much more interested in personal roles such as father, wife, and close friend. These personal relationships are much more important than work and economic goals.
4. *Aspiration and work.* Anglos believe the sky's the limit. You can become whatever you want if you work hard enough for it. Hispanics are more inclined to follow in their fathers' footsteps. Work is sufficient when it satisfies present needs.
5. *Individuality and competition.* Anglos prize individualism standing out, being first, being best. Hispanics enjoy group membership, togetherness, group well-being.

Zintz also points out conflict areas that exist between Anglos and Indians of the Southwest. Examples include:

1. *Relationship to nature.* Anglos believe in dominating nature, in controlling it to suit peoples' needs. Indians (Pueblos and Navajos) live in harmony with nature, adjusting to it and observing its natural laws.
2. *Time orientation.* Like the Hispanics, Indians have a present, here-and-now orientation, rather than a future orientation. They do not see the point of punctuality or looking toward a possible "rainy day."

3. *Success and individualism.* Anglos strive for individual success. Indians blend with the group, finding success in being a good person, not very different from anyone else.

4. *Sharing vs. saving.* Anglos stress saving, for tomorrow, for a rainy day, and so forth. Indians feel it is much better to share what one has with others. Be generous with others and they will remember and be generous with you.

These cultural differences illuminated by Zintz suggest areas where normal minority-group behavior often contrasts with normal Anglo behavior. The few examples given here merely illustrate that point. Perceptive teachers, those who recognize cultural differences and their implications, can use this knowledge to advantage, and they can remain alert for additional behaviors that are potential areas of concern.

What Teachers Know

Experts make a great contribution to our knowledge about human nature, but teachers know a lot on their own. You don't work with students day after day without learning how they think, feel, and act; without learning what pleases and displeases, excites and bores, thrills and frustrates them; without learning much about the needs, defenses, aspirations, and growth patterns that motivate their behavior.

Teacher knowledge about student nature can best be described in conjunction with age levels of students in school. Patterns of behavior change in accord with those levels. We will briefly examine the behavior traits evident to teachers' eyes of students at the primary, intermediate, junior high, high school, and adult levels.

Primary Grade Level (ages four to nine)

Many kindergarten children come to school when they are four. They are still babies in many ways. They parallel play, talking and playing individually while alongside other students. They tire easily, get fussy, cry, and need to rest. They fall, sprawl, and crawl about the floor. They can't tell much difference between work and play, and they require close supervision and special attention. Some play well together; others are spoiled, and expect to have their own way.

Teacher discipline at this level stresses two or three rules, and students break those rules regularly. They must be reminded of the rules, continually and patiently. Students respond very well to personal attention and praise. They accept adult authority without question, although they often seek to circumvent it.

This pattern continues into grades one and two. Increasingly, students become socialized to schools, to raising hands, standing in lines, and following rules. They continue to respond well to praise, affection, and various forms of behavior modification that include the personal touch.

Intermediate Grade Level (ages nine to twelve)

As students move into grade four they are becoming much more independent. They still like the attention and affection of teachers. Hugging may no longer be so eagerly sought; holding hands with the teacher may take its place. At the same time, discipline can occur effectively without the emotional involvement of the teacher.

Students recognize the logic of rules, their necessity, and their enforcement. They recognize and accept sensible consequences as the natural result of breaking rules. They can help establish the rules, and should discuss their value and enforcement frequently.

Intermediate students continue to respond well to behavior modification programs. Now, however, the reinforcers can be marks and tangible objects, rather than teacher approval and compliments. Students in the fifth and sixth grades consider the verbal reinforcers used by primary teachers to be silly. They still like genuine compliments, pats on the back, and recognition for their good efforts.

These students no longer blindly accept teacher authority. They may talk back and drag their heels. They will insist that both rules and punishments be sensible and they will raise a fuss if the rules and consequences are not administered consistently and impartially.

Junior High Grades (ages twelve to fifteen)

Discipline is difficult with students in their junior high years. It takes a special person to be able to maintain control, teach the students, and retain personal mental health all at the same time.

Teaching junior high students is difficult for six reasons: (1) students are entering the storm and strife years of adolescence; (2) mysterious things are happening to their bodies, things that worry, perplex, excite, and otherwise fill their minds; (3) excitement about members of the opposite sex is beginning to erupt; (4) the process of psychological weaning from adult dependence is under way; (5) experimentation with numerous role models and life experiences has accelerated; and (6) new curriculum, class organization, and teaching styles require significant adjustments. These six factors combine to fill students' minds to bursting, and leave little room for learning English, math, and history. Students show increasing rebelliousness;

their awe for teacher authority has waned. Students poke defiantly at the outer boundaries of rules, to see how far they will stretch and what will happen if they are broken just a bit.

Good discipline requires rules that are reasonable in every way. Those rules must be enforced or else chaos will result. Teachers have to use a combination of humor, grim demeanor, behavior modification, and authority to keep order. It is essential that order be kept, otherwise students lose respect for authority, and the climate for learning is destroyed.

High School Grades (ages fifteen to eighteen)

The high school years mark a time of settling down for most students. The majority begin to find themselves. They reach a truce with their bodily and emotional metamorphoses, and they get at least a tentative fix on the future. Those who become further alienated from the mainstream of personalities, customs, and institutions tend to leave school and reach out in other directions.

A new level of relationship with adults emerges. As adolescents gain increased independence, the love-hate syndrome begins to fade. They come more to respect adults as significant people in their lives, and recognize their dependence on them. But the dependence is now quasi legal; that is, formalized, recognized, understood, and accepted. It is not the utterly personal, authoritative dependency of former years.

These changes call for a style of discipline that approaches an adult-to-adult relationship. This relationship does not imply an egalitarian system where teacher and students have equal status. The teacher is still boss, makes the rules, enforces them, apprehends transgressors, and doles out punishment. But the entire process is built on clear, rational grounds, and students can be talked with as adults, as well as juveniles.

Adult Level (ages eighteen and up)

Discipline at the college and adult school level takes a noticeably different turn. Students are mature. Often some of them are older than their instructors. They expect to be treated as adults and talked to as adults. Their respect for authority, which reached a low point during the junior high years, has risen again, and is of two kinds. First, there is respect for the position of instructor regardless of who fills it. Second, there is initial respect for the person who fills the position. That respect can grow greatly if the instructor is knowledgeable, skilled in teaching, and adroit in human relations. It can shrink to zero if the instructor lacks those qualities.

Adult students, unfortunately, require discipline, too. You might not think they would since they are in class by choice. No one makes them attend, and presumably they are there to learn as much as possible. But ideals are not always matched by realities. In the majority of cases, college-age adults attend required classes necessary for obtaining the degree they seek. But even when in classes they truly want to take, adults rarely give it their all without some coercion from the instructor. We all want to take the easier way sometimes. We want to talk with others instead of listening to the teacher, and would rather watch TV than complete our assignments. That's adult human nature.

Adults, however, are easier to control than younger students. Requests from the instructor usually suffice, or an occasional stern lecture may help. Serious private talks are the most drastic acceptable step. Some instructors badger students and ridicule them publicly. That practice is unacceptable under any circumstances. Students who do not perform to minimum expectancies simply suffer the consequences, which are usually lowered grades.

What Teachers Should Remember

Much of this chapter has been filled with intimations of student misbehavior and teacher reactions. It is of course necessary to remember how students behave, and how poor behavior can be forestalled, guided, and corrected. But concentrating solely on misbehavior tends to make students look bad and teachers inept.

There are several positive things teachers should remember. Keeping these points uppermost in mind helps produce a positive attitude, a feeling of correctness about working with learners, a sense of being in charge, and a self-assurance that one's efforts are leading in positive directions. Here are some such points:
1. Most students want to learn, even when they pretend they don't.
2. Most students truly appreciate, admire, and like teachers who are kind and who try to help them.
3. Most students have positive attitudes toward school. (Sometimes they consider it cool to pretend they don't.)
4. Most students need and want an adult to be in charge of their learning.
5. Almost all students want a fair, reasonable, and consistently enforced set of rules in the classroom.
6. Most students resent class troublemakers.
7. All parents want their children to learn.
8. Most parents are strongly on the side of teachers.
9. Most parents think fairly strict discipline is desirable.

10. A large majority of adults who have children in school think teachers are doing a fine job.

These facts help put discipline in proper perspective. They show that the discipline necessary for best learning is needed and wanted by students and their parents. They show that students and parents appreciate teachers' efforts in setting the tone for and maintaining class discipline. They show that parents and students will support reasonable systems of discipline.

These positive aspects of discipline are not always easy to keep in mind, especially when unpleasant situations arise. Occasional reminders help, such as positive slogans posted in the room and discussions with the class about fair rules and good behavior. Student practice in complimenting and helping other students is valuable, too. These kinds of reminders keep teachers and students on an even keel. They help everyone realize that teachers and students are working toward the same end—the best learning, accomplished within the most pleasant circumstances possible.

References

Davis, A. *Social Class Influence Upon Learning*. Cambridge, Mass.: Harvard University Press, 1948.

Dewey, J. *Democracy and Education*. New York: MacMillan, 1916.

Erikson, E. *Childhood and Society*. New York: W.W. Norton, 1950.

Freud, S. *The Ego and the Mechanisms of Defense*. New York: International Universities Press, 1946.

Havighurst, R. *Developmental Tasks and Education*. New York: David McKay, 1952.

Mead, M. *Sex and Temperament in Three Primitive Societies*. New York: New American Library, 1935.

Piaget, J. *Science of Education and the Psychology of the Child*. New York: Orion Press, 1970.

Rogers, C. *Freedom to Learn*. Columbus, Ohio: Charles E. Merrill, 1969.

Skinner, B. F. *Science and Human Behavior*. New York: Macmillan, 1953.

Zintz, M. *Education Across Cultures* 2nd ed. Dubuque, Iowa: Kendall/Hunt, 1969.

Seven Models of Discipline

Chapter 3

The Redl and Wattenberg Model: Managing the Group

Dr. William W. Wattenberg. (*Photograph courtesy of Wayne State University, Detroit, Mich.*)

Redl and Wattenberg Biographical Sketches

Fritz Redl was born in Vienna and began teaching there in 1925. He arrived in the United States in 1936 and worked as a therapist, researcher, and professor of behavioral science at Wayne State University. In 1973 he became a consultant to the department of criminal justice at State University of New York at Albany, dealing with deviant juveniles. His writings in the field of education consist of *Mental Hygiene in Teaching* (1951) *Discipline for Today's Children* (1956) and *When We Deal With Children* (1966).

William W. Wattenberg was born on January 5, 1911. He received his master's degree (1932) and Ph.D. (1936) from Columbia University. His field of study was educational psychology, which he has taught at Northwestern University, Chicago Teacher's College, and currently at Wayne State University. Dr. Wattenberg's writings in the field of educational psychology include: *On the Educational Front* (1936), *Mental Hygiene in Teaching* (1951), *The Adolescent Years* (1955), and *All Men Are Created Equal* (1967).

In their book *Mental Hygiene in Teaching,* Redl and Wattenberg offer teachers insights into forces—psychological and social—that affect student behavior in the classroom. They also offer specific disciplinary techniques that teachers can use in everyday situations. These techniques help teachers maintain classroom control and strengthen emotional development in students.

Redl and Wattenberg's Key Ideas

1. People in groups behave differently than they do individually. Group expectations influence individual behavior, and individual behavior affects the group. Teachers need to be aware of the characteristic traits of group behavior.
2. Groups create their own psychological forces that influence individual behavior. Teacher awareness of *group dynamics* is important to effective classroom control.
3. Group behavior in the classroom is influenced by how students perceive the teacher. Students see teachers as filling many psychological roles.
4. Dealing with classroom conflict requires diagnostic thinking by the teacher. This thinking involves (1) forming a first hunch, (2) gathering facts, (3) applying hidden factors, (4) taking action, and (5) being flexible.
5. Teachers maintain group control through various *influence techniques.* These techniques include (1) supporting self-control, (2) offering situational assistance, (3) appraising reality, and (4) invoking pleasure and pain.

6. *Supporting-self-control* techniques are low keyed. They address the problem before it becomes serious. They include eye contact, moving closer, encouragement, humor, and ignoring.
7. *Situational-assistance* techniques are necessary when students cannot regain control without assistance from the teacher. Techniques to provide assistance include (1) helping students over a hurdle, (2) restructuring the schedule, (3) establishing routines, (4) removing the student from a situation, (5) removing seductive objects, and (6) physical restraint.
8. *Appraising-reality* techniques involve helping students understand underlying causes for misbehavior and foresee probable consequences. Teachers "tell it like it is," offer encouragement, set limits, and clarify situations with post-situational follow-up.
9. *Pleasure-pain* techniques involve rewarding good behavior and punishing bad behavior. Punishment should be used only as a last resort because it is too often counterproductive.

Group Life

Understanding motivations, the basic causes behind behavior and conflict, is half the battle of classroom control. Our knowledge of individual behavior is growing daily. Teachers know more than ever before about why individuals behave as they do. They understand how individual physical, intellectual, and emotional development interact to produce individual behavior. They know that outward behavior has roots in recognized needs. They know that students are continually torn between their personal desires and society's expectations.

However, we must recognize that teachers seldom deal with students on a purely individual basis. There are too many students to allow this luxury. Teachers must concern themselves with groups—the entire class, large groups, and smaller groups. This does not mean that they cannot use their valuable insights into individuals. They have to transfer those insights into group behavior. This leaves them with a major problem: group psychology is different from individual psychology. People simply behave differently when in groups.

Redl and Wattenberg provide a helpful view of groups and group behavior. They view the group as an organism. "A group creates conditions such that its members will behave in certain ways because they belong to it; at the same time, the manner in which the parts function affects the whole (Redl and Wattenberg 1959, p. 267). In other words, group expectations strongly influence individual behavior, and individual behavior, in turn, affects the group. Redl and Wattenberg describe several roles that are available to individuals in groups. Here are some of the roles that can cause trouble in the classroom.

Leader

A leadership role is available in almost every group. The role varies according to the group's purpose, makeup, and activities. Within the same group, different people may act as leaders in different activities. For example, a student who is a leader in physical education may fill a different role in music.

Group leaders tend to share certain qualities. They are above average in most respects (intellect, responsibility, social skills, and socioeconomic status). They generally have a highly developed understanding of others, and they embody group ideals.

Teachers need to be aware that the leaders they appoint are not necessarily the group's natural leaders. This mismatch can lead to conflicts within the group.

Clowns

Clowns are individuals who find themselves in the position of being the group's entertainers. Students may take this role to hide feelings of inferiority. They may feel that they have to make fun of themselves before others have a chance to. Clowns can hinder the group and they can help it. Sometimes, supporting the disruptive antics of the group clown is a group's way of expressing hostility to the teacher. At other times, clowning can be beneficial to both teachers and groups, especially when students are anxious and need release from tension.

Fall Guys

A fall guy is an individual who takes blame and punishment in order to gain favor with the group. Members of the group feel free to misbehave knowing that they can set up the fall guy to suffer the penalties. Teachers need to be aware of this kind of manipulation and focus their corrective actions on the instigators.

Instigators

Instigators are individuals who cause trouble, but appear not to be directly involved. These individuals often solve their inner conflicts by getting others to act them out. They may even feel that they are benefiting the victim in some way. Teachers need to look into frequent conflicts carefully to see if there is an unnoticed instigator. It may be necessary to point out this role to the group, as it is often undetected by them. The group may need help in recognizing and discouraging this role.

All of these roles are played by individuals in groups because they feel the group expects or enjoys them. By playing a role, an individual finds a place within the group, and becomes a functioning part of the organism.

Group Dynamics

We saw how roles and role expectations influence behavior. Membership in groups can affect individuals in other ways, too. Groups create their own psychological forces that strongly influence individuals. These forces are called group dynamics. Redl and Wattenberg describe some of the dynamics that cause difficulties in the classroom.

Contagious Behavior

When deciding how to handle individual misbehavior, teachers must consider the possibility of its spreading. Once they have evaluated its potential to spread, they may firmly decide to squelch it immediately. Or, they may decide it is safe to ignore the behavior or use a low-pressure technique, such as suggesting the correct behavior.

Often, one student's misbehavior shows what other students are itching to do, too. Once the ice is broken, other students may follow, especially if the instigator has high status.

Teachers can reduce contagion by giving attention to negative factors that foster it including poor seating arrangements, boredom, restlessness, lack of purpose in lessons, and poor manners in students. On the positive side, we should remember that desirable behavior can be as contagious as disruptive behavior. Teachers can enthusiastically encourage it, reinforce it, and give status to those who behave appropriately.

Scapegoating

Scapegoating takes place when a group seeks to displace its hostility onto an unpopular individual or subgroup. The group will select a target person who is weak or outcast, often unable to cope with normal occurences in the classroom. Scapegoating has undesirable consequences for everyone concerned. Teachers must guard against it and stifle it when it occurs. At the same time, they should use an approach that does not cause increased dislike for the target.

Teacher's Pets

When a group believes that a teacher is playing favorites, it reacts with jealousy and resentment. These emotions manifest themselves in hostile behavior toward the favored individual or group. Hostility may also be directed toward the teacher. When teachers need to give individual students extra help, they should be sure that the actions are seen as impartial, necessary, and professional.

Reactions to Strangers

It is common in most schools for strangers to enter the classroom occasionally. Teachers notice a marked change in student behavior when this occurs. Unknown visitors increase tension for teachers and students alike.

If the stranger is a new student, the group code may become exaggerated in order to show the newcomer how to act. For example, if the group prizes cooperation, they might go to great lengths to be helpful to the newcomer and each other. On the other hand, the group may set off a series of behaviors intended to test the new child. Individuals or subgroups may vie for friendship, offer status positions, or taunt each other.

If the stranger is an adult, the students may rally to support their teacher, if that person is liked and respected. If they do not respect their teacher they may misbehave rudely and boisterously. All teachers are well advised to set up a standard procedure to be followed whenever a stranger enters the classroom.

Teachers should note the class reactions when a stranger enters the room. Extreme behaviors provide clues to underlying motivations and feelings that are operating within the group.

Group Disintegration

Groups serve many purposes, and good group behavior is highly desirable. Teachers hope to establish groups that will prosper, grow in maturity, and serve everyone well. Even the strongest group, however, will show strain in time.

Consider Mrs. Brown's discouraging situation. Early in the year, she had a strong class group. They worked well together, pulling toward goals as one. Lately there has been a decline in cohesion. When directing group lessons, Mrs. Brown notices that some children are looking out of the window, a small group is discussing the football game, someone else is writing a letter to a friend. Group members must be coerced into participating, one individual at a time.

This situation is familiar to many teachers. They are at a loss as to what to do, how to correct the situation. They don't know what is causing the group to fall apart. Redl and Wattenberg suggest that when a formerly effective group begins to disintegrate teachers should ask themselves the following questions.

1. Are there long, unnecessary periods of waiting where students could be getting more direction?
2. Are the assigned tasks relevant and within the students' ability?
3. Is there too much emphasis on competition between groups?
4. Are there too many unexpected changes in leadership, environment, schedules, and so forth?
5. Are classroom activities stimulating and thought provoking?
6. Are students given ample opportunity to experience success, or are there too many failure situations?
7. Is there more criticism than praise from the teacher?

Each of these factors can cause problems within the group. As they appear, control problems appear with them. Group disintegration causes insecurity among members, especially weaker ones, in terms of knowing their place and their expected roles. This, in turn, causes deviant behavior and loss of mutual support within the group.

Group dynamics are psychological forces that influence individuals' behavior as members of a group. They are the forces behind the group's unwritten codes of conduct. When these codes run counter to teachers' codes, conflict occurs. Teachers are powerful, and they may seem to win out. However, the group code usually prevails under the surface, forming lasting attitudes that are the opposite to what the teacher desired.

Psychological Roles of Teachers

The ways in which groups and individuals behave in the classroom are greatly influenced by how they perceive the teacher. Like it or not, teachers fill many different roles and present many different images. Some of these roles and images are:

1. Teachers are representatives of society. They reflect and develop values, moral attitudes, and thinking patterns of the community.
2. Teachers are judges. They judge the quality of students' work, behavior, and progress.
3. Teachers are a source of knowledge, a resource from which to extract information.
4. Teachers help students to learn by removing learning obstacles and facilitating problem solving.
5. Teachers are referees. They arbitrate and make decisions when disputes arise.

6. Teachers are detectives, maintaining security in the classroom and handing out consequences.
7. Teachers are models. They model values, manners, and beliefs that students should imitate.
8. Teachers reduce anxiety by maintaining standards of behavior, consistent environments, and schedules.
9. Teachers support student egos by building self-confidence and bettering self-images.
10. Teachers are group leaders. They facilitate harmonious and efficient group functioning.
11. Teachers are surrogate parents. They are a source of approval, affection, and advice.
12. Teachers are also adversaries to parents. They introduce different attitudes and values to round out children's viewpoints.
13. Teachers are targets for hostility. When hostility cannot be appropriately expressed to other adults, it may be displayed onto teachers.
14. Teachers are friends and confidants. They can be talked to and confided in.
15. Teachers are objects of affection, of crushes and hero worship.

As you can see, teachers are assigned many roles by students. Sometimes they have little choice about those roles. Usually, however, they can decide in part on the roles and on how and when to assume them. They may assume some roles wholeheartedly and avoid others completely, depending on how they wish to relate to students. Sometimes they may adopt or avoid certain roles, if they are aware of a strong group need. In any event, teachers need to be sure that they are steady and consistent in the roles they do assume.

Diagnostic Thinking in the Classroom

So far we have examined several of Redl and Wattenberg's findings about group makeup and functioning. We explored group dynamics and how they affect class behavior. We saw how group expectations cause role-playing behaviors in individuals. We noted some of the many ways teachers are perceived. Given these elements and motivations for group behavior, how do teachers act upon them? How do they apply their understandings in the classroom?

Redl and Wattenberg suggest that a general approach for meeting challenging situations depends on *diagnostic thinking*. Diagnostic thinking is not magic. Diligence and persistence are necessary for making it an effective tool. As teachers practice diagnostic thinking, it becomes second nature and allows them to add insights about psychological forces that influence group behavior and, in turn, affect efficient classroom management. Redl and Wattenberg's diagnostic-thinking approach involves *first hunch, fact gathering, hidden factors, acting,* and *flexibility.* They describe the approach this way.

When conflicts first become apparent, it is natural to form a first hunch. This hunch is not based on specific data gathered from the incident. It is based on general feelings about the incident. This feeling gives teachers a beginning direction for acting on the problem.

Next, the teacher will want to gather facts. Is there a student on the floor? Is he pointing and screaming at someone else? Is there something broken?

After gathering the obvious facts, teachers should add any hidden factors they may be aware of. Hidden factors might consist of background information on the students involved, knowledge of psychological or mental development, or knowledge of a previously volatile situation.

When teachers believe they have the facts, motivations, and other hidden factors behind a conflict, they can then act on what they know. This is likened to testing a hypothesis. They apply a solution and see whether it works. The teacher's solution may or may not solve the problem. After observing the effect of their actions, teachers may want to revise their appraisal or solution.

When teachers think diagnostically, they must strive to be flexible. They may have assessed the situation incorrectly. By their actions, they may have altered its dynamics. This creates a new situation that requires further action. Redl and Wattenberg suggest that a single action is not enough. Teachers must act in a series of steps, that ultimately resolve the problem situation.

Redl and Watternberg offer a final word of advice: Feelings are very important. Teachers should not rely solely on their own. They should try to put themselves in the students' place, see how the students feel, and vary their actions accordingly.

Influence Techniques

Redl and Wattenberg have given much attention to the kinds of acts that teachers find useful in resolving problem behavior. Acts are only a part of diagnostic thinking, yet they are the obvious manifestations of the entire process. The remainder of the chapter is devoted to an examination of these types of acts, referred to as influence techniques.

Every teacher employs several different techniques to maintain classroom control. Some of these techniques are based on school disciplinary policies; some are adopted because they accommodate teachers' personalities and attitudes toward students; and others are used because they have worked well in the past. Some are very effective and some are not effective at all. Many techniques are applicable in one situation but not in others.

Situations arise regularly that call for corrective action. Teachers use a variety of means for making those corrections. Some shout, some remove students from the class, some suggest alternative behaviors, some ignore the misbehavior. Redl and Wattenberg urge teachers to learn to ask themselves a series of rapid-fire questions before they take action:

1. What is the motivation behind the misbehavior?
2. How is the class reacting?
3. How is it related to interaction with the teacher?
4. How will the student react when corrected?
5. How will it affect future behavior?

Answers to these questions help ensure that teachers understand the situation. They are then better able to choose a corrective technique that has positive influence on the student's behavior. Redl and Wattenberg suggest four categories of influence techniques, selected in accord with the questions listed above. The categories are (1) supporting self-control, (2) offering situational assistance, (3) appraising reality, and (4) invoking the pain-pleasure principle. All of these techniques are much more effective when students know exactly what the issues are and how they are expected to behave. Expectations and consequences must be quite clear to all students from the beginning.

The following are Redl and Wattenberg's suggestions within each of the four categories of influence.

Supporting Self-control

Most students, most of the time, want to behave correctly, in ways that will gain the teacher's approval. They do not misbehave because they want to be unpleasant. When misbehavior occurs, it is due to some other reason. Often is is nothing more than a lapse in self-control. In such situations the best corrective technique is to help students regain control of their own behavior.

Techniques for supporting self-control are low-keyed. They are not forceful, aggressive, or punitive, but aim at helping students help themselves. Teachers should use them when they feel that students are on the verge of losing control. In this way behavior is checked before it becomes unacceptable.

Redl and Wattenberg describe five techniques for supporting self-control. The first technique is *sending signals*. With this technique teachers use signs that show they know what is going on and that they don't approve. Examples are frowning, shaking the head, and making eye contact. These signals are most effective during the earliest stages of misbehavior.

If students fail to respond to a signal, teachers may want to try *proximity control*. By moving closer to the offender, teachers communicate that they are aware and want to help. This way the student can draw strength from the nearness of the teacher and use that strength to regain control. It is usually enough simply to move closer to the student, but sometimes it may require a friendly touch on the shoulder or head.

Sometimes students who have good self-control will begin to misbehave when they lose interest in an assignment. Teachers can correct this by going to students and *showing interest* in their work. A teacher might say to one, "I see you've finished the first five problems. I'll bet you'll finish them all before the end of the period." This technique is not effective, of course, if the student is lost or feels unable to do the assignment.

A pleasant way to make students aware of a lapse in control is with *humor*. It is important that this humor be gentle and always accompanied by a smile from the teacher. An example of humor would be, "My, there is so much chattering, I forgot for a minute that this was a classroom!" Sarcasm and ridicule must not be used. They are not supporting techniques, they are punishing techniques.

Ignoring is often an effective support technique, especially if a student is testing a situation. When the teacher ignores inappropriate behavior it often clues other children in the class to follow suit. This approach discourages misbehavior motivated by a need for attention. Teachers should be careful when using this technique, as it could be interpreted by students as insecurity or indecisiveness.

Techniques that support self-control are useful, but they also have disadvantages. When used in the early stages of misbehavior, they can eliminate the need to dole out penalties. They give students opportunities to work on controlling their own behavior. Supporting techniques should be tried first when problems arise. However, these techniques are effective only in situations where misbehavior is mild or just beginning. If supporting techniques don't get the message across, firmer, more direct techniques will be required.

Providing Situational Assistance

When misbehavior reaches the point that students cannot regain self-control, the teacher must step in with assistance, to guide students back to the right course. Redl and Wattenberg describe several techniques for providing situational assistance.

Suppose an assignment has been made. Susan begins working, only to discover she has no understanding of the procedure involved.

She begins to talk to a neighbor. In this case, the teacher simply needs to *help the student over a hurdle*. The teacher does not attack Susan because she isn't working. Instead Susan is helped to overcome the obstacle that is interfering with self-control.

A common cause of problem behavior is restlessness or over-excitement stemming from previous activities. In these cases, teachers can *restructure the schedule or situation*. Have the students been made to sit too long? Were there too many exciting activities in too short a time? Teachers can restructure situations by changing the nature of activities, changing the focus of attention, or finding new ways of doing the same old things.

On the other hand, a lack of established routines can also cause unruly behavior. Students don't know what they should be doing, or when. They never know what to expect. Teachers assist in this situation by *establishing routines* and adding consistency to daily activities. Routines are especially helpful in activities that are apt to become complex or confusing, or where there are many people involved.

If one student has temporarily lost self-control and is disturbing the rest of the class, the teacher might decide to *remove the student from the situation*. This should always be done in a nonpunitive way. The teacher should emphasize that the student is only exiled until self-control is regained. When a student must be removed from the group, it is important to follow up later with a private talk. Feelings of both teacher and student should be discussed.

Sometimes a lapse in self-control may cause a student to become a danger to himself and others. When this happens, the teacher may have to use *physical restraint*. When restraint is used as a situational assistance technique, it is not rough or punitive. It is only supporting, containing, or restraining until control is regained.

Attractive objects or activities can sometimes overpower self-control. The teacher simply needs to *remove the seductive object* from the student. This is a temporary measure and should be explained to the child as such.

Unexpected or exciting events can cause students to forget about self-control. If teachers anticipate and plan for such events, they can prevent control problems. They can explain the unknown and set behavior standards in advance. There is no need to describe a situation in endless detail. It is good to leave a little room for interest and anticipation. Advance standards can be set for unexpected events such as visitors, substitutes, a sick student, fire drills, and so forth. In each case, a routine method of dealing with the situation can set the tone for an efficient, controlled classroom.

In short, situational assistance comes into play when students are unable to maintain their own self-control and require teacher assistance to regain it. The strengths of the techniques described are:

1. They allow anticipatory planning before a crisis.
2. They allow students to keep their energy and attention focused on learning.
3. They reduce confusion.
4. They show a desire on the part of the teacher to be helpful and promote kindly feelings.

Their weaknesses are:
1. Teachers may be fooled into thinking a calm surface means they have alleviated deeper problems.
2. Too much teacher intervention causes students to depend more on the teacher and less on themselves for controlling their behavior.

Reality Appraisal

Education is supposed to help people follow reason and intelligence rather than emotions and impulses. Teachers can help by calling on students to look at a behavior situation, see the underlying causes, and foresee the probable consequences. Redl and Wattenberg have outlined a variety of techniques for helping teachers conduct effective reality appraisal with students.

The key to reality appraisal is that teachers must make it very clear to students which behaviors are unacceptable and what the consequences will be for those behaviors. Then when students misbehave the teacher simply says, "These are the rules. You broke the rules. Therefore, you suffer the consequences."

Too often teachers overlook the simplest method for dealing with students, which is "to tell it like it is." Teachers do this by explaining exactly why behavior is inappropriate and outlining clear connections between conduct and consequences. Don't underestimate students' ability to understand statements such as: "If everyone talks at once, no one gets heard;" or "Pushing in line can cause injuries;" or "If you don't keep up with assignments, you can't progress." Students will often take it upon themselves to abide by rules when they understand their reasons. Teachers who use this technique are considered fair and just.

When teachers give criticism, they should strive to express it in ways that reveal encouragement. The teacher deals with the student's self-image by giving insights into areas where personal standards are not being met. Criticism should be offered in such a way that it stimulates efforts to try harder; it should not frustrate by setting unreasonable expectations. Care should be taken so that correction will not attack personal values, humiliate, or lower the student's prestige. The teacher's role is to support, not to attack or blame.

Students will often misbehave for no other reason than to test limits. They need the security of knowing exactly how far they will be able to go. This is related to the technique of telling it like it is, in that *setting limits* tells a child what is expected of him and why. Teachers should remember that setting limits and enforcing rules are separate issues. Making threats while setting limits indicates that the teacher expects violations.

Clarity and consistency are vital to setting limits. Teachers should explain why certain limits are needed or, better yet, ask students to discuss their opinions. Often students already know the answers.

Post-situational Follow-up. During disturbing incidents emotions run strong. Teacher and student are apt to say inappropriate things. It is difficult for both parties to listen to what is being said. Redl and Wattenberg believe discussions about an incident should be held sometime after the incident, when both parties are calmer and better able to talk over what happened. This talk is not a time for lecturing or scolding, but rather a time to sort out causes and feelings. It is important that the student understand why the teacher acted in a particular manner. It may be possible to decide how to handle similar incidents in the future. Appraising the reality of a situation helps students develop and promote their own values. It enhances their ability to see underlying aspects of themselves and others.

Invoking the Pain-Pleasure Principle

Teachers may support self-control, offer situational assistance, and help appraise reality and still encounter behavior problems. Such problems call for stronger techniques that increase appropriate behavior and deter inappropriate behavior.

Rewards and Promises. Rewarding any behavior increases the probability that that behavior will be repeated. When students are praised their self-esteem grows. They learn to repeat good behavior because it makes them feel good about themselves. One danger of rewards is that they may cause students to behave for the reward only. Teachers need to observe behavior carefully to be sure this isn't the case in their classrooms. Rewards should be paired with verbal praise describing exactly what behavior is being rewarded and why that behavior is valuable.

Threats. Often, teachers make threats for potential misbehaviors before they occur. These statements usually take on an "If you don't . . . I will. . . ." quality. Teachers should never make threats unless they have the full intention of carrying them out. Not following through on threats is one of the easiest ways to lose classroom control.

Threats can be useful, but they have more disadvantages than advantages. Students may view threats as rejection. Threats make people anxious and anxiety, in turn, interferes with learning. Other students may see threats as a challenge. They may want to try the teacher out. Instead of making threats, teachers can simply state which behaviors are unacceptable and explain exactly what the consequences will be for those behaviors. This lends security to the classroom and aids students in developing their own self-control.

Punishment. When students lose the battle between self-control and emotions, it might become necessary to resort to punishment. Punishment should consist of planned, unpleasant consequences, the purpose of which is to modify behavior. Punishment should not come in angry outbursts that indicate lack of self-control on the teacher's part. Neither should they be actions taken to get back at misbehaving students, or to teach them a lesson.

Even when punishing teachers should try to get across the idea that they like the students and are trying to help them. Students should be made to see punishment as a natural and understandable consequence of unacceptable behavior. If students sense good intentions from the teacher, they will be at least partly angry at themselves for losing self-control, not at the teacher who helps them regain it.

Punishment is not the best technique for maintaining control. It should be used as a last resort, only when all other techniques fail. That is because there are many things that can go wrong when punishment is used, such as:

1. The teacher uses punishment as revenge or as a release for tension.
2. The punishment ends up being too extreme for the crime.
3. Students who are punished frequently lose the ability to control their own behavior. They become dependent on someone else to do it for them.
4. Students may draw punishment to raise their status with peers.
5. Students being punished may be physically or mentally incapable of the control demanded by the teacher.
6. Too much punishment can cause victims to become hardened to its effects. They may learn to justify misconduct if they are willing to suffer the consequences.
7. If punishment is too drawn out or delayed too long the child may lose sight of the connection between misbehavior and punishment.
8. Punishment may have detrimental effects on self-concept, group status, or relations with teachers.
9. Physical punishment causes the teacher to model aggressive, violent behavior as the way to solve problems.

Redl's Suggestions

How can teachers tie together the quantities of advice presented by Redl and Wattenberg? Perhaps this is best done through examining the following series of suggestions, presented in Fritz Redl's book *When We Deal with Children:*

1. Give students a say in setting standards and deciding consequences. Let them tell how they think you should handle situations that call for punishment.
2. Keep students' emotional health in mind at all times. Punished students must feel that the teacher likes them. *Always* talk to students about their feelings after the situation has calmed down.
3. Be helpful, not hurtful. Show students you want to support their best behaviors.
4. Punishment does not work well. Use it as a last resort. Try other approaches first.
5. Don't be afraid to change your course of action, if you get new insights into a situation.
6. Remember: mistakes in discipline need not be considered disastrous, unless they are repeated.
7. Be objective, maintain humor, and remember that we are all human.

References

Redl, F. "Disruptive Behavior in the Classroom," *School Review* 83:569–94, August, 1975.

Redl, F. and Wattenberg, W. *Mental Hygiene in Teaching*. New York: Harcourt, Brace and World, 1959.

Redl, F. and Wineman, D. *The Aggressive Child*. New York: Free Press, 1957.

Wattenberg, W. "Ecology of Classroom Behavior," *Theory into Practice* 16:256–61, October, 1977.

Chapter 4

The Kounin Model: Withitness, Alerting, and Group Management

Professor Jacob Kounin *(Photograph courtesy of Wayne State University, Detroit, Mich.)*

Kounin Biographic Sketch

Dr. Jacob Kounin was born in Cleveland, Ohio on January 17, 1912. He received his master's degree (1936) from Western Reserve University, and his Ph.D. (1939) from Iowa State University. In 1946 he was appointed to an assistant professorship at Wayne State University, where he is currently a full professor teaching educational psychology. Dr. Kounin has made numerous presentations to the American Psychological Association, the American Educational Research Association, and many other organizations. He is a consultant to twelve institutions and a visiting professor at four universities.

The concepts of discipline and group behavior described in this chapter have grown from careful, scientific, research. Kounin designed and directed this research in an attempt to gain knowledge about group management and discipline techniques for the classroom teacher.

Dr. Kounin is best known for his work, *Discipline and Group Management in the Classroom,* a book that grew out of two decades of research. In the earlier years his studies focused on group management, with particular emphasis on how handling the misbehavior of one student affected students who were not misbehaving. Kounin observed that a general effect occurred in the group, which he called the *ripple effect.*

From ripple-effect studies came subsequent research on disciplinary and group-management techniques. This research involved videotapes of eighty elementary school classrooms. Kounin analyzed thousands of hours of tape and discovered several dimensions of group management that promoted work involvement and reduced the amount of misbehavior. We will examine the most significant of those dimensions in the sections that follow.

Kounin's Key Ideas

1. When teachers correct misbehavior in one student, it often influences the behavior of nearby students. This is known as the ripple effect.
2. Teachers should know what is going on in all parts of the classroom at all times. Kounin calls this phenomenon *withitness.*
3. The ability to provide smooth transitions between activities and to maintain consistent momentum within activities is crucial to effective group management.
4. Teachers should strive to maintain group alertness, and to hold every group member accountable for the content of a lesson, which allows optimal learning to take place.

5. Student satiation (boredom) can be avoided by providing a feeling of progress and by adding variety to curriculum and classroom environment.

Let's see what Kounin has to say about each of these key ideas.

The Ripple Effect

Kounin's research on the ripple effect started innocently one day
when a college student was reprimanded for reading a newspaper
during the lecture. Immediately afterward, there occurred a difference
in the behavior of students who had not been targets of the repri-
mand. They reacted by sitting up straighter, paying closer attention,
and refraining from deviant behavior.

The way in which teachers issue desists (remarks intended to
suppress misbehavior) influences behavior in students who witness
the desist. The effect of the desist ripples from the target student outward to others.

Kounin tested the ripple effect in four settings—college, kindergarten, high school, and summer camp. In the college study, he set up
an experiment to test the effect of a supportive desist (offering help to
correct the deviant behavior), versus a threatening desist (chastising
the deviant). Both caused a ripple effect. In the kindergarten study,
Kounin again tried to find whether the quality of the desist influenced the degree of conforming behavior. The three qualities of desists were:

1. Clarity—the desist carried information that named the deviant,
specified the behavior that was unacceptable, and listed the reasons for the desist.
2. Firmness—an "I-mean-it" attitude was projected with follow
through until the child stopped the misbehavior.
3. Roughness—the desist included anger, threats, physical handling, and punishment.

Kounin found that increased clarity tended to increase conforming behavior in students who witnessed the desist. Firmness in
the desist increased conformity only in students who were themselves
misbehaving at the time. Roughness did not improve behavior; it
simply upset the audience children, making them anxious, confused,
and restless. It was also noted that the ripple effect was very pro-
nounced on the first day of school but tended to diminish as the year
wore on.

In the summer camp study, Kounin attempted to measure the ripple effect with children from seven to thirteen years of age. He could
find no measurable effect, and decided that this was due to the fact

that misconduct at camp was considered more trivial than misbehavior at home or school. It carried fewer consequences. Thus, children in summer camps did not take desists seriously.

In the high school study, Kounin found that the type of desist had no effect on the amount of misbehavior exhibited by the audience students. He found that an extremely angry outburst caused some emotional discomfort for students witnessing the desist. What did influence behavior in high school was the degree to which the teacher was liked. High motivation to learn coupled with high regard for the teacher created maximum work involvement and minimum misbehavior.

From these studies one can conclude that the ripple effect, in itself, is powerful at the elementary level. It becomes weak at the secondary and college levels where it depends on the popularity or prestige of the teacher.

Withitness

Kounin coined the term withitness to describe the trait of teachers having eyes in the back of their heads. This trait conveys to students that the teacher knows what is going on in all areas of the classroom at all times. Kounin felt that this was communicated more effectively by teachers' behavior than by their words. Further, it was effective only if students were convinced that the teacher really knew what was going on.

Kounin found two elements of withitness that contributed to its effectiveness. The first is the ability to select the correct student for a desist. Suppose Bob and Bill are teasing Mary while the teacher is directing a small group. Mary finally says in a loud voice, "Stop that, you two!" The teacher tells Mary to go sit alone and ignores the instigators of the incident. This tells the students that the teacher does not know what's going on. The second element is attending to the more serious deviancy when two are occurring simultaneously. Here is an illustration: Jill is playing with a toy at her desk. Meanwhile, James and Eric are pushing each other violently around the drinking fountain. The teacher looks up and says, "Jill, bring that toy up to me and then get back to work." The teacher failed to take any action against the fight at the drinking fountain. If mistakes like these occur often, students begin to get the idea that the teacher is not truly aware. This encourages them to engage in misbehavior without fear of getting caught.

Timing also influences withitness. A major mistake in timing is to wait until the misbehavior spreads before taking action. A student throws a paper ball at the wastebasket. Another student sees this and decides to try it. Three or four others join in until there is a virtual basketball game in progress. Teachers who display withitness correct misbehavior as soon as it occurs. This shows students that the teacher knows exactly what is going on and will not tolerate misbehavior.

Another timing mistake is to allow the misbehavior to increase in seriousness before stopping it. Let's return to the example of the two boys at the drinking fountain. James went there to get a drink. Eric pushed his way in front of James. James pushed him out of the way claiming he was there first. Eric hit James. James hit back. They scuffled. The teacher waited too long to intervene. If she had been aware of what was happening, she could have spoken to Eric when he first butted in. In this way, she would have conveyed her withitness to the students.

Kounin found that if children perceive that teachers are withit (in that they choose the right culprit and correct misbehavior at once), they are less likely to misbehave. Withitness was found to induce more work involvement and less misbehavior, especially in teacher-directed lessons. Handling the correct deviant on time was more important to classroom control than was the firmness or clarity of a desist.

Overlapping

In his videotape studies, Kounin became aware of a group-management technique which he labeled *overlapping*. Overlapping is the ability to attend to two issues at the same time. Here is an example: A teacher is meeting with a small group and notices that two students at their seats are playing cards instead of attending to an assignment. The teacher could:
1. Stop the small group activity, walk over to the card players, stand there until they are back on task, and then attempt to reestablish the lesson in the small group; or
2. Have the small group continue while addressing the card players from where the small group is sitting and continue to monitor the students at their seats while conducting the small group lesson.

Teachers are interrupted often while they are working with a group. A student might approach with a paper that must be looked at before the student can go on. Teachers skilled in overlapping can check the paper while glancing at the small group and adding encouraging remarks such as, "go on," or "that's correct." Thus, the teacher has attended to two issues simultaneously.

Not surprisingly Kounin found that teachers who were adept at overlapping were also aware of a broader scope of happenings in the classroom. They were more withit. Overlapping loses its effectiveness if the teacher does not also demonstrate withitness. If students working independently know that the teacher is aware of them and able to deal with them, they are more likely to stay on task.

Movement Management

Kounin's research revealed an important relationship between student behavior and *movement* within and between lessons. He did not mean physical movement of students or teachers. He meant lesson *pace, momentum,* and *transitions.* Teachers' ability to move smoothly from one activity to the next and to maintain momentum within an activity has a great deal to do with their effectiveness in the classroom. In smooth transitions student attention is turned easily from one activity to another. Student concentration is kept on the task at hand.

Kounin discovered two transition mistakes—*jerkiness* and *slowdowns*—both of which encourage student misbehavior.

Jerkiness

When activities do not flow smoothly from one into the other, the transition is called jerky. Kounin identified four causes of jerkiness. A first cause of jerky transitions is a teacher behavior called *thrusts.* Thrusts occur when the teacher suddenly bursts into an activity with a statement or directions, but the group is not ready to receive the message. For example, suppose students are working on an art project. The teacher is doing desk work. Without looking up to see if the group is ready to receive a message, the teacher says, "Put your supplies away and get ready for reading." Half of the class doesn't hear and the other half starts to move around in confusion. Their attention was not directed to the teacher who thrust a message onto the group without assessing their readiness to follow directions, causing nonconformance and confusion.

A second cause of jerky transitions is a behavior called *dangles.* Kounin described dangles as the practice of leaving one activity dangling in midair to start another activity, and then returning to the first activity. Example: The class has just begun a math lesson. The teacher calls on three students to go to the board. On their way up she suddenly asks, "How many of you brought your money for the field trip?" She then counts the raised hands, goes to her desk and writes the number down. The class is distracted from the math lesson. Many students are now talking about the field trip. It is difficult at this point to bring them back to the business at hand.

A third cause of jerkiness is *truncations,* the same as dangles, except that the teacher never returns to the first activity. Let's say a teacher asks the class to get out their spelling books. As they begin, she says, "Did we practice for the Christmas play yesterday? No? Oh dear, we need to do that right now." Spelling is forgotten, left dangling in midair. If it is resumed later it will be difficult for the students to figure out where they left off and how to begin again.

A fourth cause of jerkiness is *flip-flops*, another variation of dangling. When a flip-flop occurs, teachers totally terminate one activity, begin a second, and then return to the first. Mrs. Smith has the students put away their math assignment and get out their library books. After a few minutes she interrupts their reading and asks, "How many of you got to number ten on your math assignment today?"

Jerky transitions interrupt smooth flowing from one activity to another. They cause confusion, unnecessary activity, noise, and nonconformance. They provide an opportunity to misbehave. It is difficult for students to turn their attention from one task to another. It is even more difficult for them to get down to work and concentrate on the new task. Smooth transitions help them direct their attention appropriately and keep it focused.

Slowdowns

If jerkiness is at one end of the transition continuum, slowdowns are at the other end, and are just as bad. Slowdowns are delays and waste time between activities. They occur because of two phenomena: *overdwelling* and *fragmentation*—both of which impede progress and allow friction to occur.

Overdwelling

Kounin found the biggest cause of slowdowns is overdwelling, or spending too much time giving directions and explanations. Everyone can remember a time when the teacher began a task with elaborate directions and long drawn out explanations. They went far beyond what was required for understanding how to proceed.

Some teachers have a tendency toward overdwelling on student behavior. This is commonly known as nagging. To correct misbehavior, these teachers lecture on and on beyond what was quite adequate to stop the misbehavior and convey their displeasure. Such teachers may even lecture long and hard about misbehavior that has not occurred. Students usually turn off this sort of nagging and begin thinking of other things while the teacher talks.

Kounin labeled another type of overdwelling *actone overdwelling*. Actone overdwelling occurs when teachers concentrate more on details than on the main idea of the lesson. Suppose Miss Anderson is doing a math lesson with the class. She writes some problems on the board for the children to copy. As they are copying, she stops them saying, "Make sure there is a one-inch margin on your paper. Skip lines between problems. Number each problem. Don't put more than three problems on a line. Put a box around the answer." The teacher has drawn attention away from the concepts being taught by focusing attention on details. This slowed the activity and caused students to lose sight of the main focus of the lesson.

Related to actone overdwelling is *prop overdwelling*. This happens when teachers devote more time and attention to physical props than to the lesson. Let's look at an art lesson. After the materials are passed out, Mrs. Crisp says, "Everyone hold up your paint container. Do you have a fourth of a cup? Now everyone should have two brushes. Is there anyone who doesn't have a big and a little brush? Measure your paper. It should be exactly $8\frac{1}{4}'' \times 11\frac{1}{2}''$. Put your paint on your right, your brushes on your left, and the paper in the middle. Be sure to hold your brush exactly like this." By the time the teacher gets around to the activity, the students have lost interest. The sooner the students can involve themselves in activity, the less time they have to be doing something they shouldn't.

You can see how overdwelling causes students to lose interest in the main idea of the activity. They begin to feel they already know the information the teacher is passing on. They quit listening and find something else to do, often something inappropriate. Teachers should practice giving the minimum amount of instructions necessary for the lesson.

Fragmentation

Slowdowns in class momentum also result from fragmentation. Fragmentation consists of breaking down an activity into several unnecessary steps when it could be easily handled as a whole. During a science lesson the teacher began, "Row one may get up and get their beakers. Row two may get theirs. Now row three. Now, row one may line up to put some salt in their beakers. Row two may follow them," and so forth. When each row had gotten the salt, the teacher then had them go row by row to get some water. This left the rest of the class sitting at their desks with no direction. At best they were doing nothing. Probably they were dreaming up something with which to entertain themselves.

Another type of fragmentation was evident in that same science lesson. Kounin called it group fragmentation. After every child had the necessary elements in their beakers the teacher proceeded. "Okay Roy, now pour the vinegar into the water while we watch. Now Susie, it's your turn. Patti, you're next." The teacher had individuals doing the activity singly when it would have made more sense to have the class do it together. It is always better to involve as many students as possible in an activity. This helps focus attention and promotes involvement, decreasing the possibility of boredom and misbehavior.

Transitions may seem minor at first, but they are not. Kounin found that *teachers' ability to manage smooth transitions and maintain momentum was more important to work involvement and classroom control than any other behavior-management technique.*

Group Focus

Teachers have few opportunities to work exclusively with one student. Mostly they work with groups. Sometimes the group is the entire class. Sometimes it is one to several small groups working at the same time.

Kounin found that the ability to maintain a concerted group focus is essential to a productive, efficient classroom. Maintaining this group focus depends on (1) *group format,* (2) *degree of accountability* of each student for the content of the lesson, and (3) effective focus of group *attention.* Let's explore each of these factors.

Group Format

Group format refers to organization that produces active participation by all students in the group. Optimal format increases the amount of concurrent activity by all members. For instance, students may be reading along in a book or counting on an abacus. When responses are called for, teachers may ask the group to respond in unison. Or they may ask one student to work a problem on the board while the remainder of the group does it in a workbook. This is an effective behavior-control technique. It eliminates group waiting for one member to perform. Every member is participating in the lesson, actively involved in learning.

Accountability

The second element, degree of accountability, is related to group format. Accountability refers to each student in the group being responsible for the concept of the lesson. To enhance accountability, teachers must show awareness of how each student is progressing. Kounin recommends many techniques for holding all members of a group accountable. Some of them are:

1. All students hold up props for the teacher to see. For instance, they may arrange words in alphabetical order on a pocket chart.
2. The teacher asks all members to observe and check on accuracy while one member performs.

3. The teacher asks all members to write the answer, and then at random calls on several students to respond.
4. The teacher circulates and observes the responses of nonreciters.
5. The teacher calls for a unison response and then checks individuals at random.

Group accountability has much in common with overlapping. The teacher is able to deal with the entire group, and yet let individuals know that she is aware of their progress. When students perceive that the teacher will definitely and immediately hold them accountable for the content of the lesson, they are more likely to pay attention and stay involved in the activity.

Attention

Attention is a third element in effective group focus. Group alerting involves focusing the attention of all group members on the activity at all times. Kounin advocates the following for maintaining attentive group focus:

1. The teacher attracts attention by looking around the group in a suspenseful manner, or saying, "Let's see who can. . . ."
2. The teacher keeps in suspense who will be called on next and avoids a predictable pattern of response.
3. The teacher varies unison responses with individual responses.
4. Nonreciters are alerted that they may be called on in connection with a reciter's response ("Listen to Jim as he reads and see if you can guess who took the crystal ball.").

All of these practices draw the attention of the group to the lesson. Every member of the group is alerted. The teacher tries hard to keep the group on their toes.

Kounin also examined some common mistakes that contribute to nonattention within the group, some of which mistakes are:

1. The teacher focuses on one student at a time and excludes the other members from the lesson.
2. The teacher chooses a reciter before asking a question, causing others to stop listening because they know they won't have to respond.
3. The teacher calls on students to respond in a predictable sequence, such as going clockwise around a circle. Students then only need to be ready to respond after their neighbor. This allows them an opportunity to focus their attention elsewhere when it is not their turn to respond.

Of these three elements of group focus, Kounin found the ability to maintain group attention the most important. Teachers who held the attention of every member throughout the lesson were more successful at inducing work involvement and preventing misbehavior.

The element of group accountability was found to be more effective in teacher-directed lessons than when students were working independently. Accountability and group attention usually accompanied each other.

Being able to alert a group and hold it accountable is an important technique for teachers. When students pay attention and know that they may at any time be held accountable for the information presented in a lesson, they have little time to engage in inappropriate activity.

Avoiding Satiation

Satiation means getting filled up with something, getting enough of it, getting bored. Kounin uses the term to describe a change in the dynamics of an activity due to repetition. He found that repetition often causes less involvement in and liking for an activity. As students become increasingly satiated, certain behavior changes result. For instance, students may introduce spontaneous variations into the activity. If made to write multiplication facts ten times each they may after a time, start writing the top line of the problem across the paper, then add the times sign, then add the bottom digit, and so forth, rather than writing each problem separately.

Satiation causes careless work that results in increased errors. Students begin to do the work mechanically, devoting little thought to the process. The result is a breakdown in meaning. When students break up an activity in a different way to add variety, they may also lose their grasp on the process or concept being learned. Satiated students tend to become less involved with an activity, or they may try to escape from it. This is often shown in behaviors such as looking out the window, tying shoes, poking a neighbor, or sharpening a pencil. They look for anything to initiate some new type of stimulation. Teachers can eliminate these effects by providing progress, challenge, and variety.

Progress

Kounin studied many different classrooms to determine why some teachers induced more satiation than others. One element found effective in slowing the rate of satiation was a feeling of progress. Students who felt they were making definite progress took longer to become satiated. Those who did the same task over and over, without any feeling of progress, satiated quickly.

Challenge

Kounin also noticed that teachers who offered challenges throughout a lesson prevented satiation. They provided challenges in many different ways. One way was to show enthusiasm for the lesson with remarks like, "I have a special magical math formula to teach you today." Another way was to elicit positive feelings about the lesson by saying something like, "I know you'll all get the answer to the next one!" Teachers might make comments such as, "Don't be fooled by this one. It's tricky!" These techniques work if the teacher is genuinely enthusiastic and positive—students pick up on genuine teacher interest and follow its cues.

Variety

Variety is the spice of life, and is the spice of any lesson. Kounin feels that variety plays a crucial role in reducing satiation. The first thing teachers can do is vary the content of classroom activities. They might have a quiet reading time followed by an active physical-education session, followed by math and then a spelling game. Students may become satiated simply because they are having to sit and work quietly for extended periods of time. This can be avoided by varying quiet times with active ones. Teachers should consider changing the daily class schedule from time to time.

Within a lesson, teachers may wish to change the level of intellectual challenge. Sometimes the students are simply listening. Other times they may practice a skill or demonstrate comprehension of a concept. The teacher may challenge them by having them engage in abstract thinking or exhibit some sort of creativity. All of these require a different level of intellectual functioning.

Teachers should also vary the way they present their lessons. They can demonstrate, direct an activity, participate along with the students, circulate among the students, or observe students working on the activity. Students enjoy variety in styles of presentation as well as variety among lessons, even when covering the same material over and over.

Variety can be provided in learning props. One activity may call for routine props such as pencils and paper. Other activities can call for props like tape recorders, slides, a live snake, or a musician. Doing multiplication facts on a calculator once in a while can make them appear to be a completely new activity.

As we know, Kounin stresses the need to pay attention to the group focus. We may start a lesson with the entire class, break into subgroups, and then reconvene with the whole class again. Thus, the focus changes from the teacher to the students, and back to the teacher again. This provides variety through movement and different kinds of thinking.

Conclusion

The techniques presented in this chapter are advocated by Kounin to create an effective classroom environment and promote optimal learning. As you can see, none of them requires a punishing attitude or harsh responses from the teacher. All of them require effective and efficient group-management techniques.

Teachers must be able to deal with the entire class, subgroups, pairs of students, and individuals, often at the same time. Kounin does not feel that teachers' personality traits are particularly important in classroom control. What is important, he says, is teachers' ability to manage groups. To do this they must:

1. Know what is happening in every area of the classroom at all times, and communicate that fact to the students.
2. Be able to deal with more than one issue at the same time.
3. Correct the appropriate target before misbehavior escalates.
4. Be able to use the ripple effect to advantage.
5. Initiate and maintain smooth and consistent momentum.
6. Maintain group focus through alerting and accountability.
7. Provide nonsatiating learning programs by including progress, challenge, and variety.

Reference

Kounin, J. *Discipline and Group Management in Classrooms.* New York: Holt, Rinehart and Winston, 1970.

Chapter 5

The Neo-Skinnerian Model: Shaping Desired Behavior

B. F. Skinner (*Photograph courtesy of Harvard University News Office, Cambridge, Mass.*)

Skinner Biographical Sketch

B. F. Skinner is generally acknowledged to be one of the greatest living psychologists. Many consider him the greatest psychologist of all time. His work has had prodigious influence in both psychology and education.

Skinner was born in Pennsylvania in 1904. He earned his Ph.D in psychology at Harvard University in 1931. Most of his subsequent career was spent at Harvard. There he conducted his experimental studies in learning, working mostly with rats and pigeons, but sometimes with humans, too. Earlier behaviorism was concerned with stimulus-response connections in learning. Skinner looked at the learning process in the opposite way, investigating the effects on learning of stimuli provided *after* an act was performed. He found that with some of those stimuli the organism repeated a given act more frequently. He called those stimuli reinforcers. Providing reinforcers in a systematic way was called reinforcement, and the process through which behavior was shaped in desired directions was called behavior shaping.

Skinner became widely recognized for using the process of behavior shaping to teach pigeons to do complicated acts. This teaching was often done inside a glass-walled enclosure that came to be known as a Skinner Box.

Skinner's work was not confined to laboratory animals, however. He drew worldwide attention for his ideas about raising infants inside glass enclosures called air cribs where the child was kept dry, warm, and comfortable, with all needs attended to. He raised his own daughter in an air crib.

Skinner drew much attention, too, with the publication of his novel *Walden Two* (1948), which described the workings of a utopian community built on principles of reinforcement. It is still widely read, and has served as a model for communes in various places.

In 1971 Skinner's book *Beyond Freedom and Dignity* was published, and again world attention turned to him. He challenged traditional concepts of freedom and dignity as inadequate, insisting they are outmoded, useless, and incorrect. We are not free to choose, he asserted. Our choices are made, instead, on the basis of what has happened to us in the past; that is, on the reinforcements we have received for prior actions. Instead of concentrating on free choice, we should turn our efforts to providing conditions that improve human behavior in general.

Teachers have benefited most from Skinner's fundamental work in reinforcement as a means of controlling and motivating student behavior. That work has been enlarged, extended, and modified by numerous psychologists and educators. Its various applications to classroom practice are commonly called *behavior modification*, a technique which has been refined during the past two decades. Most teachers consider it to be one of the most valuable tools available for improving the learning and behavior of school students.

Skinner's Key Ideas

The model presented here is called neo-Skinnerian to indicate that it is made up of newer applications of Skinner's basic ideas. Skinner, himself, never proposed a model of school discipline. Other writers have taken his ideas on learning and adapted them to controlling the behavior of students in school. The following ideas reveal the essence of the neo-Skinnerian model:

1. Behavior is shaped by its consequences, by what happens to the individual after performing an act.
2. Behavior is strengthened if followed immediately by reinforcers. Technically, a reinforcer is a stimulus that increases the likelihood that the individual will repeat the act. We commonly think of reinforcers as rewards.
3. To say that a behavior is strengthened is to say that the individual has become more likely than before to repeat it.
4. Behavior is weakened if it is not followed by reinforcement.
5. To say that a behavior is weakened is to say that the organism has become less likely than before to repeat the behavior.
6. Behavior is also weakened if followed by punishment. Punishment is *not* the same thing as negative reinforcement.
7. Systematic use of reinforcement (rewards) can shape individuals' behavior in desired directions.
8. In the early stages of learning, constant reinforcement produces the best results. Constant means that the behavior is reinforced every time it occurs.
9. Once learning has reached the desired level, it is best maintained through intermittent reinforcement, reinforcement that is provided only occasionally, on an unpredictable schedule.
10. When applied to classroom learning and discipline, this process of behavior shaping through reinforcement is called behavior modification.
11. Behavior modification is perhaps the most powerful tool available for strengthening desired classroom learning and behavior.
12. Behavior modification is applied in these two ways: (a) The teacher observes the student perform a desired act; the teacher rewards the student; the student tends to repeat the act. (b) The teacher observes the student perform an undesired act; the teacher either ignores the act or punishes the student, then praises a student who is behaving correctly; the misbehaving student becomes less likely than before to repeat the act.

13. Behavior modification successfully uses various kinds of reinforcers. They include social reinforcers, such as verbal comments, facial expressions, and gestures; graphic reinforcers, such as marks and stars; activity reinforcers, such as free time, free reading, and collaborating with a friend; and tangible reinforcers, such as food, prizes, and printed awards.

Remember that this model of discipline was not proposed by B. F. Skinner, but rather is bits and pieces of work done by many different people. It is a powerful model for classroom teachers, one that can be easily modified and implemented with students of all ages and backgrounds. We will examine the model in the following manner: a general description; what the model is good for; dangers of punishment; types of reinforcers; systems of behavior modification; a taxonomy of uses; formulating a plan of behavior modification; and implementing a plan of behavior modification.

The Neo-Skinnerian Model

The neo-Skinnerian model of discipline makes systematic application of the scientific principles of reinforcement toward improvement of the behavior and learning of classroom students. These principles of reinforcement apply equally well to students of all ages, from all backgrounds. Some of the specific reinforcers, as well as ways of applying reinforcement, have to be modified in accord with the ages and interests of the students. The basic principles, however, apply consistently.

Skinner established precise definitions of terms he used, such as operant behavior, reinforcing stimuli, schedules of reinforcement, successive approximations, positive reinforcement, and negative reinforcement. Those terms are necessary to an understanding of the model. We needn't be worried, however, about the precise, scientifically acceptable definitions. Teachers can use the model just as well if they keep these basic concepts in mind.

Operant behavior is simply behavior that the student produces. It comes not as reflex or reaction but as purposeful, voluntary action. These behaviors are any of the incredible variety of actions that individuals are able to perform in voluntary ways.

Reinforcing stimuli are stimuli that the individual receives immediately after performing an operant behavior. We can think of reinforcers as rewards. When we see a student exhibit any behavior (operant) that we think especially worthy of attention we can immediately give that individual a reward. Receiving the reward pleases the student, who will likely repeat the behavior in hopes of getting further reward. The process of supplying these rewards is called reinforcement.

Schedules of reinforcement were important in Skinner's experimental work. Different schedules were shown to produce different effects. Constant reinforcement, provided every time a desired act is seen is most effective in establishing new learnings. The individual works hard and fast to earn rewards. Once new learning is acquired it can be maintained indefinitely by using intermittent reinforcement, in which reward is supplied only occasionally. The individual knows that reward will come sooner or later, and keeps on trying.

Successive approximations simply means actions that come closer and closer to the goal in mind. You have to work toward many learnings and behaviors in gradual ways, taking one small step at a time. Successive approximations are small-step improvements leading to the overall learning. Teachers usually must reinforce the small improvements if the student is to progress.

Positive reinforcement is the process of supplying a reward that the student wants, something that will spur greater effort. For classroom purposes we needn't confuse ourselves about positive and negative reinforcement. We can simply call all rewards reinforcement.

Negative reinforcement is a term that is misunderstood by most classroom teachers. They think of negative as meaning harsh, some kind of punishment that will suppress behavior. Negative reinforcement increases the likelihood of behavior, just as positive reinforcement does. Negative means taking away something that the student doesn't like. That, in turn, increases learning and good behavior. It is easy to use negative reinforcement in the experimental laboratory with rats, but not easy to use it in school settings.

What Behavior Modification is Good For

Since the beginning of human history parents and teachers have used punishment to motivate learning in the young. Learners did what they were supposed to do or suffered harsh lectures, even beatings, from their teachers. This punitive system of motivation has persisted to the present day, and is still evident in some classrooms.

Skinner found in his experiments with learning that animals worked harder and learned more quickly if given rewards for doing something right than if given punishment for doing wrong. This made sense for rats and pigeons because we don't have any way to tell them what we want them to do. Punishment doesn't help them at all—it doesn't give them any guidance.

When the notion of providing rewards for doing something right was applied to school students an interesting fact came to light. Students, like rats and pigeons, responded better to positive rewards than they did to punishment. There were, and are, exceptions, but generally speaking, rewards spurred interest and effort. Moreover, they helped clarify what was expected.

Behavior modification is based almost entirely on rewards. It gives teachers power to work with students in positive ways. It lets them get away from harshness and punishment, which neither students nor teachers like. It allows them to maintain control within classroom environments that are warm, supportive, and positive, instead of cold, harsh, and punitive. This coincides with a growing trend toward humaneness in all walks of life.

Behavior modification, then, is good for speeding the learning of academic material as well as good personal behavior. It has the advantage of allowing the teacher to work in warm, supportive ways, emphasizing the positive and reducing the negative. It is also good for helping students build behavior that grows in small steps. A little reward for each step accomplished keeps the pigeon pecking and the boy writing.

The Dangers of Punishment

This discussion is giving punishment a black eye, as well it should, for the most part. However, a word must be said in defense of punishment before we go on to malign it further.

We need to realize that punishment is effective for stopping bad behavior. Positive reinforcement can be ineffective or too slow if, for instance, one student is beating another over the head with an encyclopedia. Life and limb cannot be adequately protected by finding a student who is sitting quietly and saying, "Thank you, Susan, for not hitting anyone with an encyclopedia." Instead, we must do whatever is necessary to stop the beating and suppress it permanently, even if that means punishing the offender.

On the other hand, we have found that while punishment suppresses unwanted behavior, it produces side effects that override our best educational intents. If the student sees punishment as unwarranted, malicious, or excessive, bad feelings result toward teacher, school, and classmates that are very hard to overcome. Those feelings may produce counterattacks, or sometimes withdrawal. Always they teach that might makes right, that muscle is more important than mind.

For those reasons we try to use punishment as little as possible, and to try the positive approach first. At the same time, we have to be realistic. Positive reinforcement doesn't tell a person what he is doing wrong. The first step in correcting misbehavior is to be sure that students know what they are doing wrong. The second step is to be sure they know how to do it right.

Punishment depicted as natural consequences is an effective middle ground between harsh punishment and positive reinforcement. Students are punished for misbehavior, but only after they have been fully informed of what is expected of them. They know how to behave acceptably and what will happen to them if they choose not to behave as desired. Then the punishment is seen as a natural consequence of inappropriate behavior, which the student voluntarily chooses.

Types of Reinforcers

Bear in mind that reinforcers, rewards, can be anything that an individual wants badly enough to do something to earn it. They can range from such mundane things as a breath of fresh air to such rarities as Pulitzer prizes. Many of the things that students want cannot be dispensed in school, and while that puts limitations on what teachers can use as reinforcers, they still have a powerful arsenal at their disposal. Reinforcers commonly used in schools fall into four categories: social, graphic, activity, and tangible.

Social reinforcers consist of words, gestures, and facial expressions. Many students work their fingers to the bone just to get a smile, a pat, a kind word from the teacher. How rewarding those winks can be, those nods, agreements, and thank you's. Some examples are:

† Verbal—OK. Wow! Excellent. Nice going. Exactly. Right. Thank you. I like that. Would you share that? Good for you.

† Nonverbal—Smiles, winks, eye contact, nods, thumbs up, touches, pats, walk beside, stand near, shake hands.

Graphic reinforcers include marks of various kinds, such as numerals, checks, happy faces, and special symbols. Teachers make these marks with felt pens and rubber stamps. They may enter them on charts. They may punch holes in cards kept by the students. They may attach stars or stick-ons that are available in quantity and variety.

Activity reinforcers include those activities that students prefer in school. Any school activity can be used as a reinforcer if students prefer it to another. Examples of activities that usually reinforce academic learning are:

† For younger students: Being a monitor, sitting near the teacher, choosing the song, caring for the pet, sharing a pet or toy.

† For middle students: Playing a game, free reading, decorating the classroom, having extra recess time, going to an assembly.

† For older students: Working with a friend, being excused from a test, working on a special project, being excused from homework.

Tangible reinforcers are real objects that students can earn as rewards for desired behavior. Such reinforcers are more powerful for some students than other types of reinforcers. They are widely used with students who have special behavior problems. Many elementary teachers use tangible reinforcers regularly. Examples of inexpensive reinforcers are: fruit, popcorn, peanuts, raisins, stapled notebooks, chalk, crayons, felt pens, pencils, badges, decals, pennants, used books, old magazines, stationery, posters, rubber stamps, certificates, notes, letters, and plastic tokens.

Systems of Behavior Modification

Behavior modification is best approached in a systematic way. Even if done randomly it works, but less effectively. A random approach has been used for decades, based on teachers' praising students for doing good work. That fact caused many teachers to say, when behavior modification was first being introduced, "But I've always done that." In truth, however, few teachers systematically reinforced as a means of shaping desired behavior. They used praise on a hit and miss basis. Behavior modification is maximally effective when used in an organized, systematic, consistent way.

Systems of behavior modification are legion. Every teacher adds a personal twist. Such flexibility is a strength because it allows teachers to apply reinforcement in ways that match their personalities and those of their students. The multitude of systems fit roughly into five categories: (1) informal "catch 'em being good," (2) rules-ignore-praise (RIP), (3) rules-praise-punishment (RPP), (4) contingency management, and (5) contracting. The following sections explain the nature and procedures of each.

Catch 'em being good. This approach rests solely on rewarding students who are doing what is expected. The teacher says, "Class, take out your math books." Several students get their books at once. Others waste time talking. The teacher picks out students who did as directed and says, "Thank you, Helen, for being ready. Thank you, Ted. I like the way Ramon got his book immediately." This strategy has two benefits. First, it reinforces the proper behavior of Helen, Ted, and Ramon, and second, it shapes behavior of other students. They quickly get out their books and are ready for math.

The catch-'em-being-good approach is highly effective in primary grades. Through third grade, teachers need use little else. In intermediate grades it begins to lose its effectiveness, and by junior high, students find it laughable. Other systems of behavior modification must be used for them.

Rules-Ignore-Praise. The RIP approach is used as follows. The teacher, perhaps in collaboration with the students, formulates a set of rules for class behavior. Those rules are made very clear and understandable to the students. They may be written on a chart and posted at the front of the room. This list is kept short—five or six rules. Students with practice and reminders can keep that many in mind.

Once the rules are established the teacher watches for people who are following them. Students who do so receive praise and every student is praised as often as possible. Student behavior that breaks the rules is ignored. That is, no direct attention is given to that student. No reinforcement comes from the teacher. Instead the teacher immediately finds a student who is following the rules and praises that student.

This system works well at the elementary level, but it is not good at the secondary level. Students speak derisively of peers who are receiving public praise, calling them pets and kiss-ups. Moreover, secondary students when misbehaving are not shaped well through praise given to others. They are already getting enough positive reinforcement in the form of peer attention, teacher attention, and laughter.

Rules-Reward-Punishment. The RPP approach builds limits and consequences into behavior modification. As with RIP, it begins with rules and emphasizes rewards. But it does not ignore inappropriate behavior. This added factor of limits and consequences makes this approach especially effective with older students and with students who have behavior problems.

The rules phase is the same as described earlier. Rules, as few in number as possible, are established, understood, and put on written display. The teacher becomes very directive about compliance. Students who follow the rules will be rewarded in various ways. They will receive praise, if appropriate. They will receive laudatory notes to take home to their parents. They will earn points that count toward a larger reward, either for the individual or for the class as a whole.

Students are clearly informed about what will happen if the rules are broken. They realize that they may choose to break the rules. That is their prerogative. But if they do so, they simultaneously choose the consequences that follow and punishers are invoked immediately, in accord with procedures described fully and carefully to the class. Thus, the teacher does not punish misbehavior; students punish themselves. They have chosen to behave in ways that bring undesired consequences.

This system is very effective with older students. It clearly sets expectations, rewards, and punishments. Students know they choose what they will receive and that the responsibility for good behavior rests directly on their shoulders. This approach is fully elaborated in chapter 9.

Contingency management. *Contingency management* involves an elaborate system of tangible reinforcers. It is especially effective with behavior-problem students and with the mentally retarded.

Often called *token economies,* contingency management systems use tokens that students earn for desired behaviors such as staying in their seats, raising their hands, finishing their work, improving over past performance, and so forth. The tokens may be exchanged for tokens of higher value. They may be cashed in for prizes such as food, toys, comic books, magazines, badges, privileges, and activities. In actual practice the tokens often become sufficiently reinforcing in themselves. Students have no desire to cash them in, preferring simply to have the tokens in their possession. Plastic discs and poker chips are often used for tokens. Discs of different colors are assigned different values. Some teachers print up play money in different denominations and special certificates of value.

Teachers who use token economies must be sure to award the tokens fairly and consistently. They must have an adequate supply of tokens, provide a manageable way for students to keep their tokens, and be sure that counterfeiting and extortion do not occur. They must set aside a time every few weeks for students to cash in their tokens. Students can buy white elephants that other students have brought from home, the teacher can obtain free materials from various shops and stores, and vouchers can be made available for special activities and privileges. Each object and voucher has its price in tokens. Some teachers like to have auctions, where students bid for the items available.

This plan should be explained carefully to the principal, the parents, and the students before it is implemented. That ensures that everyone approves and knows what is going on. It prevents many problems that might otherwise appear.

Contracting. The use of *contracts* has been quite successful, especially at the intermediate and secondary levels. Contracts specify work to be done or behavior to be established, with deadlines for completion. They indicate what the payoff will be for successful accomplishment. They tell what input the teacher will give. They lend an air of legality, promise, and responsibility. Student and teacher both sign the agreement. Sometimes parents cosign with the student.

Contract forms can be drawn on duplicating masters and quantities can be run off for later use. For older students quasi-legal terminology adds a pleasing touch, as do filigree and official stamps of gold foil or contact paper. While contracts are fun to use, they must be seen as serious commitments, the terms of which must be lived up to by all who have signed.

Taxonomy of Uses

David K. Gast has developed a taxonomy of uses for behavior modification that helps teachers implement their programs more effectively. His taxonomy includes the following functions: informal maintenance, informal facilitation, informal correction, systematic maintenance, systematic facilitation, and systematic correction. Here is what he meant by each of those uses.

1. Informal Maintenance—Aimed at behavior, but not at any specific problem. The teacher gives positive verbal reinforcers as students behave appropriately to maintain desired behavior.
2. Informal Facilitation—Aimed at class learning. Verbal reinforcers, smiles, and pats help students stay on task, complete their work, and contribute to discussions.
3. Informal Correction—Aimed at gentle shaping of behavior when students stray a bit from what is expected. The teacher uses verbal and behavioral reinforcers plus occasional simple tangible reinforcers.
4. Systematic Maintenance—Focused on class behavior. The teacher employs a systematic procedure of points, marbles, and so on, for rewarding desired behavior. This is done continually to reinforce self-control, manners, and courtesy.
5. Systematic Facilitation—Focused on learning. Points are awarded as students stay on task, complete work, and help others. The points enable the individual or group to earn privileges or desired activities.
6. Systematic Correction—Aimed at improving undesired behaviors. Points, tokens, and other tangibles are provided to students who abide by class rules. The points can be applied to a total for the class to be used to buy privileges and activities. Applying the points toward the class total brings peer pressure to bear on personal behavior.

Planning and Implementing Behavior Modification

Teachers who intend to use behavior modification should spend some time planning in advance. This planning requires two things: analysis of the behaviors you want to change, and implementing a specific plan for changing those behaviors.

Analysis. Analysis consists of identifying the behavior to be changed, deciding exactly what is wrong with it at present, and deciding what you would like it to be. Analysis should extend to *antecedents* and consequences. Antecedents are conditions in the classroom that encourage misbehavior. They might include distractions, boredom, poor models, awkward transitions between lessons, and so forth. Consequences are the results brought about by the inappropriate behavior. They are the rewards that reinforce the behavior, spurring it on. They might include attention from teacher and peers, gaining power through bullying, or getting one's own way.

Analysis of behavior can be done quickly, within fifteen minutes. Notes should be made as reminders of observations and decisions.

Implementation. Implementation is making the behavior modification plan and putting it into action. The plan follows from the analysis of behavior, and should be written in outline form, providing reminders of specific things to be done. It should mention target behavior, antecedents, and consequences. The plan is a guide for teacher use, but provisions can be made for students to use it, too.

Target behaviors are the new behaviors you want to see in the students. Systematic reinforcement shapes the behavior in the direction desired. If the target behavior is to stop talking out in class, you reward people who raise their hands and wait to be called on before they speak. You may decide to use verbal praise such as, "Thank you, Mary, for raising your hand." If the target behavior is to stay on task for the entire work period, you reward students for staying at work. The rewards are given frequently at first. Later, longer periods on task are needed to bring reward.

The plan calls for correcting antecedent conditions including uncertainty about rules, forgetfulness, poor peer models, inadequate teacher model, awkward times between lessons, poor pacing, boredom, frustration, and lack of interesting activities. When their interference is removed the plan has a much better chance of success.

Students who chronically misbehave are receiving rewards of some sort for their misbehavior. As previously mentioned, those rewards might include teacher and peer attention, laughter, sense of power, getting one's own way, and so forth. Those consequences must be changed so that misbehavior brings negative consequences rather than positive ones. Negative consequences range from ignoring (from both teachers and students) to isolation from the group. Positive consequences, meanwhile, must be supplied for desired behavior. You can always find someone doing what they are supposed to do, even by accident. You reinforce that person verbally, stating what it is they have done right. Example: "John, you got right to work. Good going." Then, as the chronically misbehaving person begins to show the first improvement, you make a point of reinforcing the behavior. Example: "Thank you, Sammy, for remembering to get right to work." Ordinarily teachers supply the reinforcers that shape desired behavior, but students can learn to reinforce each other. They can even learn to reinforce themselves. Students reinforce each other continually, but without intending to do so. Sometimes this reinforcement shapes behavior in desirable directions, sometimes in negative directions. When group effort is being rewarded by the teacher, peer pressure and reinforcement help shape desired behavior. Suppose, for example, that the class is earning points when everyone is on task. If a student begins to misbehave, the class stops receiving points. Peer pressure is quickly brought to bear to stop the misbehavior.

Students can learn to reinforce themselves, a tactic that is very powerful. Suggestions for self-reward have been put forth by several people, including Ogden Lindsley, Michael Mahoney, and Carl Thoresen.

Lindsley has popularized a technique called *precision teaching* which involves the graphing of student performance, whether academic or personal behavior. While the graph documents the performance it has a great additional advantage in the positive reinforcment that comes from the graphic evidence. As students see themselves improving, they strive to improve further, trying hard to surpass their previous achievements.

Older students can graph their own performances. In this way, they are providing their own rewards, reinforcing their own behavior. Students often outdo themselves to have the chance to chart improvements. They are proud to keep the graphs and show them to their parents.

Mahoney and Thoresen have described a system in which students set up their own systems of reward and punishment, which they apply as consequences to their own behavior. Kindergarten students who finish their art work may go on their own to the play area. Fifth graders who have not disrupted for the entire math period may go to the reinforcement area and pick up a permit for ten minutes of *free* reading. Secondary students who complete assignments accurately before they are due allow themselves to work together with a friend.

Self-rewarding is, of course, subject to misuse. Students won't always earn the reinforcement they select. In this event, teachers must first inspect the student's work or behavior, then signal an okay for reinforcement. The student then selects the reinforcer.

Behavior Mod Forever

Teachers who begin using behavior modification in a systematic way rarely stop. They love its powerful results. They come to see it not as manipulating students but as freeing them to behave in ways that bring success and positive recognition. Systematic attention and reinforcing become natural parts of the teaching act. They become automatic—after a while teachers don't even have to think of them. That natural spontaneity makes reinforcement even more effective. Students feel that the teacher is simply kind, considerate, and friendly, not designing or manipulative.

Teachers like what works; behavior modification works. It helps students and it makes teaching easier and more enjoyable. If you asked teachers to name the single most valuable control technique, many would doubtless say, "Behavior mod. Give me behavior mod forever."

References

Axelrod, S. *Behavior Modification for the Classroom Teacher.* New York: McGraw-Hill, 1977.

Becker, W. et al. *Teaching 1: Classroom Management.* Chicago: Science Research Associates, 1975.

Gast, D. in C. Charles, et al. *Schooling, Teaching, and Learning: American Education.* St. Louis, Mo.: C. V. Mosby, 1978.

Mahoney, M., and Thoresen, C. "Behavioral Self-Control—Power to the Person," *Educational Researcher* 1:5–7, 1972.

"Precision Teaching in Perspective: An Interview With Ogden R. Lindsley," *Teaching Exceptional Children* 3:114–119, Spring, 1971.

Skinner, B. F. *Walden Two.* New York: Macmillan, 1948.

———. *The Technology of Teaching.* New York: Appleton-Century-Crofts, 1968.

———. *Beyond Freedom and Dignity.* New York: Knopf, 1971.

Chapter 6

The Ginott Model: Addressing the Situation with Sane Messages

Haim Ginott, author and child psychologist. (*Photograph by United Press International Inc.*)

Ginott Biographical Sketch

Haim G. Ginott is best known for his book *Between Parent and Child* (1965). In that book and in a sequel, *Between Parent and Teenager* (1968), he offered solutions to communication breakdowns that occur between parents and their offspring. Ginott believed that adults vitally impact children's self-esteem through the messages they send. In an attempt to make that impact positive, he developed specific skills for dealing with parent-child conflicts. As a fundamental principle, Ginott emphasized addressing the situation while avoiding attacks on the child's character, that is, I like you, but I don't like what you are doing.

In a later book, *Teacher and Child* (1972), Ginott showed how those ideas could be extended to the classroom. Teachers, like parents, hold the power to make or break children's self-concept. *Teacher and Child* deals with methods of communication that maintain a secure, humanitarian, productive classroom environment.

Haim Ginott was born in Tel Aviv in 1922. He received his doctorate in education from Columbia University in 1952 and went on to become a professor of psychology at New York University Graduate School and a professor of psychotherapy at Adelphi University. He also served in Israel as a UNESCO consultant, was a resident psychologist on television's Today Show, and wrote a weekly syndicated column, entitled "Between Us," that dealt with interpersonal communication. Dr. Ginott died November 4, 1973.

Ginott's Key Ideas

The following is a list of key ideas advocated in Ginott's model of discipline. The remainder of the chapter elaborates on these concepts.
1. Discipline is a series of little victories.
2. The most important ingredient in discipline is the teacher's own self-discipline.
3. The second most important ingredient is using sane messages when correcting misbehaving students. Sane messages are messages that address the situation and do not attack children's characters.
4. Teachers at their best use congruent communication, communication that is harmonious with students' own feelings about situations and themselves.
5. Teachers at their worst attack and label students' characters.
6. Teachers should model the behavior they hope to see in their students.
7. Inviting cooperation from students is vastly preferable to demanding it.

8. Teachers should express anger but in appropriate (sane) ways.
9. Labeling students disables them.
10. Sarcasm is always dangerous; praise often is. Use both with great care.
11. Apologies from students should be accepted with the understanding that they intend to improve.
12. The best teachers help students to build their own self-esteem and to trust their own experience.

The Ginott Model of Discipline

Teachers are a decisive, powerful element in the classroom. They create and maintain its environment. They have the power to humanize or dehumanize their students. Their effectiveness depends on their ability to establish an emotional climate that promotes optimal learning. Children who are in constant emotional turmoil cannot learn. To reduce this turmoil, Ginott advocates using *congruent communication*, a way of talking that is harmonious and authentic in which teacher messages to students match the students' feelings about situations and themsleves. Ginott claims that the principle of congruent communication is the crucial factor in classroom climate. Teachers must constantly endeavor to use it. When they do so, they convey an attitude of helpfulness and acceptance and are continually aware of the impact of their messages on students' self-esteem. Congruent communication incorporates many different elements that we see expressed in Ginott's descriptions of teachers at their best and at their worst.

Teachers at Their Best/Worst

Ginott writes at length about teachers at their best and at their worst. At their best, they use congruent communication; at their worst, they do not. At their best, teachers strive to:
1. Send sane messages, addressing the situation rather than the child's character.
2. Express anger appropriately.
3. Invite cooperation.
4. Accept and acknowledge student feelings.
5. Avoid labeling (it is disabling).
6. Correct students by directing them appropriately.
7. Avoid the perils of praise.
8. Be brief when correcting students.
9. Be models of humane behavior.

At their worst, teachers:
1. Are caustic and sarcastic.

2. Attack children's character.
3. Demand cooperation.
4. Deny feelings.
5. Label the students as lazy, stupid, and so forth.
6. Give long and unnecessary lectures.
7. Lose their tempers.
8. Use praise to manipulate students.
9. Are poor models of humane behavior.

Let's look at some of Ginott's suggestions for helping teachers function at their best.

Sane Messages

Sane messages address situations rather than students' characters. They *accept* and acknowledge how students feel. Sanity, according to Ginott, depends on people's ability to trust their own perception of reality. Too often, adults send insane messages, telling children to distrust or deny their feelings or inner reality. They blame, preach, command, accuse, belittle, and threaten. In doing so, they tell children to deny their feelings about themselves and to rely on others for judgement of their self-worth.

Ginott repeatedly reiterates his cardinal principle of the sane message: when a child gets in trouble the teacher should always address the situation and never judge a child's character or personality. By simply describing the scene of concern, teachers allow students to appraise the situation, consider what is right and wrong, and decide how they feel about themselves.

Here is an example of a sane message. Two children are talking during a quiet time, violating class rules. The teacher says, "This is a quiet time. It needs to be absolutely silent." An insane message, according to Ginott, would be, "You two are being very rude. You have no consideration for others."

The way teachers respond to students shows how they feel about them. Responding can build or destroy self-concept. Poor teacher responses can contradict a student's perception of himself. Good teacher responses simply state the facts, letting children decide for themselves if their behavior is in keeping with their self-images.

Expressing Anger

Teaching is a tough job. Fatigue, frustration, and conflict make teacher anger inevitable. Most people, adults and students alike, expect teachers to be saints. This expectation, says Ginott, is wrong and self-defeating. Teachers should never deny human feelings, either their students' or their own. Their behaviors should always be genuine. That includes how they talk, behave, and respond to students. However, they need to learn to express anger, even displeasure, without damaging the student's character.

When situations arise that cause teachers to feel angry, they should simply (and sanely) describe what they see. They address the situation and tell how they feel about it. When telling how they feel, Ginott encourages the use of I-messages. "I am angry." "I am disappointed." These I-messages are much more appropriate expressions of anger than are you-messages. "You are no good." "You are lazy and messy." "You never think of anyone but yourself." I-messages tell how the teacher feels about the situation. You-messages attack the student.

When angry, good teachers state their demands clearly and firmly, avoiding language that insults or humiliates. Their messages are as brief as possible. It is important that they be good models of civilized behavior. When tempted to explode with wrath, they should ask themselves, "Am I dealing with anger in the same way I expect my students to? Am I modeling behavior I want to see replicated in my classroom?"

One last item about expressing anger. Ginott points out that an anger situation is one of those times when teachers have the full attention of students. They afford an opportunity to enrich vocabulary by expressing anger in eloquent terms, such as, "I am appalled, indignant, chagrined. I see inexcusable and intolerable behavior. I wish to terminate the situation at once." The teacher conveys two messages, one about the students' behavior and another about the power of descriptive language. Ginott notes that using words that students understand only vaguely increases the shock value of teacher expressions of anger.

Inviting Cooperation

We all depend on others, but if that dependency is too strong it creates problems. This is true when students are made too dependent on teachers. They often become lethargic and indecisive, even resentful and hostile. Ginott recommends reducing dependency problems by providing many opportunities for students to behave independently. One of the various ways Ginott suggests to promote independence is to present students with several solutions to a problem and let them decide on the one they want to adopt. This helps them feel they have some control over happenings in the classroom. They can also decide how they want to proceed in applying the solution they have chosen. Given these opportunities to make decisions they come to depend less on the teacher for motivation and direction. Too, they are more likely to live up to standards of behavior they have set for themselves.

Ginott urges teachers to invite cooperation rather than demand it. One of the ways to issue the invitation is to decide with the class before an activity is started what kinds of personal behavior are required during the activity. Another is to stop an activity that has gotten out of control and say, "We can watch the movie in silence, or we can do another math assignment. You decide." If the students continue to disrupt the activity, the teacher must follow through with the alternative, making it clear that it was the students' decision.

Teachers who don't invite cooperation must use ordering, bossing, and commanding. Ginott stresses the need to avoid direct commands, which almost always induce hostility. Again, Ginott says to describe the situation and let the students decide on their own what their course of action should be. Too often, teachers use long, drawn out directions or explanations such as, "Close your library books. Put them in your desks. Get out your math book. Get out a pencil. Turn to page 60. Start on the assignment." Ginott suggests a simple declaration such as, "It is now math time. The assignment is on page 60." With those kinds of messages, teachers show that they respect students' ability to behave autonomously. They invite cooperation, promote self-choice, and foster responsibility. Self-image increases with independent choice of productive behavior.

Accepting and Acknowledging Feelings

Students are in an awkward position in that they recognize that they have their own feelings about themselves and about situations, but at the same time are also told how they *should* feel by adults. Ginott sees teachers in a crucial position for helping students sort out feelings. Ginott would like to see teachers minimize student confusion by withholding their own opinions and merely acting as sounding boards for students with problems.

Young children's perception of reality is much different from that of adults. Youngsters routinely exaggerate the truth, and their opinions often have no base in reality. Teachers should not argue with children's perceptions, even when they are wrong. This only causes feelings of belittlement and rejection. Instead, teachers should strive to acknowledge and understand children's feelings. Here is an example. Suppose Juan comes running in from the playground crying, "Jose threw a ball at me and hit me in the head on purpose. Everyone started laughing at me. No one likes me." The teacher could argue with the child's experience and deny his feelings, saying, "That's silly. I'm sure it was an accident. The others were laughing at something else." Or she could respond with sympathy and understanding, offering no judgment of the situation. She could say, "You seem very upset. You feel that no one likes you. Your feelings are hurt when others laugh at you." In this way, the child's feelings are acknowledged and respected. He is not put on the defensive or told how he should feel.

Ginott suggests that the teachers add another comment to such situations: "How can I help you?" This provides an opportunity for the child to come up with a solution to the problem, and reveals the teacher's confidence in the child's ability to cope. By acknowledging feelings and offering to be helpful the teacher does not deny feelings, reject opinions, attack a child's character, or argue with a child's experience. Children must have an opportunity to decide how they feel and what they are going to do about it.

Children's fears are another matter that should be treated carefully. Adults have the tendency to make light of them. When they do this, they tell children that their feelings are not real. Adults also may cause them to believe that people are not supposed to feel that way. Ginott says to avoid the standard adult phrase, "There is nothing to be afraid of," which only makes children feel worse. They are now stuck with both the original fear and a new fear of showing fear. Telling children not to be afraid, angry, or sad does not dispel those emotions, but it does cause them to doubt their own inner feelings. It causes them to doubt the teacher's ability to understand, and teaches them that adults are not to be trusted during times of trouble.

Labeling is Disabling

By now you realize that Ginott is adamant about there being no place in the classroom for labels, diagnoses, or prognoses of students' character. Frequently, teachers are heard delivering statements such as, "You're lazy, irresponsible, and sloppy. You'll never amount to anything, if you don't change."

Labeling is disabling, Ginott avows, because it tells students how to think of themselves. When subjected to these messages often enough they begin to believe them. They start to live up to a negative self-image. This is especially true when adults attempt to predict a student's future. When teachers tell students to forget about going to college they may do just that. The very art of teaching demands that teachers open vistas, encourage growth and achievement, provide enlightenment, and stimulate imagination. Labeling and diagnosing a student's character only limits visions of the self and the future.

In difficult situations, teachers can avoid labeling, while striving to be helpful and encouraging. They can offer statements like, "Your grades are low, but I know if we work together we can improve them." "You want to be a veterinarian? Did you know there is a career information section in our media center?" Statements such as these do not tell students what you think they can or can't do. They encourage students to set goals for themselves and they assure them that the teacher will support and assist in the attainment of those goals. When teachers believe in students, the students begin to believe in themselves.

Correction is Direction

Through every day, situations arise in the classroom that require correcting comments from the teacher. Tim and Paul may throw erasers. A group of boys may discuss baseball at the listening table. Bryan is staring out of the window instead of doing his math. In these situations Ginott would recommend directing as a method of correcting. Teachers would describe the situation and then offer acceptable, alternative behavior. Often students simply need to be told what they could be doing differently. In the case of Tim and Paul the teacher might say, "Erasers are not for throwing. This is spelling time." Or, "There is too much conversation at the listening table. If you are finished there, return to your seat and take out a library book."

When correcting misbehavior, teachers should avoid attacking students' character. They should not rant and rave about what they dislike in it. When teachers tell what they see and suggest acceptable alternatives, students know how the teacher feels about the current behavior and exactly how they are supposed to behave differently. They become more likely to follow the teacher's suggestions and correct their behavior on their own.

Sarcasm

Ginott has a short word of advice for teachers who are tempted to use sarcasm in the classroom—don't. Many adults use sarcasm as a form of wit. Teachers often do so with students intending only to be clever and witty. More often than not, however, their sarcasm sounds clever only to themselves and not to the students receiving the comments. Too often sarcasm produces hurt feelings and damaged self-esteem. Students seldom understand sarcasm, and feel that they are being made fun of or belittled. It is better to avoid sarcasm altogether than to risk hurting feelings.

The Perils of Praise

Who would ever think that praise could damage a student's self-concept? Don't we all need to be told we are great, terrific, valuable? Ginott makes some provocative observations about praise. He does not deny its value, but he sees a danger there, too. The danger is that teachers can use it to manipulate students' feelings about themselves. As with negative comments, praise can have detrimental effects on forming a positive self-image. Ginott warns teachers about the use of judgmental praise—that is, praise that makes judgments about a student's character. Statements such as, "You're a good boy," or "You're terrific," create a dependence on others for approval and validation of self-worth.

Again, Ginott is emphatic about the importance of describing the circumstances and letting a student decide what behavior is appropriate. When praising, teachers need to concentrate on applauding specific acts without including adjectives about the personality.

An example of Ginott's point is seen in these comments that Mrs. Richards, a teacher, wrote on a student's paper: "This is an exceptional description of human emotions. This paper truly has poetic qualities." She did not make the mistake of attributing qualities of the paper to the student's personality. In that way she allows students to come to their own conclusions about themselves from the remarks on their papers.

Another way teachers use praise inappropriately is by telling students that they are good because they know the correct answer. A logical conclusion could then be drawn by other students—that they are bad because they don't know the answer. Ginott says, "Knowledge does not make one good. The lack of it does not make one bad." Appropriate responses for correct answers are, "Fine," "Exactly," or "That's correct." These comments carry no evaluation of the student's personality.

Praising good behavior has its drawbacks, too. When teachers praise students for behavior they are supposed to show it may appear that they are surprised by good behavior. This implies that they expect poor behavior. Sometimes, children decide to live up to negative expectations. Teachers should express their feelings of appreciation without words that evaluate the students' behavior. Ginott would have the teacher say, "Thank you for entering quietly," or "I enjoyed working with you in art today." He would not want them to say, "You were so good at the assembly," or "You can really behave if you want to." Ginott insists that evaluative praise inevitably puts teachers in a judgmental position. It causes them to appear condescending. Persons on a higher-status level are at liberty to praise those on a lower level, but not vice versa. Students would seem disrespectful if they said, "You're doing a fine job, Mr. Green. Keep it up." Since teachers are in a position of authority their value judgments carry much weight.

This evaluative praise can be used to manipulate student behavior. When teachers give profuse praise they are trying to assure repetition of a desired behavior. Students, especially older ones, sometimes resist such obvious manipulation. They feel that the praise is not sincere, but is only delivered to coerce them into desired behavior.

Praise is not a villain—used correctly, it can be productive. Such is the case when teachers describe their own feelings, or describe the efforts of students. They honestly recognize them without making value judgments about their personalities. Thus, praise should recognize and show appreciation for students' efforts yet let the students make their own evaluations about themselves. The function of praise is to support, motivate, and encourage, not to judge.

Discipline

Ginott describes discipline as "a series of little victories." It is not one thing that a teacher does one time. It is small step, ongoing, never ending. Ultimately it produces student concern, self-direction, and responsibility.

Teachers can influence behavior with threats and punishment, which generate ill will, rebellion, and subversive behavior. Or, they can influence behavior through compassion and understanding, which can turn volatile situations into victories for teachers and students alike. Students often misbehave in order to get reactions from adults. These negative reactions support students' negative opinions of themselves and also their opinions of adults. Good teachers choose words that do not confirm negative expectations.

Ginott states that the most important ingredient of effective discipline is the teacher's own self-discipline. Teachers do not lose their tempers, insult others, or resort to name calling. They are not rude, sadistic, or unreasonable. Instead, teachers strive to model the behavior they expect of students in their classrooms. They are polite, helpful, and respectful. They handle conflicts in a calm and productive manner. In the face of crisis, good teachers show reasonable behavior, not uncivilized responses. Children always wait and watch to see how adults handle difficult situations. You can bet that they will imitate the teacher's behavior.

Ginott presents many vignettes on discipline. His vignettes describe disciplinary methods that are inappropriate as well as those that are appropriate. Teachers using inappropriate discipline:

1. Lose their tempers. Example: Resort to shouting, slamming books, and using verbal abuse.
2. Resort to name calling. Example: "You are like pigs!" "Clean that up!"

3. Insult students' character. Example: "Johnny, you are nothing but lazy!"
4. Demonstrate rude behavior. Example: "Sit down and shut up!"
5. Overreact. Example: Mary accidentally drops a sheaf of papers she is handing out. Teacher: "Oh for heaven's sake! Can't you do anything right?"
6. Display cruelty. Example: "Watch carefully on your way home from school, Jack. You're a little bit short on brains."
7. Punish all for the sins of one. Example: "Since certain people couldn't listen during the assembly, we will have to miss the next one."
8. Threaten. Example: "If I hear one more voice, we will all stay in at recess."
9. Deliver long lectures. Example: "It has come to my attention that several students think the trash can is a basketball hoop. We can throw things on the playground. In the classroom. . . ."
10. Back students into a corner. Example: "What are you doing? Why are you doing that? Don't you know any better? Apologize at once!"
11. Make arbitrary rules. These rules involve no student discussion or input.

Teachers using appropriate discipline:
1. Recognize feelings. Example: "I can see that you are angry because you have to stay after school."
2. Describe the situation. Example: "I see coats all over the closet floor. They need to be hung up."
3. Invite cooperation. Example: "Let's all help to be quiet, so we can go to the puppet show."
4. Are brief. Example: "We do not throw paper."
5. Don't argue. They stick to a decision, but remain flexible enough to change it if they are wrong. Arguing is always a losing proposition.
6. Model appropriate behavior. They always show through example how they want students to behave.
7. Discourage physical violence. Example:"In our class we talk about our problems. We do not hit, kick, or pull hair."
8. Do not criticize, call names, or insult. Example: A child interrupts the teacher's conversation. Teacher: "Excuse me. I will be with you as soon as I finish this conversation."
9. Focus on solutions. Example: "I am seeing unsportsmanlike conduct on the playground. What can we do about that?"
10. Allow face saving exits. Example: "You may remain at your desk and quietly do spelling, or you may sit by yourself in the back of the room."

11. Allow the children to set their own standards. Example: "What do we need to remember when we are using paint?"
12. Are helpful. Example: Matthew: "Roger and Joe are teasing me!" Teacher: "You sound upset. What would you like me to do?"
13. De-escalate conflicts. Example: Student (crumpling a paper): "I'm not going to do this assignment. It's too hard!" Teacher: "You feel this assignment is too difficult. Would you like me to go over a few problems with you?"

Summary of Ginott's Views

It is a teacher's job to provide an environment conducive to optimal learning. An important part of this environment is the social-emotional atmosphere in the classroom. Teachers must be aware of students' feelings. They must realize that their messages have strong impact on students' feelings and self-esteem.

Ginott believes teachers can be most effective if they strive to use congruent communication—language that fits situations and feelings. When teachers learn to address a situation instead of attacking a child's character, they communicate (1) that they know what is happening, (2) what they want changed, and (3) that they are aware of the student's feelings. They do not tell children how to feel about themselves or the situation.

Teachers should always be aware of emotions, both in themselves and in their students. When angry, they should express their anger, but in a calm and productive manner. By doing so they teach children how to handle their own anger. When children express emotions, they should never be denigrated or punished. Teachers should simply describe the emotions they see with statements like, "I know that you are upset," or "Sometimes your feelings get hurt when others are thoughtless." When teachers recognize emotions in themselves and their students, they teach students to recognize and deal with their emotions in a constructive way.

Teachers should keep in mind that students are people, too. Being bossed or labeled gives students justification for being rebellious or hostile. Teachers should provide choices, ask for cooperation rather than demand it, and always offer to be helpful. They should think to themselves, "How do I want my students to relate to me and each other?" They should always be the best model of behavior they want to see in their classrooms.

References

Ginott, H. *Between Parent and Child*. New York: Avon Books, 1965.
_____ . *Between Parent and Teenager*. New York: Macmillan, 1969.
_____ . *Teacher and Child*. New York: Macmillan, 1971.

Chapter 7

The Glasser Model: Good Behavior Comes from Good Choices

William Glasser, M.D., President, Institute for Reality Therapy, Los Angeles.
(Photograph courtesy of the Institute for Reality Therapy.)

Glasser Biographical Sketch

William Glasser, a Los Angeles psychiatrist, has received national acclaim in both psychiatry and education. His book *Reality Therapy: A New Approach To Psychiatry* shifted a long-standing focus in treating behavior problems. Instead of seeking to uncover the conditions in one's past that contribute to inappropriate behavior (the psycho-analytic approach), Glasser attends to the present, to the reality of the situation. He believes it is what one does right now that matters, and that this present reality is what psychiatrists should deal with.

Glasser extended his ideas in *reality therapy* to the school arena. His work with recalcitrant students further convinced him that teachers can help students make better choices about their school behavior. Teachers should never excuse bad student behavior. Poor background or undesirable living conditions do not exempt students from their responsibility to learn and behave properly in school. This point of view together with practical advice for carrying it out forms the core of Glasser's book *Schools Without Failure* (1969), one of the more influential educational books of recent times.

William Glasser was born in Cleveland, Ohio in 1925. He first became a chemical engineer, later turning to psychology and then to psychiatry. Since 1957 he has been in California working in private practice, assisting in correctional agencies, developing programs in school districts, and lecturing widely about his ideas for working with school students.

Glasser's Key Ideas

The following points are keys to understanding Glasser's views on classroom discipline, which are elaborated in the remainder of the chapter.

1. Students are rational beings. They can control their behavior.
2. Good choices produce good behavior. Bad choices produce bad behavior.
3. Teachers must forever try to help students make good choices.
4. Teachers who care accept no excuses for bad behavior.
5. Reasonable consequences should always follow student behavior, good or bad.
6. Class rules are essential. They must be enforced.
7. Classroom meetings are effective vehicles for attending to matters of class rules, behavior, and discipline.

The Glasser Model

Glasser's views about discipline are simple but powerful. Behavior is a matter of choice: good behavior results from good choices and bad behavior results from bad choices. A student's duty is to make good choices. A teacher's duty is to help students make those good choices.

Many educators, psychologists, and psychiatrists look into peoples' backgrounds for underlying causes of inappropriate behavior. Psychoanalysts delve far back into infancy and early childhood. Psychologists and educators look into the social environments within which people live. They search there for conditions that cause people to behave inappropriately in school.

Often you will hear teachers say, "What can you expect? Sammy comes from a broken home." Or, "Sara was an abused child." Or, "Edmund's family lives in poverty." Glasser does not deny that such conditions exist, or that they influence behavior. He simply says that humans, unlike dogs and parakeets, have rational minds and can make rational choices. They can understand what acceptable school behavior is and they can choose to behave in acceptable ways.

But to make good choices students must come to see the results of those choices as desirable. If bad behavior choices get them what they want, they will make bad choices. That's where the teacher comes in—helping students see that they are choosing to act the ways they do. The teacher forces them to acknowledge their behavior and make value judgments about it. The teacher refuses to accept excuses for bad behavior, always directing attention instead to what would be more acceptable.

Glasser's model of discipline is built around those basic ideas. Behavior is a matter of choice; background and poor upbringing do not make poor behavior acceptable. Students choose to act the way they do, and teachers can help students make better choices. The essence of discipline is helping students make good choices.

What School Offers

School offers students a chance to be successful and to be recognized for that success. It offers many students the only chance they have for genuine esteem, love, and the resultant feeling of self-worth. Self-worth produces success identity. Success identity mitigates deviant behavior, and the road to success identity begins with a good relationship with people who care. For students who come from atrocious backgrounds, school may offer the only chance to find a person genuinely interested in them.

Yet students often resist entering into quality relationships. They may fear teachers, distrust adults in general, or obtain peer rewards by disdaining teachers. Teachers must thus be very persistent. They must never desist in their efforts to help students, which is how they best show that they care. Glasser repeatedly points out that students can't begin to make better, more responsible choices until they become deeply involved emotionally with people who can, with people such as teachers.

What Teachers Should Do

Glasser sees a teacher's role in discipline as:
1. Stressing student responsibility continually.
2. Establishing rules that lead to class and individual success.
3. Accepting no excuses for bad behavior.
4. Calling on students when they misbehave to make value judgments about their behavior.
5. Identifying suitable alternatives to bad behavior.
6. Ensuring that reasonable consequences naturally follow whatever behavior the student chooses.
7. Persisting always; never giving up.
8. Continually reviewing rules, responsibilities, and problems within classroom meetings.

Let us examine what Glasser advises within each of these role elements.

1. Student Responsibility is Stressed Continually.

Since good behavior comes from good choices, and since students ultimately must live with the choices they make, their responsibility for their own behavior is always kept in the forefront.

Discussions in which this responsibility is explored and clarified occur in classroom meetings. These meetings (See number 8) occur as regular parts of the curriculum. Students sit in a tight circle with the teacher and discuss matters that concern the class.

Throughout the school day the teacher calls attention, directly and indirectly, to the responsibilities discussed in the classroom meeting. This continual attention to student responsibility accomplishes two things, both essential in Glasser's view of good discipline. First, it emphasizes that good behavior is good choice, which students can and should make. Second, it cements the caring bond between teacher and student. Bit by bit the message gets through that the teacher truly cares about students and their good behavior.

2. Rules are Established That Lead to Class and Individual Success.

Glasser considers class rules to be essential. He writes disparagingly of programs and classes that attempt to operate without rules, in the mistaken belief that rules stifle initiative, responsibility, and self-direction. He stresses that rules are especially essential for students who have done poorly in school. Permissiveness for them tends to be destructive. It fosters antagonism, ridicule, and lack of respect for teachers and others.

Rules should be established by teachers and students together, and should facilitate personal and group achievement. They should be adapted to the age, ability, and other realities of the students. One thing is essential: rules must always reinforce the basic idea that students are in school to study and learn. Furthermore, rules should constantly be evaluated to see whether they are useful. When no longer useful they should be discarded or changed. So long as they are retained, however, they must be enforced.

3. No Excuses are Accepted for Bad Behavior.

For discipline to be successful, Glasser says, teachers must accept no excuses. He uses this no-excuse dictum in two areas. The first has to do with conditions outside the school. What goes on there does not excuse bad behavior in school. They may, indeed, cause bad behavior, but that doesn't make it acceptable. The teacher must never say, "We can excuse Bill's behavior today because he has had trouble at home. It's okay if he yells and hits."

The second area in which Glasser says teachers should accept no excuses concerns student commitment. Once a student has decided on a course of good behavior and has made a commitment to it, the teacher must never accept excuses for the student's failing to live up to that commitment. A teacher who accepts an excuse says, *in effect,* that it is all right to break a commitment, that it is all right for students to harm themselves. Teachers who care, Glasser says, accept no excuses.

4. Students are Called on to Make Value Judgments about Their Bad Behavior.

When students exhibit inappropriate behavior, teachers should have them make value judgments about it. Glasser suggests the following procedure when a student is misbehaving:

Teacher:	"What are you doing?" (asked in warm, personal, unthreatening voice)
Student:	(Will usually give an honest answer, if not threatened.)
Teacher:	"Is that helping you or the class?"
Student:	"No."
Teacher:	"What could you do that would help?"
Student:	(Names better behavior. If can think of none, teacher suggests appropriate alternatives and lets student choose.)

By following this procedure consistently, teachers can cause students to doubt the value of their misbehavior, make better choices responsibly, and thus gradually make a commitment to choosing behaviors that bring personal success instead of failure.

5. Suitable Alternative Behaviors are Identified.

Misbehaving students will sometimes be unable to think of appropriate behaviors they might select. The teacher should then suggest two or three acceptable alternatives. The student chooses one and reinforces the notion of choice and responsibility.

The student is then expected to abide by the choice made. The teacher accepts no excuses for not doing so, although if the choice proves untenable the student is allowed to make another choice.

6. Natural Consequences Must Follow Whatever Behavior the Student Chooses.

Glasser stresses that reasonable consequences must follow whatever behavior the student chooses. These consequences will be desirable if good behavior is chosen. They must be undesirable if poor behavior is chosen.

Never, says Glasser, should teachers manipulate events so that these reasonable consequences do not occur as a natural course of events. If the student consciously selects an inappropriate behavior that calls for, let us say, isolation from the group, then isolation should occur promptly, without exception. Natural and reasonable consequences of bad behavior should not be physically punishing, nor should they employ caustic language, ridicule, or sarcasm. They must be undesirable, however, something unpleasant to the student. On the other hand, consequences of good behavior should be pleasant or personally satisfying in some way.

The knowledge that behavior always brings consequences and that individuals can largely choose behavior bringing pleasant as opposed to unpleasant consequences builds the sense that people are in charge of their own lives and in control of their own behavior.

7. Teachers are Persistent: They Never Give Up.

Caring teachers work toward one major goal—getting students to commit themselves to desirable courses of behavior. Commitment means constancy. It means doing something repeatedly, intentionally, sure that it is right. It doesn't mean doing that thing part of the time and not doing it part of the time.

To convey this idea and to help implant it in students, teachers themselves must be constant. They must always help students make choices. They must always have them make value judgments about their bad choices. They must always see tomorrow as a new day and be willing to start again. In short, caring teachers never give up in helping their students toward self-discipline. Even when progress is slow, they persevere because they know it is the students' best hope for ultimately gaining maturity, respect, and an identity of success.

8. Rules, Responsibilities, and Problems are Continually Reviewed in Classroom Meetings.

At the heart of his views about discipline Glasser places what he calls the classroom meeting. A classroom meeting is a whole-class discussion of topics relevant to the students. It explores problems and suggests solutions; it does not place blame. It is carried out with students and teacher seated in a close circle, an arrangement that has come to be known as the Glasser circle.

Glasser advocates three types of classroom meetings. He would have them all be as regular a part of the curriculum as English or math. The three types of classroom meetings are Social problem-solving meetings, Educational diagnostic meetings, and Open-ended meetings. The first of these meetings attempts to solve problems that arise among people living and working within the school setting. It is a natural place to consider matters related to discipline. The second type has to do with problems of curriculum, instructional activities, and learning. The third deals with any topic of intellectual concern to the students.

Discussions within classroom meetings deal with two things only—identifying the problem and seeking plausible solutions. Students are never allowed to find fault with, place blame on, or seek to punish others. Students are encouraged to make judgments about the matters under consideration. The teacher stays in the background, giving opinions sparingly and participating in a way that reflects student attitudes back to the group for examination. Glasser stresses that the meetings require practice in order to be successful, and that unless they are openly focused on finding solutions they will surely fail.

Glasser Revisited

Up to this point, the ideas presented in Glasser's model of discipline were all put forth in *Schools Without Failure*. More than a decade has passed since its publication. One naturally wonders whether his views have remained constant since so many social changes have occurred during the intervening years. Through 1977 Glasser had changed his views little if at all. He summarized them succinctly in his article "10 Steps to Good Discipline," which appeared in *Today's Education* (November-December, 1977).

In that article Glasser made the point that his suggestions work only in school situations within which students choose to be. That is, they don't work well if students are being held against their wills, which unfortunately they are in some cases. Given a group of students who are not actively struggling against being in school, teachers have a good chance to establish excellent discipline. They must begin by striving to make school a good place to be where, Glasser says, they provide, support, and promote the following conditions:

1. *People are courteous.* Adults have the main responsibility. They do not, nor do they allow students to, yell, denigrate others, or use sarcasm.
2. *The sounds of joy are heard.* These sounds come not from frivolity but from the excitement and pleasure of significant learning and purposeful working together.
3. *Helpful communication is practiced.* People talk with each other, instead of at each other.
4. *Reasonable rules exist, to which everyone agrees.* These rules make group work maximally efficient and enjoyable for everyone. They are flexible and everyone has a say in formulating them.
5. *School administrators actively participate in a system of discipline that teaches self-responsibility.* They themselves model desired behavior. They support efforts of teachers. And always try to help students take responsibility for their own behavior.

Glasser reiterates specific duties of teachers in fostering "good places" and student self-responsibility. He reminds teachers to:

- *Be personal.* Say, "I care enough to get involved."
- *Refer to present behavior.* The past does not count.
- *Stress value judgments.* Have students evaluate their behavior.
- *Plan alternatives.* Work with students to develop better behaviors and allow them time to prove themselves.
- *Be committed.* Follow up; check back; pay attention; reinforce.
- *Don't accept excuses.* Don't allow students to make excuses. Instead, help them replan their behavior.
- *Don't punish.* Make students be responsible. Punishment lifts responsibility from them. They should make restitution and replan their behavior.
- *Never give up.* Hang in there longer than students expect you to. Firm results take between one and two months to achieve.

These principles constitute a general way of dealing with students.

Glasser also makes explicit suggestions for dealing with misbehavior. His 1977 article goes into greater detail than did *Schools Without Failure.* Previously, teachers were left wondering what to do if students defied them when asked to make value judgments about their behavior. Glasser clarifies the procedure:

A. Student is misbehaving.

Teacher: What are you doing? Is it against the rules? What should you be doing?

Student responds in negative, rather than positive way.

Teacher: I would like to talk with you privately at (time).

B. Private conference between teacher and student.

Teacher: (repeats) What were you doing? Was it against the rules? What should you have been doing?

C. Student later repeats the misbehavior.

Teacher calls for another private conference.

Teacher: We have to work this out. What kind of plan can you make so that you will follow our rules?

Student: I'll stop doing it.

Teacher: No, we need a plan that says exactly what you *will do*. Let's make a simple plan that you can follow. I'll help you.

D. Student later repeats misbehavior; does not abide by own plan.

Teacher assigns student "time out." This is isolation from the group. Student is not allowed to participate with group again until making a committment to the teacher to adhere to the plan.

If student disrupts during time out, he is excluded from the classroom. (A contingency plan should be set up in advance with the principal.)

E. Student, after returning to class, disrupts again.

Teacher: Things are not working out here for you and me. We have tried hard. You must leave the class. As soon as you have a plan you are sure will allow you to follow the rules of the class, let me know. We can try again. But for now, please report to the principal's office. (Principal was informed in advance of this possibility.)

F. If student is out of control, principal notifies parents and asks them to pick up student at school, immediately.

G. Students who are repeatedly sent home are referred to a special school or class, or to a different community agency.

Throughout, Glasser's confrontation plan stresses these elements: (1) positive approach, (2) simple plan of behavior, (3) responsibility placed on the student, and (4) willingness of the teacher to help. At the same time, teachers do not accept excuses for misbehavior, nor do they cave in to disruptive pressure from students.

In short, teachers do their best to help students behave successfully. But when their efforts fail, the misbehaving student should be removed from the class. Learning must not be disrupted for anyone. This emphasis on helping, together with the acknowledgement that a large part of discipline is the student's responsibility, makes Glasser's model of discipline an attractive one for teachers.

References

Glasser, W. *Reality Therapy: A New Approach to Psychiatry*. New York: Harper and Row, 1965.

_____ . *Schools Without Failure*. New York: Harper and Row, 1969.

_____ . "10 Steps to Good Discipline," *Today's Education*, November-December, 1977.

Chapter 8

The Dreikurs Model: Confronting Mistaken Goals

Rudolf Dreikurs, M.D. (*Photograph courtesy of Alfred Adler Institute, Chicago, Ill.*)

Dreikurs Biographical Sketch

Rudolf Dreikurs was born in Vienna February 8, 1897. After receiving his M.D. from the University of Vienna he began a long association with the renowned psychiatrist Alfred Adler. Their studies dealt with family and child counseling. Rudolf Dreikurs came to the United States in 1937, and eventually became the director of the Alfred Adler Institute in Chicago. He was also a professor of psychiatry at Chicago Medical School. He continued to focus on family-child counseling throughout his career. Dreikurs became known as an expert in the field of classroom behavior through his books *Psychology in the Classroom* (1957), *Maintaining Sanity in the Classroom* (1971), and *Discipline Without Tears* (1972). These books are valuable to teachers for their explanations of motivation behind student behavior. They also provide information for dealing with student behavior. Dr. Dreikurs died May 31, 1972.

Dreikurs' Key Ideas

1. Discipline is not punishment. It is teaching students to impose limits on themselves.
2. Democratic teachers provide firm guidance and leadership. They allow students to have a say in establishing rules and consequences.
3. All students want to belong. They want status and recognition. All of their behaviors indicate efforts to belong.
4. Misbehavior reflects the mistaken belief that it will gain students the recognition they want.
5. Misbehavior is associated with four mistaken goals: attention getting, power seeking, revenge, and desire to be left alone.
6. Teachers should identify mistaken goals and then act in ways that do not reinforce them.
7. Teachers should strive to encourage students' efforts, but avoid praising their work or characters.
8. Teachers should teach students that unpleasant consequences will always follow inappropriate behavior.

The Nature of Discipline

Discipline is essential to smooth functioning in schools and society. Too often adults have an either-or concept of discipline. Either children behave, or they walk all over you. Most people think of discipline as punishing actions used against children in times of conflict or misbehavior.

Children form stereotyped ideas about discipline, too. Generally, they see it as arbitrary rules set up by adults to show who is in charge. They may view discipline as a complex game with rules they don't understand. Some see it as punishment given without reason. These children soon decide that being punished justifies retaliation, rebellion, and hostility.

Discipline is not punishment. Punishment is physical pain, humiliation, isolation, and revenge; it is a force imposed on one from an outside source. Dreikurs claims that "it teaches what not to do, but fails to teach what to do."

Discipline requires freedom of choice and the understanding of consequences. It is not imposed by authority figures, but rather, on individuals by themselves. By choosing to behave in certain ways individuals learn to gain acceptance from others and, consequently, acceptance of themselves.

Discipline in the classroom means setting limits for students until they are able to set limits for themselves. It involves allowing students freedom to choose their own behavior. They can do this because they understand exactly what consequences will follow any behavior chosen. Good behavior brings rewards. Poor behavior *always* brings undesired consequences. When teachers teach this concept to students they are teaching students to behave in ways that are acceptable to society. This helps students promote their own welfare in all living situations.

Teaching self-discipline requires a positive, accepting atmosphere. Students must feel the teacher likes and respects them. They must understand that the teacher wants what is best for them. Students must also be allowed input into establishing rules and consequences. They should always understand the reasons for rules because this allows a sense of personal commitment and involvement. It provides recognition of the need for limits.

Dreikurs believes that establishing discipline in the classroom must involve teaching the following concepts:

1. Students are responsible for their own actions.
2. Students must respect themselves and others.
3. Students have the responsibility to influence others to behave appropriately.
4. Students are responsible for knowing what the rules and consequences are in their classroom.

Dreikurs also believes that teachers who are most effective in establishing discipline are those who teach democratically. Let's explore the qualities of different types of teachers.

Types of Teachers

Autocratic teachers force their will on students to prove they have control of the class. They motivate students with outside pressure instead of stimulating motivation from within. They need to feel power and a sense of superiority over students. This attitude and approach tend to perpetuate problem behavior. More and more, students are rejecting authority figures. They seek a democratic atmosphere in which they are treated as human beings and react with hostility to the autocratic teacher.

Permissive teachers are equally ineffective. They, too, generate problem behavior because the atmosphere they allow is not based on everyday reality. Students in a permissive classroom are not learning that living in society requires following rules. They are not learning that failure to follow rules results in consequences. They do not learn that acceptable behavior requires self-discipline. They are confused because they believe they can do whatever they want, and yet things do not go smoothly for them.

Discipline and control must be present in classrooms if learning is to occur. Students *want* guidance and leadership. They are willing to accept guidance if it is not forced on them and if they believe they are being listened to. This does not mean they want to run the show.

Democratic teachers are neither permissive nor autocratic. They provide firm guidance and leadership by establishing rules and consequences. They motivate students from within. They maintain order and at the same time, they allow students to participate in decision making. Democratic teachers teach that freedom is tied to responsibility. They allow students freedom to choose their own behavior. They also teach students that they must suffer the consequences if they choose to misbehave. In this way, students learn to behave in ways that get them what they want.

Students who fail to develop self-discipline limit their choices. They choose inappropriate behavior because they do not understand that it always brings negative consequences. Freedom grows from discipline. If students understand that consequences follow behavior they are freer to choose behavior that will get them what they want. Discipline involves teaching students to establish inner controls that allow them to choose behavior compatible with their best interests. Teaching self-discipline eliminates the need for constant corrective actions by the teacher.

The following are key elements established by Dreikurs to foster a democratic classroom. Democracy requires:

1. Order.
2. Limits.

3. Firmness and kindness. Firmness from teachers shows they respect themselves. Kindness shows they respect others.
4. Student involvement in establishing and maintaining rules.
5. Leadership from the teacher.
6. Inviting cooperation—eliminating competition.
7. A sense of belonging to a group.
8. Freedom to explore, discover, and choose acceptable behavior through understanding the responsibilities and consequences associated with it.

Remember: Autocratic teachers motivate from without. Democratic teachers motivate from within.

Mistaken Goals

Dreikurs makes three very strong points in his writings. First, students are social beings who want to belong. All of their actions reflect their attempts to be significant and gain acceptance. Second, students can choose to behave or misbehave. Their behavior is not outside their control. Putting these two beliefs together, Dreikurs makes his third point: students choose to misbehave because they are under the mistaken belief that it will get them the recognition they seek. Dreikurs calls these beliefs mistaken goals.

All people want to belong, to have a place. They try all kinds of behavior to see if it gets them status and recognition. If they do not receive recognition through socially acceptable means they turn to mistaken goals, which produce antisocial behavior. Antisocial behavior reflects the mistaken belief that misbehavior is the only way to receive recognition.

Dreikurs identified four mistaken goals: *attention getting, power seeking, revenge seeking,* and *desire to be left alone.* These goals identify the purposes of student misbehavior. They are usually sought in sequential order. If attention getting fails to gain recognition, the student will progress to power-seeking behavior. If that is not rewarded they move on to getting revenge, and then to seclusion. Let's examine each of these mistaken goals more closely.

Attention Getting

When students discover that they are not getting the recognition they desire, they may resort to getting attention through misbehavior. These students are trying to seek proof of acceptance through what they can get others to give them, in this case, attention. They want the teacher to pay attention to them and provide them with extra services. They disrupt, ask special favors, continually need help with assignments, refuse to work unless the teacher hovers over them, or ask irrelevant questions. Some good students can also make unusual bids for attention. They can function only as long as they have the teacher's approval. If this approval is not forthcoming, they may resort to less acceptable ways of getting attention.

Giving attention to misbehaving students does not improve their behavior, it reinforces it. Their need for attention increases. Furthermore, it causes them to be motivated by outside forces, rather than from within.

If attention-getting behavior does not provide students the recognition they seek, they will turn to the next mistaken goal, power.

Power Seeking

Power-seeking students feel that defying adults is the only way they can get what they want. Their mistaken belief is: if you don't let me do what I want, you don't approve of me. A need for power is expressed by arguing, contradicting, lying, temper tantrums, and hostile behavior. If these students can get the teacher to fight with them they *win*, because they succeed in getting the teacher into a power struggle. Whether or not they actually get what they want doesn't matter. What does matter is that they upset the teacher. Should the teacher win the contest of wills, it only causes the student to believe more firmly that power is what matters in life. If students lose these power struggles, they move on to more severe misbehavior, getting revenge.

Revenge Seeking

Students have failed to gain status through getting attention or establishing power. Their mistaken goal now becomes: I can only feel significant if I have the power to hurt others. Hurting others makes up for being hurt.

Students who seek revenge set themselves up to be punished. They are vicious, cruel, and violent. When adults punish them, they have renewed cause for revenge. The more trouble they cause for themselves, the more justified they feel. They consider it a victory to be disliked.

Underneath their bravado, these individuals are deeply discouraged. Their behavior only elicits more hurt from others. They feel totally worthless and unlovable, and these feelings cause them to withdraw to the next mistaken goal, a desire to be left alone.

Desire to be Left Alone

At this level students feel entirely hopeless, and see themselves as total failures. There is no need to try anymore. They withdraw from any situation that can cause further feelings of failure. They guard what little self-esteem they have left by removing it from tests. Their mistaken belief is: if everyone leaves me alone, nobody will discover how worthless I am.

Students with this goal play stupid. They refuse to respond to motivation and passively refuse to participate in classroom activities. They don't interact with anyone. Dreikurs calls them "blobs." This goal is very difficult for students and teachers to overcome.

All of the mistaken goals are based on the belief that they provide a way to achieve significance. Most mistaken goals are pursued one at a time, but some students switch from goal to goal.

What Can Teachers Do?

The first thing teachers can do is identify the student's mistaken goal. The easiest way for teachers to do this is to note their own responses to the misbehavior. Their responses indicate what type of expectations the student has. If teachers feel:

- Annoyed, it indicates attention-getting behavior.
- Defeated or threatened, it indicates power seeking behavior.
- Hurt, it indicates revenge.
- Helpless and defeated, it indicates students' desire to be left alone.

Another way to identify mistaken goals is to observe students' reactions to being corrected.

If they:	Then their goal is:
1. Stop the behavior and then repeat it	getting attention.
2. Refuse to stop or increase the behavior	power seeking.
3. Become violent or hostile	getting revenge.
4. Refuse to cooperate, participate, or interact	desire to be left alone.

After the teacher has identified the mistaken goals, they should confront students and point out their faulty logic. By doing this in a friendly, nonthreatening way, teachers can usually get students to examine the purposes behind their behavior.

Dreikurs would have teachers ask students the following questions, in order, and observe reactions that might indicate a mistaken goal:

1. Could it be that you want me to pay attention to you?
2. Could it be that you want to prove that nobody can make you do anything?
3. Could it be that you want to hurt me or others?
4. Could it be that you want me to leave you alone?

These questions have three effects. They open up communication between teacher and student, they improve behavior because they remove the fun of provoking the teacher, and they take the initiative away from the student, allowing the teacher to implememt actions to change behavior.

When teachers know which mistaken goals are being acted on they can begin to take action that will defeat the student's purposes and initiate new, constructive behavior. Here is what Dreikurs recommends teachers do in each case of mistaken goals.

Attention Getting

When teachers discover students operating under the mistaken goal of attention getting, they can either agree to go on giving attention, or they can refuse to grant attention or services by ignoring students when they are bidding for attention. Students who seek attention cannot tolerate being ignored. They would rather be punished, belittled, or humiliated, anything as long as they are getting someone to give them something. So, they create behavior that cannot be ignored by the teacher. Teachers who fall for this behavior nag, coax, scold, and otherwise reinforce the student's need for attention.

When teachers perceive that students are making undue bids for attention they should consistently and without fail ignore all such behavior. If they do so, the students will not get what they need from their behavior and will be forced to find new ways to gain recognition.

In addition to ignoring, teachers should strive to give attention to these students any time they are not demanding it. This encourages students to develop motivation from within instead of depending on attention from without.

Sometimes it is not feasible for teachers to ignore behavior that is disrupting the class. In these cases, teachers need to give attention in ways that are not rewarding to the student. The teacher may call the student's name and make eye contact without any comments. Or the teacher may describe the behavior without any trace of annoyance. Example: "I see that you are not finishing your assignment."

One technique that has been partially effective is to privately confront the student with his goal and ask, "How many times do you think you will need my attention in the next hour?" The student will usually not know what to say. The teacher might then say, "If I give you attention fifteen times, will that be enough?" This will sound like an exaggeration to the student. Then when the student misbehaves the teacher responds by saying, "Joel, number one." "Joel, number two," and so forth. The teacher does not comment on the behavior or scold, which would give Joel the attention he seeks, but simply lets him know that his behavior is being observed yet not given in to.

By encouraging students to seek attention through useful behavior teachers teach them that they can receive recognition through good efforts and accomplishments. This helps them to feel pride in themselves. Learning to function for self-satisfaction can be one of the most valuable lessons taught in school.

Power Seeking

Most teachers react to power struggles by feeling their authority threatened. They fight back, refusing to let students get the best of them. By fighting and winning struggles teachers only cause students to become more rebellious and hostile, and to think about getting revenge. Dreikurs believes that teachers do not have to fight with students and that they do not have to give in, either. The best thing for them to do is to not get involved in power struggles in the first place. They should withdraw as an authority figure. The student cannot meet a goal of power if there is not one to fight with. Teachers may admit to the student and the class that they recognize the need for power. One way is to stop the entire class and have them wait for the disruptive behavior to cease in which case the student is in conflict with his peers and not the teacher.

Teachers can also redirect students' ambitions to be in charge by inviting them to participate in making decisions or by giving them positions of responsibility. A teacher might take a student aside and say, "The language at p.e. is very unsportsmanlike. The others look up to you. Do you think you could help out by setting an example?"

Or, in the same situation, the teacher may say, "I have a problem. It concerns the language I am hearing. What do you think I should do?" In this way, they admit that the child has power but refuse to to be engaged in conflicts.

Teachers may also wish to confront the behavior openly. When a disruption begins they would say, "I cannot continue to teach when you are doing that. Can you think of a way in which you could do what you want and I could still teach?" If they can't think of any ways, be prepared to suggest some alternatives.

By withdrawing as a power figure, teachers take fuel from a student's fire. Students cannot be involved in a power struggle with themselves. They will not receive status or recognition if they cannot get the best of the teacher. Teachers who withdraw thwart the purpose of power-seeking behavior.

Revenge Seeking

The goal of revenge is closely related to the goal of power. Some students feel they should be allowed to do whatever they please and consider anyone who tries to stop them an enemy. These students are very difficult to deal with because they do not care about consequences. Consequences only give them justification for revenge.

It is difficult for teachers to care for students who are out to hurt them. These students feel the need to hurt others because they have been hurt themselves. What they need most is understanding and acceptance. Teachers can best provide this by calling on the class to support and encourage these students. Sometimes this is best accomplished by selecting a student with high esteem to befriend the troublemaker and help him develop constructive behavior. Or the teacher may be able to set up situations that allow revengeful students to exhibit talents or strengths, helping to persuade these students that they can behave in ways that bring acceptance and status.

This is a very difficult thing to ask of a class. Students who seek revenge at first reject efforts made by others. Teachers must encourage their students and persuade them that their efforts will pay off. It is awful for any student to feel unliked by everyone. It takes persistence and patience on everyone's part to change such a situation.

Desire to be Left Alone

Students who wish to be left alone usually think of themselves as thoroughly inadequate. They want their teacher to believe that they are too hopeless to deal with. Teachers often believe exactly that, and promptly give up. After all, the students are not troublemakers—they are not disruptive or hostile. They are simply blobs. Students who adopt this goal usually do so for one of the following reasons:

1. They are overly ambitious. They cannot do as well as they think they should. If they cannot be the best, they will not put forth any effort at all.

2. They are overly competitive. They cannot do as well as others. They feel that they are not good enough. They withdraw from being compared.
3. They are under too much pressure. They cannot do as well as others want them to. They don't feel good enough as they are. They refuse to live up to anyone's expectations.

In each case, discouraged students feel like failures. They feel worthless and inadequate. They want to keep others from discovering exactly how useless they are.

Teachers must *never* give up on these students. They must forever offer encouragement and support for even the smallest efforts. Encouragement is especially needed when the student is making mistakes. It is not the achievement but the effort that counts. Every attempt should be made by teachers and peers to make these students feel successful.

Teachers should also be very sensitive to their own reactions to these students. Any indication of defeat or frustration on the teacher's part reinforces the student's conviction of worthlessness and desire to be left alone is only increased. One failure does not mean a student is forever a failure, and teachers must help encourage students to see that fact.

Four Cases of Mistaken Goals

1. Mrs. Morton's class was doing independent seat work. Every few minutes Sally raised her hand to ask for some kind of direction. She wanted to know if she should number the sentences. Should she put her name on the paper? Was this right? Mrs. Morton became very exasperated. She'd had to explain things dozens of times to Sally. Finally she told Sally she would not help her during seat work anymore. She would explain the directions to the class once, and if Sally did not understand them she would have to wait and do the assignment at recess. Mrs. Morton then totally ignored all Sally's requests for help. She did however, immediately encourage Sally when she saw her working without teacher assistance.

This is an example of attention-getting behavior. The best clue was the teacher's reaction to Sally's behavior. She was annoyed. But Mrs. Morton did the best thing in this instance. She ignored Sally's bids for attention and reinforced her ability to work independently. She established logical consequences for Sally's inability to work independently.

2. Jerry and another student were wrestling near dangerous equipment in woodshop class. They knew this was against the rules and would result in their being removed from the class. Mr. Graves ap-

proached them and asked them to leave. Jerry refused. Mr. Graves was tempted to remove him, physically. Instead, he walked to the front of the room and told everyone to turn off their machines and put their work down. He told the students that woodshop could not continue because Jerry was behaving in a dangerous way around equipment and was refusing to leave the room. The class stood and waited, not without directing a few glares at Jerry. Jerry soon chose to leave the woodshop.

This is an example of power-seeking behavior. Mr. Grave's first reaction was to feel his authority was threatened. He was tempted to get into a power struggle with Jerry. However, he refused to be drawn into a fight. He freely admitted to the class that Jerry had the power to stop them from continuing. Jerry then had no one to struggle against. His power-seeking behavior was thwarted.

Later, Mr. Graves offered Jerry the job of shop foreman. It would be his job to see that everyone behaved in a safe way around dangerous equipment. That put Jerry in a position of authority and met his need for power in a constructive way.

3. Julie was looking at a book the teacher had brought in to read to the class. Cindy came over and grabbed it away, saying she wanted to read it. Miss Allen gave the book back to Julie and told Cindy to go sit in the hall. When Miss Allen was cleaning up the room after school she found the book torn into pieces. She was shocked and hurt by Cindy's behavior. Miss Allen had punished Cindy and Cindy had taken revenge. Her revenge hurt Miss Allen, which was exactly what Cindy intended.

Miss Allen might have better handled the situation by suggesting that Julie and Cindy sit down and read the book together. Cindy might have been able to show Julie that she was an excellent reader. Julie might have shown Cindy that sharing could be fun. Cindy might have had an opportunity to feel accepted.

4. Mr. Redding gave the class an assignment to write a story. Everyone was writing busily, except for Kathy who was staring at her blank paper. Mr. Redding walked over to her and said, "Kathy, you can start by writing your name on your paper." Kathy did not pick up her pencil, but she kept staring at her paper. Mr. Redding felt frustrated, he did not feel like coaxing Kathy. He wanted to give up. Instead he said, "Sometimes writers need time to think before they write. I know you'll start writing when you're ready."

Kathy wanted to be left alone. If she had wanted attention she would have responded to the teacher. Instead she acted as if he were not there, hoping he would go away. Mr. Redding did not give up as Kathy wished him to. He offered encouragement and let her know that he had faith in her ability to do the assignment.

Encouragement

Teachers traditionally have used a variety of undesirable discipline techniques when confronted with disruptive behaviors. They have threatened, humiliated, and punished. They have waited for misbehavior, and then pounced. The results have been resentment, rebellion, and hostility. Today's teachers need new approaches for effective classroom control, many of which are being explored. One of the most promising is encouragement. Dreikurs believes that encouragement is a crucial element in the prevention of problem behavior. Through encouragement teachers make learning seem worthwhile and help students develop positive self-concepts.

Encouragement consists of words or actions that convey teacher respect and belief in students' abilities. It tells students that they are accepted as they are. It recognizes efforts, not achievements. It gives students the courage to try, while accepting themselves as less than perfect. Teachers should be continually alert for opportunities to recognize effort, regardless of its results.

Encouragement facilitates feelings of being a contributing and participating member of a group. It helps students accept themselves as they are. It draws on motivation from within and allows them to become aware of their strengths.

Praise is not the same thing as encouragement. Praise is given when a task is well done. It promotes the idea that a product is worthless unless it receives praise. Students learn to perform to receive praise from without, and fail to learn to work for self-satisfaction. Praise encourages the attitude, "What am I going to get out of it?" Here are some examples showing the differences between praise and encouragement:

Praise	*Encouragement*
You're such a good girl for finishing your assignment.	I can tell that you have been working hard.
I am proud of your behavior at the assembly.	Isn't it nice that we could all enjoy the assembly!
You play the guitar so well!	I can see that you really enjoy playing the guitar.

Dreikurs outlines the following points for teachers who want to encourage students:
1. Always be positive; avoid negative statements.
2. Encourage students to strive for improvement, not perfection.
3. Encourage *effort*. Results don't matter if students are trying.
4. Emphasize strengths and minimize weaknesses.

5. Teach students to learn from mistakes. Emphasize that mistakes are not failures.
6. Stimulate motivation from within. Don't exert pressure from without.
7. Encourage independence.
8. Let students know that you have faith in their abilities.
9. Offer to help overcome obstacles.
10. Encourage students to help classmates who are having difficulties. This helps them appreciate their own strengths.
11. Send positive notes home, especially noting effort.
12. Show pride in students' work. Display it and invite others to see it.
13. Be optimistic and enthusiastic—it's catching.
14. Try to set up situations that guarantee success for all.
15. Use encouraging remarks often, such as these:

    a. You have improved!
    b. Can I help you?
    c. What did you learn from that mistake?
    d. I know you can.
    e. Keep trying!
    f. I know you can solve this, but if you think you need help. . . .
    g. I understand how you feel, but I'm sure you can handle it.

There are some pitfalls, too, in using encouragement. The teacher should *not*:

1. Encourage competition or comparison with others.
2. Point out how much better the student *could* be.
3. Use "but" statements such as, "I'm pleased with your progress, but. . . ."
4. Use statements such as, "It's about time."
5. Give up on those who are not responding. Always encourage consistently and constantly.
6. Praise students or their products.

Logical and Natural Consequences

No matter how encouraging teachers are, they will still encounter behavior problems. Dreikurs advises setting up logical and natural consequences to help deter misbehavior and motivate appropriate behavior. Consequences are not punishment. Punishment is action taken by the teacher to get back at misbehaving students, and show them who is boss. Punishment breeds retaliation and gives students the feeling that they have the right to punish in return. Consequences are actions that follow behavior in a natural and logical way. They are not weapons used by the teacher. They teach students that all behavior results in some corresponding action: good behavior brings rewards and unacceptable behavior brings unpleasant consequences.

Dreikurs identifies two types of consequences—natural and logical. Natural consequences are those that students experience only as a result of their behavior. They are not due to the intervention of another. For example, if a student kicks his desk and breaks his foot, he experiences a natural consequence of his behavior. Logical consequences are arranged by someone else, in this case, a teacher. If a student throws papers on the floor, that student will have to pick them up. Logical consequences imposed by the teacher are very effective except when dealing with power-seeking behavior. In that case natural consequences control students' behavior.

Consequences must be explained, understood, and decided upon by students. If they are sprung on students at the time of conflict, they will be considered punishment. When applying consequences, teachers should not act as self-appointed authorities. They should simply represent the order required by society and enforce the rules established by the students.

Consequences are only effective when applied consistently. If teachers apply them while in a bad mood, or only to certain students, students will not learn that misbehavior *always* carries unpleasant consequences. They will misbehave and gamble that they can get away with it. Students must be convinced that consequences will be applied each and every time they choose to misbehave. They will have to consider carefully whether misbehaving is worth it. Sometimes it takes time to break old habits of behavior but teachers should never get discouraged and give up on invoking consequences.

Applying consequences allows students to make their own choices about how they will behave. They learn to rely on their own inner discipline to control their actions. They learn that poor choices invariably result in unpleasant consequences. It's nobody's fault but their own. Students also learn that the teacher respects their ability to make their own decisions.

Consequences should relate as closely as possible to the misbehavior, so students can see the connection between them. For example;

1. Students who damage school property have to replace it.
2. Failure to finish an assignment means you must finish it after school.
3. Fighting at recess results in no recess.
4. Disturbing others results in isolation from the group.

Teachers should not show anger or triumph when applying consequences. They should simply say, "You chose to talk instead of doing math, so you must finish your math after school." When students choose to misbehave, they choose to suffer the consequences. It has nothing to do with the teacher.

References

Dreikurs, R. *Psychology in the Classroom.* 2nd ed. New York: Harper and Row, 1968.

Dreikurs, R. and Cassel, P. *Discipline Without Tears.* New York: Hawthorn Books, 1972.

Dreikurs, R., Grunwald, B., and Pepper, F. *Maintaining Sanity in the Classroom.* New York: Harper and Row, 1971.

Chapter 9

The Canter Model: Assertively Taking Charge

Lee and Marlene Canter. (*Photography courtesy of Lee and Marlene Canter of Canter and Associates, Culver City, CA.*)

The Canters' Biographical Sketches

Lee and Marlene Canter have done extensive research into the traits of teachers known to have good control in their classrooms. Their research led to the formulation and testing of a control system they call *assertive discipline*. Their approach, which they began to disseminate in the mid-1970's, has been widely acclaimed by teachers and administrators. As of 1980 Canter and Associates had trained more than 100,000 teachers and administrators nationwide in the techniques of assertive discipline.

By profession, Lee Canter is a specialist in child guidance. He has worked in a number of child-guidance agencies that attend to behavior problems in the young. He is now director of Canter and Associates, an organization that provides training in assertive discipline.

Marlene Canter collaborated with her husband in the research that led to assertive discipline. She coauthored their book *Assertive Discipline: A Take-Charge Approach for Today's Educator* (1976), and she has been a teacher of the learning disabled in schools in Los Angeles, Carmel, and Irvine, California.

Assertive discipline is an approach to classroom control intended to help teachers take charge in their classrooms. It provides the means for interacting with students in calm yet forceful ways. It enables teachers to put aside yelling and threatening, offering instead a positive power that prevents their giving in or giving up. This power combines clear expectations, insistence on correct behavior, and consistent follow-through, overlaid with the warmth and support that all students need.

Assertive discipline is built around principles from assertion training as they affect interactions with school students. The result is a positive approach that allows teachers to deal constructively with misbehaving students while maintaining a helpful, supportive climate for best student growth.

The Canters' Key Ideas

The following list presents the key ideas that form the core of assertive discipline. They provide a summary of the assertive model of discipline. These ideas are explained in greater detail in subsequent sections of this chapter.

1. Teachers should insist on decent, responsible behavior from their students. Students need this type of behavior, parents want it, the community at large expects it, and the educational process is crippled without it.
2. Teacher failure, for all practical purposes, is synonymous with failure to maintain adequate classroom discipline.

3. Many teachers labor under false assumptions about discipline. They believe that firm control is stifling and inhumane. It is not. Firm control maintained correctly is humane and liberating.
4. Teachers have basic educational rights in their classrooms including:
   a. The right to establish optimal learning environments.
   b. The right to determine, request, and expect appropriate behavior from their students.
   c. The right to receive help from administrators and parents when it is needed.
5. Students have basic rights in the classroom, too including:
   a. The right to have teachers who help them limit their inappropriate, self-destructive behavior.
   b. The right to have teachers who provide positive support for their appropriate behavior.
   c. The right to choose how to behave, with full understanding of the consequences that automatically follow their choices.
6. These needs, rights, and conditions are best met through assertive discipline, in which the teacher clearly communicates expectations to students and consistently follows up with appropriate actions but never violates the best interests of the students.
7. This assertive discipline consists of the following elements:
   a. Identifying expectations clearly.
   b. Willingness to say, "I like that," and, "I don't like that."
   c. Persistence in stating expectations and feelings.
   d. Use of firm tone of voice.
   e. Maintenance of eye contact.
   f. Using nonverbal gestures in support of verbal statements.
8. Assertive discipline enables teachers to do such things as:
   a. Say no, without feeling guilty.
   b. Give and receive compliments genuinely and gracefully.
   c. Express thoughts and feelings that others might find intimidating.
   d. Stand up for feelings and rights when under fire from others.
   e. Comfortably place demands on others.
   f. Firmly influence students' behavior without yelling and threatening.
   g. Work more successfully with chronic behavior problems.
9. Teachers who use assertive discipline do the following:
   a. Employ assertive response styles, as distinct from nonassertive or hostile response styles.
   b. Eliminate negative expectations about student behavior.
   c. Establish and communicate clear expectations for positive student behavior.

    d. Use hints, questions, and I-messages rather than demands for requesting student behavior.

    e. Use eye contact, gestures, and touches to supplement verbal messages.

    f. Follow through with promises (reasonable consequences, previously established) rather than with threats.

    g. Be assertive in confrontations with students, including statements of expectations, consequences that will occur, and why the action is necessary.

10. To become more assertive in discipline teachers should do the following things:

    a. Practice assertive response styles.

    b. Set clear limits and consequences.

    c. Follow through consistently.

    d. Make specific assertive discipline plans and rehearse them mentally.

    e. Write things down; don't trust the memory.

    f. Practice the broken-record technique for repeating expectations.

    g. Ask school principals and parents for support in the efforts to help students.

The Need for Assertive Discipline

Discipline is a matter of great concern in schools. It remains so, year after year. Teachers hold it as their greatest concern in teaching. It is the overwhelming cause of teacher failure, burn out, and resignation. Parents and the community name school discipline far more than any other factor as the area in which they would like to see improvement. Discipline remains a source of sore concern for several reasons. Among those reasons are a general decline in our society's respect for authority, a decline in parents' insistence that their children behave acceptably in school and elsewhere, and a laxity within law enforcement and legal circles in dealing with juvenile offenders. But teachers and school administrators have to share some of the blame, too. The societal conditions just mentioned make discipline more difficult, yet much of the control problem can be laid at the feet of teachers and administrators who hold mistaken ideas about discipline.

    Those mistaken ideas include the following: good teachers can handle discipline problems on their own without help; firm discipline causes psychological trauma in students; discipline problems disappear when students are given activities that meet their needs; misbehavior results from deep-seated causes, which are beyond the influence of the teacher. Such mistaken ideas about discipline cause teachers to be hesitant about controlling misbehavior. They are afraid they will do ethical or psychological harm and become reluctant to confront misbehaving students. Teachers hesitate to take action and by the time they realize that action is necessary, the situation in the classroom is out of hand.

These mistaken ideas must be supplanted with correct ideas about discipline including: we all need discipline for psychological security; we need discipline as a suppressant to acts that we would not be proud of later; we need discipline as a liberating influence that allows us to build and expand out best traits and abilities; discipline is necessary to maintain an effective and efficient learning environment.

The Basis of Assertive Discipline

Canter and Canter (1976, p.9) say that an assertive teacher is one who clearly and firmly communicates needs and requirements to students, follows those words with appropriate actions, responds to students in ways that maximize compliance, but in no way violates the best interests of the students.

The basis of this assertive posture is *care*—caring about oneself to the point of not allowing others (students) to take advantage; caring about students to the point of not allowing them to behave in ways that are damaging to themselves. Such care can only be shown when the teacher takes charge in the classroom. The manner must be positive, firm, and consistent. It must be composed. It cannot be wishy-washy. Neither can it be hostile, loudly abusive, or threatening. These negative postures are doomed to failure. The calm, positive manner shows students that teachers do care about them, about their needs, and about their proper behavior. It provides the climate of support that best assists students' own self-control.

A climate of care and support rises up from what Canter and Canter (p.2) call basic teacher rights in working with students:
1. The right to establish optimal learning environments for students, consistent with the teacher's strengths and weaknesses.
2. The right to expect behavior from students that contributes to their optimal growth, while also meeting the special needs of the teacher.
3. The right to ask and receive help and backing from administrators and parents.

The climate of care also has origins in what Canter and Canter (p. 8) call rights of students, when under the teacher's guidance:
1. The right to have a teacher who will limit inappropriate and self-destructive behavior.

2. The right to have a teacher who will provide positive support for appropriate behavior.
3. The right to choose one's own behavior, with full knowledge of the natural consequences that follow that behavior.

The climate of positive support and care is best provided, Canter and Canter believe, through the careful application of principles of assertion training to classroom discipline. Such application produces assertive discipline. It removes teacher inertia and hostility, replacing those traits with firm positive insistence. While certainly not a cure-all for problems that occur in the classroom, assertive discipline greatly helps teachers establish and maintain the sort of working climate that meets students' needs as well as their own. Canter and Canter (p. 12) say that assertive discipline provides the following helps for teachers:
1. Identify situations where assertiveness will help both teacher and students.
2. Develop more consistent and effective communication with students.
3. Gain confidence and skills for making firmer and more consistent demands on students.
4. Reduce hostile teacher behavior, replacing it with the more effective positive, firm, composed insistence.
5. Gain confidence and skills for working more effectively with chronic behavior problems in the classroom.

Five Steps to Assertive Discipline

The material Canter and Canter present in *Assertive Discipline: A Take-Charge Approach for Today's Educator* suggests that teachers can easily incorporate the basics of assertive discipline into their own behavior. A series of five steps is implied for this implementation, which appear to be (1) recognizing and removing roadblocks to assertive discipline, (2) practicing the use of assertive response styles, (3) learning to set limits, (4) learning to follow through on limits, and (5) implementing a system of positive assertions. These five steps are explained and discussed in the paragraphs that follow.

Step 1. Recognizing and Removing Roadblocks to Assertive Discipline

All teachers have within themselves the potential for expressing their educational needs to students. They also have the potential for obtaining student compliance with those needs. Most teachers have difficulty, however, with both the expression of needs and the acquisition of compliance that can be attributed to a group of "roadblocks" that hinder teachers in their efforts to be assertive. The first step in learning to use assertive discipline is to recognize and remove these roadblocks. Most of the roadblocks have to do with *negative expectations* about students: we expect them to act bad. We feel they cannot do otherwise, that conditions of health, home, personality, or environment prohibit normal behavior. This negative expectation must be recognized as false, and it must be supplanted with positive expectations.

The first thing we must realize, say Canter and Canter (p. 56), is that "problems or no problems, no child should be allowed to engage in behavior that is self-destructive or violates the rights of his peers or teacher." Thus, we learn never to tolerate improper behavior in students, even when we feel they are afflicted with such conditions as:

- Emotional illness (Students are too sick to behave normally, therefore all behavior must be tolerated.)
- Poor heredity (Bad from the beginning, students are unable to be otherwise because of genetic makeup.)
- Brain damage (Damage to the nervous system makes appropriate behavior impossible.)
- Socioeconomic background (Deprivation and poverty have so dehumanized the students that they can't be expected to behave in a civilized way.)

The second thing we must do is recognize this simple fact: we can influence in positive ways the behavior of all students under our direction, no matter what their problems. Recognition of this fact helps remove the roadblocks associated with negative expectations and we come to accept the following realities:

1. All students need limits, and teachers have the right to set them. Teachers who fear that students will not like them if they set limits and stick to them have not paid attention to human psychology. Most of us admire and respect teachers who have high expectations, set high standards, and stick to them. We seldom respect teachers (or like them in the long run) if they take a laissez faire approach to teaching.

2. Teachers have a right to ask for and receive back-up help from principals, parents, and other school personnel. All teachers hold a fear in the back of their minds that they will have confrontations with students they cannot handle. They fear the student will hostilely disobey, go out of control, or even attack physically. Teachers have the right to expect back-up assistance when and if such an event occurs to keep them from being intimidated by students and help them to be more firmly insistent on appropriate student behavior.

3. We can't always treat all students exactly alike. Teachers have heard that discipline is improved when standards are applied equally, when all students are treated just alike. That is true up to a point. If students think a teacher is playing favorites, they may become res-

tive. However, we all know that people respond differently to different situations. We know that some of us require stronger motivation than others. Students realize that fact, too, and when they see that one of their peers needs special help in order to reach the same standards of conduct expected of other class members, they will be understanding and accepting. They will even help, if needed. Thus, some students may have to be put on special incentive programs or behavior-modification programs before they can live up to the standards that are expected.

Step 2. Practice the Use of Assertive Response Styles

Canter and Canter (p. 16) differentiate among three styles of responses that characterize teachers' interactions with misbehaving students: nonassertive, hostile, and assertive. The first two should be eliminated, the third should be practiced.

The nonassertive response style is typical of teachers who have given in to students or who feel it is wrong to place strong demands on students' behavior. With this style teachers do not establish clear standards of acceptable and unacceptable behavior. Or if they do, they fail to back up their words with appropriate actions. Teachers using this style are passive. They feel basically powerless to control students and hope to use their good natures to gain student compliance. They will often ask students to "please try" to do their work, behave themselves, do better next time. They are not firm or insistent and end up resignedly accepting whatever the students decide to do.

The hostile response style is typically used by teachers who feel that they are barely hanging on to class control. They use an aversive approach, characterized by sarcasm and threats. They often shout. They rule with an iron fist and believe that to do otherwise is to invite certain chaos, to lose vital control in the classroom. Hostile responses produce several bad side effects. First, they abuse students' feelings. Second, they fail to provide for students' needs for warmth and security. Third, they violate two of the basic student rights described earlier: the right to positive limit-setting on self-destructive behavior and the right to choose their own behavior, with full knowledge of the natural consequences that will follow.

The assertive response style, which teachers should practice until it becomes a natural part of their dealings with students, protects the rights of both teacher and students. With this style teachers make their expectations clearly known to students. In a businesslike way they continually insist that students comply with those expectations. They back up their words with actions. When students choose to comply with teacher guidance, they receive positive benefits. When they choose to behave in unacceptable ways, the teacher follows through with consequences that reasonably accompany the misbehavior.

Teachers, then, should learn to eliminate nonassertive and hostile responses from their behavior, supplanting them with assertive responses. Here are examples of the three kinds of responses:

Example: Fighting

> *Nonassertive:* "Please try your very best to stop fighting."
> *Hostile:* "You are acting like a disgusting savage again!"
> *Assertive:* "We do not fight. Sit down until you cool off."

Example: Talking Out

> *Nonassertive:* "You are talking again without raising your hand."
> *Hostile:* "I hope you learn some manners. Otherwise there's going to be trouble."
> *Assertive:* "Don't answer unless you raise your hand and I call on you."

Notice in these examples that the assertive response clearly communicates the teacher's disapproval of the behavior, followed by an indication of what the student is supposed to do. The teacher is persistent in making these responses, which will be repeated as often as necessary, in the broken-record fashion. When students behave in appropriate ways the teacher is equally quick to recognize the correct behavior and acknowledge it.

In contrast to the assertive response, the nonassertive response leaves students unconvinced that they are truly expected to behave differently. The teacher may plead with them rather then firmly directing them, may fail to communicate precisely what the students are to do, may fail to back up firm directions with actions if necessary. This lack of direction and firmness, regardless of its underlying reasons, suggests to students that the teacher is afraid of them or feels powerless to deal with their behavior. Either of these notions encourages students to misbehave.

The hostile response is counter-productive, too. It attacks the student and smacks of dislike and vengeance. It wounds students in ways that are difficult to cure. It depicts the classroom as a battleground where teacher and students are pitted as adversaries, each intent upon subduing the other. Teachers who use this response style rely on you-messages, which put down the students but do not communicate clearly what is expected. They make threats that if carried out are far too severe. If the threats are made but not carried out students are reinforced in their belief that they can do as they please in the classroom.

Step 3. Learning to Set Limits

Canter and Canter (p. 65) make this point very clearly: "No matter what the activity, in order to be assertive, you need to be aware of what behaviors you want and need from the students. They say that teachers should think in terms of specific behaviors they expect from students, such as taking turns, not shouting out, starting work on time, and listening to a student who is speaking. They suggest that teachers list the various kinds of activities they provide during the day so that within each of these activities they can decide on the specific kinds of behavior they need to see in their students. Following this step, teachers should instruct students very clearly on the behaviors they have identified. For elementary teachers, signs can be made and posted at the appropriate time in front of the room. Such signs might be made for quiet time, art, group work, and so forth. The specific behavior expectations for each of those times are discussed and practiced. Secondary teachers will not need to make signs but they should clearly specify behaviors that are accepted for such different activities as individual work, group discussions, group projects, and teacher lecture and demonstration. It is often helpful to make short, succinct written lists of key do's and don'ts. These lists are posted in the classroom and referred to as necessary to provide constant reminders of behaviors that are desired and behavior that will not be tolerated.

Once a teacher's specific behavioral needs and expectations are established the next step is to decide how forcefully those needs will be communicated and how far the teacher is willing to go in following through on them. Canter and Canter suggest that students need to be told clearly and firmly what behaviors are desired and what behaviors will not be tolerated. It is not sufficient to say "be nice" or "work hard." The understanding should be so clear that students can tell a visitor exactly how they are supposed to be behaving at any given time.

Teachers must also decide on how they intend to respond to students when established expectations are either complied with or broken. Compliance calls for acknowledgment, using procedures in keeping with the ages and needs of the students. For most students verbal acknowledgment is sufficient. Sometimes tangible rewards or special privileges are needed to motivate the continuance of desired behavior. In other cases, students will not want to be singled out for praise because it embarrasses them in front of the group. For them, the teacher will need to find other means, such as knowing looks, special signals, and private conferences.

While dealing with compliance is easy, dealing with violations is more difficult. It is here that assertive discipline is most effective.

Teachers should not ignore inappropriate behavior. Instead, they should stop it, with firm reminders of what the students are supposed to be doing. They should clarify in their minds what they will do to follow through if and when students continue to misbehave. Knowing they will have to back up their words with actions, they should decide in advance what they will say and do. In particular they need to think through clearly how they will deal with students who are especially deviant, stubborn, and powerful.

Canter and Canter suggest *verbal limit setting*, combined with physical acts, as the vehicle for establishing expectations and follow-through procedures. Verbal limit setting has three key aspects, the first of which is called *requesting behavior*. Four general methods or approaches are suggested for use in requesting behavior from students. Those four methods are hints, I-messages, questions, and demands. Whenever possible, the first three should be used; demands should be used only as a last resort because they imply dire consequences if they are not met. Here is how Canter and Canter describe the four methods of requesting behavior: Hints are statements the teacher makes from time to time simply to remind students of what they are supposed to be doing, such as, "Everyone should be reading silently." I-messages tell how the behavior is affecting the teacher, such as, "It is getting so noisy I can't do my work." Questions are hints put into interrogative form, such as, "Would you please get back to your reading?" Demands direct students about what to do. Negative consequences are implied if the demand is not met; for instance, "Get back to your reading. I'd better not have to tell you again." Again, Canter and Canter (p. 74) warn of the effects of demands. In doing so, they put forth their one and only commandment of assertive discipline: "Thou shalt not make a demand thou art not preparest to follow through upon." Ask yourself, they say, just what you will in fact do if the student defies your demand. Unless you have a response ready that is assertive and appropriate to the degree of misbehavior, think twice.

The second aspect of verbal limit setting involves the way in which the hint, I-message, question, or demand is delivered. This aspect includes tone of voice, eye contact, gestures, use of student's name, and physical touch. The tone of voice you use should be firmly neutral. It should not be harsh, abusive, or intimidating. Neither should it be mirthful, implying that you are not really serious about what you say. It should be businesslike, no-nonsense, I-mean-what-I-say.

Eye contact is essential for the message to have full impact. Teachers should always look a student straight in the eye when setting limits and correcting. The students should see the intensity in teachers' eyes. There is one caution we should remember, which is that teachers should *not* insist that students look them back in the eye. It is very difficult, indeed, for a young person to look directly back at an older person when being upbraided. Moreover, in some ethnic groups, younger people show respect for older people by dropping their eyes—to insist that they look you in the eye would be to insist that they make an open show of disrespect. Nevertheless, teachers should fix students with their direct gaze when correcting them forcefully.

Gestures add much impact to verbal messages. This is especially true in Anglo-American society, compared to other societal groups, where we use so few gestures. Canter and Canter advocate using facial expressions and hand and arm movements to accent what is being said verbally. They warn us to stop short of waving fingers or fists in front of students' noses.

Use of students' names when delivering messages also adds impact since it personalizes the message making it more forceful and penetrating. This act especially assists messages delivered at a longer range—across the classroom or across the school grounds. The use of names gets the message precisely where it is supposed to go. It leaves no doubt in anyone's mind as to whom is being corrected.

Physical touch is usually extremely effective when used in conjunction with verbal messages. Light placement of the hand on the shoulder, for example, communicates forcefulness combined with sincerity. For many students it is the most powerful way to communicate genuine, positive concern. Again, however, we should remember a word of warning. You can't be sure in advance how each individual student will react to physical touch. Some may defiantly pull away. Occasionally, someone may thrust back physically. And it is not unknown for students to claim that a teacher pinched or pressed hurtfully. While physical touch is usually especially effective, it can sometimes produce undesirable consequences.

A third aspect of verbal limit setting is the use of the broken-record ploy when students seek to divert teachers from their intended message. The broken-record strategy involves insistent repetition of the original message. Here is an example:

> Teacher: Alex, we do not fight in this room. I will not
> tolerate fighting. You must not fight again.
> Student: It's not my fault. Pete started it. He hit me first.
> Teacher: I understand that might be. I didn't see. But you
> will not fight in this class.
> Student: Pete started it.
> Teacher: That may be. I'll watch. But you *may not fight in
> this class.*

You can see how the teacher was not diverted from the matter of fighting to the matter of who started it. The broken-record strategy (repetition that we do not fight in the class) maintained firm, positive insistence.

Canter and Canter (p. 88) present these reminders about using the broken record.

- Use it only when students refuse to listen, persist in responding inappropriately, or refuse to take responsibility for their own behavior.
- Preface your repetitions with, "That's not the point. . ." or, "I understand, but. . . ."
- Use it a maximum of three times.
- After the third time follow through with an appropriate consequence, if necessary.

Step 4. Learning to Follow Through on Limits

By limits, Canter and Canter mean the positive demands you have made on students. By following through, they mean taking the appropriate actions when students (1) refuse to meet the demands that were set, or (2) act in compliance with the demands. Either response calls for follow-through.

In the first case, the natural, undesirable consequences should be invoked. In the second case, the natural, desirable consequences should be invoked. Thus, the students choose their behavior but with advance knowledge of the good or bad consequences that will result from their choice.

Canter and Canter present four guidelines that help teachers follow through appropriately:

1. Make promises, not threats.
2. Establish in advance your criteria for consequences.
3. Select appropriate consequences in advance.
4. Practice verbal confrontations that call for follow-through.

Let's see what is suggested in each of these four guidelines.

1. Make promises, not threats. Assertive teachers promise; they do not threaten. A promise is a vow to take positive action when necessary. A threat is a statement that shows intent to harm or punish. Teachers have to recognize that follow-through is not always pleasant. Neither teachers nor students like the notion of staying after school or being isolated from the group. But assertive teachers recognize that limit-setting and follow-through are essential to the best interests of the student.

Promises have their pleasant side as well as their unpleasant side. Follow-through should also be provided when students behave in desired ways. They should be acknowledged or rewarded for choosing to behave in ways consistent with their own best interests.

The crucial point is this: students know what is expected of them. They can choose to behave in expected ways, or they can choose to behave in undesirable ways. If they choose the former, follow-through is pleasant for all concerned. If they choose the latter, follow-through is unpleasant for all concerned. In either case, the result does not come as a surprise out of the blue. Students have been informed of it in advance. That advance information has been given in the form of promises that the teacher has made to the class to follow through—to implement—the consequences that naturally accompany behavior chosen by the students.

2. *Establish, in advance, the criteria for consequences.* Criteria are the defining characteristics that set one thing apart from another. Your criteria for beauty, for example, are the characteristics that for you set beautiful things apart from things not beautiful. Thus, criteria for consequences are the characteristics you consider appropriate, all things being considered, for acts you will establish as your follow-through consequences. Canter and Canter (pp. 94–95) suggest the following criteria as useful to teachers who wish to establish criteria.

1. Make sure the consequence is comfortable to yourself. That is, don't punish yourself along with the students as you might do if you keep them after school, or if you assign written work that will add to your reading burden.
2. Make sure the consequence is something the students don't like, but that is not physically or psychologically harmful to them.
3. Make sure students see that the consequences you select are provided as a matter of choice for them. They earn them by what they do, good or bad.
4. Make sure the consequence can be applied immediately, when the students' behavior calls for it.

3. *Select appropriate consequences in advance.* In accord with their criteria, teachers should select several specific consequences that can be invoked when necessary. The consequences should be of both positive and negative types. Gradations of severity should be present so that the level of consequence can match the seriousness of the misbehavior.

Examples of negative consequences teachers have found most useful are time out, loss of privilege, loss of preferred activity, detention, visit to principal, and home consequences. *Time out* is the same as isolation and refers to removal from an activity or from the classroom for a period of time. Ordinarily, isolation is applied by having the student sit and work alone in a corner of the room while the remainder of the class continues its usual routine. A more powerful form of isolation is sending the misbehaving to another classroom for a while. This form should not be used except in severe cases. Students will be greatly embarrassed by having to go to another class with another teacher. However, this type of isolation is effective precisely because students greatly dislike being sent to another room. Of course, teachers make arrangements in advance for such isolation.

Loss of privilege means the students do not get to participate in something they have been looking forward to. Examples include having to forego a special assembly, field trip, performance, film, or athletic event. They include loss of special duties in the classroom, such as monitor, messenger, or audio-visual assistant. Loss of privilege is not effective unless the loss is significant. If it is something a student didn't care about anyway, its removal will produce little result.

Loss of preferred activity is similar to loss of privilege, except that it refers to normal class activities that students especially enjoy. These losses can be applied in the form of sitting out competitive games, doing seat work rather than art, music, or free reading (assuming they are preferred activities), and exclusion from planning and preparation for holiday parties, plays, feasts, and so forth.

Detention is the familiar staying in after school. Students must report to a classroom, principal's office, or special room set up for the purpose. There they complete work they were supposed to have done during the day. Again, detention is a negative consequence only when students would rather be doing something else. Sometimes students would rather stay and help the teacher than go home. If so, detention becomes a reward rather than a punishment.

Visits to the principal are another natural consequence that most students do not like. If this consequence is to be effective the visit must be unpleasant. For that reason many principals do not like to have students sent to them. They would rather present an image of the principal as a friend to students. This posture does not help teachers, however, and teachers must be able to count on the principal to back their efforts at discipline. In order to provide this backing, principals should discuss the nature of the misbehavior with the offending student and establish positive steps that will be taken to correct it. This discussion need not be harsh but it must be firm and serious. The student must be made to understand that continued misbehavior will result in removal from school.

Home consequences like visits to the principal are a form of support the teacher must be able to count on. When the best efforts of the teacher and principal do not correct a student's self-defeating behavior, the parents must step into the picture. They must arrange for negative consequences to be applied at home in the form of loss of television privileges, isolation to the bedroom, foregoing socialization with friends, extra homework, or having to do undesirable chores.

The invocation of home consequences is the most serious step normally taken in school discipline. It is a frank admission by the school that other measures, effective with the vast majority of students, have not helped this particular student behave in ways consistent with the best interests of the individual, class, and teacher. If the unacceptable behavior is not corrected through home intervention, the teacher should no longer be expected to have to work with the student. Placement with another teacher, removal from school, or placement in a school that specializes in behavior problems are possibilities for the student.

Canter and Canter point out that all these consequences should indicate one thing clearly to the student and parents: the teacher and school really care about the student. They care so much that they are prepared to use all means at their disposal to influence the student in positive directions.

Step 5. Implementing a System of Positive Assertions

Most of what has been presented so far is of a negative sort. We have considered rules and limits, and we have examined steps the teacher can take when the rules are broken. While these matters are of great concern for teachers, they reflect only one side of the discipline picture.

The other side of the picture is a positive one. It has to do with teacher follow-through when students behave in appropriate ways, when they are being good instead of being bad. Canter and Canter (pp. 118–120) name several benefits that accrue to teacher and students alike when systematic attention is given to students who are behaving appropriately:

1. Your influence with students increases. In the negative aspect of discipline students learn to limit their behavior so they can avoid unpleasant consequences. In this positive view they learn to maximize their appropriate behavior so they can enjoy consequences that meet their needs and interests. The addition of this positive side doubles a teacher's effectiveness.

2. The amount of problem behavior decreases. All students want attention. If they can't get it by being good, they will try to get it by being bad. When they learn they can get attention and other things they like through being good, the demeanor of the class changes dramatically. Instead of walking the fine line that separates barely acceptable behavior from unacceptable behavior, they move toward highly acceptable behavior. There they can get what they want.

3. The classroom environment becomes much more positive. As mentioned, the total class demeanor changes for the better when students see that good behavior will get them attention, praise, privileges, and other things they desire. They naturally become positive in their interactions with teachers and other students. That positive stance brings rewards that far exceed those that accrue from negative behavior.

What are some of the positive consequences that students are so pleased to receive? Canter and Canter (pp. 122–126) list many of them. Included are:

1. Personal attention from the teacher. Special, positive, personal attention from the teacher is one of the most rewarding experiences that students can have. Most students respond enthusiastically to that attention. It is given in the form of greetings, short talks, compliments, acknowledgments, smiles, and friendly eye contact.

2. Positive notes to parents. Often, parents are informed about their children only when they have misbehaved in school. A brief note or phone call, positive and complimentary, can do wonders for both students and parents. They can provide the added bonus of rallying parents to stronger support of the teacher and the educational program.

3. Special awards. Students respond very well to special awards given for good work, good improvement, good behavior, help given to fellow students, courteous manners, and so forth. These awards can vary from comments stamped on papers to certificates drawn or printed for the purpose.

4. Special privileges. Students will try hard to earn special privileges. These privileges need not be grandiose. They can be as simple as five extra minutes of p.e., choosing a friend with whom to work for a while, or helping their teacher correct papers.

5. Material rewards. Many effective reinforcers come in tangible form. Again, these things need not be expensive or elaborate. Adhesive stickers are prized by primary-grade students. Older students like to receive posters, pencils, and special rubber stamps. Edibles such as raisins, nuts, and popcorn are prized.

6. Home rewards. In collaboration with parents, privileges can be extended to the home. Completing homework can earn extra TV time. Reading an extra book can earn a favorite meal.

7. Group rewards. Canter and Canter discuss methods of rewarding the entire group at the same time. They include suggestions such as: (1) dropping marbles into a jar, as the entire group remains on task and works hard, and (2) writing a series of letters on the board that when completed make up a secret word, such as POPCORN PARTY, which the class then receives as a reward.

Four Final Suggestions

Canter and Canter present many suggestions that can have strong, positive effect on students, the majority of which have been noted in preceding sections of this chapter. To conclude our overview of their model of discipline, four final suggestions will be acknowledged.

Beginning the Year

Students are usually on their best behavior during the first few days of the new school year. That is an ideal time to establish a plan of assertive discipline with the class. Canter and Canter (pp. 136–139) suggest the following steps in establishing the plan:

1. Decide on behaviors you want from the students the first few days of school.
2. Decide on the negative consequences you will invoke for inappropriate behavior, as well as the positive consequences you will use to follow up good behavior.
3. On first meeting the new students, discuss and write on the board the behaviors you expect. Keep the list to five or six behaviors.
4. Ask the students to write the behaviors on a sheet of paper, take it home, have their parents read and sign it, and return it the next day.
5. Stress that no student will be allowed to break the rules. Tell the students exactly what will happen each time a rule is broken (first, second, third offense, and so on).
6. Tell students what you will do as you see them complying with the rules (such as marbles in the jar for credit toward later activities).
7. Stress that these rules help the class toward their responsibility of learning and behaving acceptably.
8. Ask students to repeat orally what is expected, what will happen for violations, and what will happen for compliance.
9. Prepare a short letter to send home to each parent, indicating your plans for behavior, your intention to keep parents fully informed of their child's progress, your need for their support, and your pleasure in collaborating with them toward the benefit of their child.
10. Implement the assertive discipline immediately.

Making Assertive Plans

Canter and Canter (pp. 146–148) have found that while most teachers make lesson plans as a routine matter virtually none make discipline plans. They believe that making discipline plans is important and helpful. They urge teachers to make discipline plans according to the following steps

1. Identify any existing or potential discipline problems.
2. Specify the behaviors you want the student(s) to eliminate or engage in.
3. Decide on negative and positive consequences appropriate to the student and situation.
4. Decide how to implement the negative and positive consequences.

Mental Rehearsal

Mental rehearsal is the process of visualizing specific situations in which you will need to respond assertively. This clear visualization and thought about assertive responding help make the process become a natural part of your behavior. This rehearsal is especially effective when done in conjunction with the assertive-discipline plans discussed in the previous section. It allows you to practice verbal confrontations in advance, thus ensuring that you will respond in firm, insistent ways rather than in a hostile, defensive, or wishy-washy manner.

Practicing Interventions

While mental rehearsal is effective, and while it is usually the only available way to practice confrontations in advance, practice with a person is more effective yet. The following is Canter and Canter's (pp. 121–122) scheme for practicing positive interventions. The same scheme is used for practicing negative interventions, recognizing that a more firm, insistent tone would be used. With a partner do this:

Step 1. Say, "I really appreciate your help in class," while looking over your partner's shoulder.

Step 2. Say, "I really appreciate your help in class," while looking your partner straight in the eye.

Step 3. Using your partner's first name say "Frank, I really appreciate your help in class," while looking him in the eye.

Step 4. Say the same thing using eye contact and first name. In addition, touch your partner on the shoulder.

Step 5. Repeat Step 1, exactly.

Step 6. Repeat Step 4, exactly.

Conclusion

This concludes the overview of the Canter and Canter model of assertive discipline. You can see that it incorporates ideas from several other models, such as behavior as choice, logical consequences rather than threats or punishments, positive reinforcements for desired behavior, and addressing the situation rather than the student's character. Its unique contribution is the view that teachers must care enough about students to limit their self-defeating behavior, that they must insistently and firmly guide students and apply natural consequences of student behavior, and that they have the right to count on full support from administrators and parents if their best efforts with students come to naught.

Reference

Canter, L. and Canter, M. *Assertive Discipline: A Take-Charge Approach for Today's Educator.* Seal Beach, Calif.: Canter and Associates, 1976.

Supplements to the Models

Chapter 10

Seriousness, Rules, and Great Expectations

Suppose you could go into any large school district and from the personnel director obtain two lists of teachers. The first list would name teachers considered to be strongest in class control and the second would name teachers considered weakest in class control. Suppose you then studied the teaching traits of people on those two lists. You would find interesting differences between them in many areas, almost certainly including the following:

1. Seriousness about teaching and learning.
2. Class rules for personal conduct and work that are clear, reasonable, and consistently enforced.
3. Great expectations, which means that the teacher fully expects students to behave well and learn rapidly, and continually conveys those expectations to the students.

These three areas of class control are fundamentally important and merit further examination.

Seriousness

Have you ever read the dictionary definitions of the word serious? If so, you might have the wrong idea about what seriousness means in teaching. In defining "serious," dictionaries use such gloomy terms as grave, solemn, demanding, weighty, dangerous, and apprehensive. You have to skip over those words to get at the meaning intended here. If you try hard you can find defining words such as earnest, thoughtful, and important. Finally, when you read explanations of synonyms for serious you find the way the term applies to good teachers. Webster's New Collegiate Dictionary puts it this way: "Serious implies a concern for what really matters."

Seriousness in teaching means exactly that: concern for what really matters in schooling. As discussed earlier, different people hold different ideas about what really matters in schooling. Although their opinions differ, they are remarkably alike in some ways. Almost unanimous agreement exists regarding (1) maximum learning in academic areas, (2) courtesy and respect for others, and (3) pursuit and development of talents and abilities. Teachers are serious about teaching and learning when they show continued concern over student progress in these three aspects of schooling.

But how do we distinguish between serious and nonserious teachers? Certainly not by asking them. Ninety-nine and nine-tenths percent of all teachers will avow complete seriousness about their work with learners.

To make the distinction we must examine what they do in their work on a day-to-day basis. Such an examination reveals that teachers characterized by seriousness continually and consistently do the ten things listed below. They show these traits in the way they talk, in the way they work, and in the way they interact with others. They even reveal them while chatting in that great gossip factory known as the teachers' lounge. Here are the traits:

Ten Traits of Serious Teachers

1. They value education.
2. They value learning.
3. They value the golden rule.
4. They prepare adequately for instruction.
5. They give their best effort in teaching.
6. They keep students on task.
7. They follow up.
8. They take the extra step.
9. They persevere.
10. They communicate with parents.

After glancing at this listing of the golden ten, one might conclude that this section has jumped from a treatise on discipline to a treatise on good teaching. That simply shows how closely the two are entwined. Teachers who are truly serious about schooling as shown by these ten traits have much better class control on the average than do teachers who lack them. A brief examination of these traits will reveal the powerful role that each plays in class control.

Value Education

To value something means to believe firmly that it is true and good. One makes this valuing known to others by (1) talking positively about it, (2) behaving in accord with it, and (3) helping others move toward it.

Serious teachers value education. They still believe firmly that education is the best path to the individual good life and the only means of perpetuating a democratic society. They make their views known, when necessary, to parents and colleagues. They make them known continually to the students they teach. They do not preach or cajole. They explain, sometimes even avow. They give real life examples of what they mean, in terms that students can understand. They help students explore realistic life goals, and show how education can lead to those goals.

Value Learning

Serious teachers value learning. They think it is good and worthwhile, whether as a practical means to a goal, as a way of forming a life habit for inquisitiveness and information gathering, or as an enjoyable end in itself. They show this value in various ways. One way is by making sure that genuine learning pervades all classroom activities. No wheel-spinning is acceptable, no busy work just to keep students occupied. Something new is to be learned regularly. A second way is by making full use of resource people, reference materials, supplemental instructional materials, and class projects that require basic learning for successful completion. A third way is to help the class present public displays of creative and productive work. Parents, teachers, and other students view the displays and presentations. A fourth way is to produce a class publication that includes samples of students' work, annotated references of subjects and topics being studied in class, and a regular listing of new and interesting information that students have acquired. A fifth way is for teachers to show that they themselves are avid learners. They can discuss their learning activities with the class, show examples, and do demonstrations. This teacher-as-learner example can be one of the most powerful influences of all. You may have heard that seeing is believing; that actions speak louder than words; and that we all learn more through imitation than through any other avenue.

Value the Golden Rule

Do unto others as you would have them do unto you. Treat others as you want to be treated. Think how you like to be spoken to and speak to others in that way. Think how you like to be recognized and thus recognize others. We could go on and on with this kind of advice. Serious teachers do go on and on with it. They have found it to be a most desirable guide to behavior, easy to understand, easy to apply, effective, and contagious. It teaches positive habits that have life-long value. It helps as much as anything else in reducing conflict in the classroom. As conflicts shrink, class control improves.

You may think it odd that serious teachers put such emphasis on the golden rule. You may be remembering teachers who appeared serious by definition number 1—stern, demanding, harsh, inflexible, frightening. If so, remember serious definition number 2—caring, determined, concerned about, dedicated. This helps remind us that one can be serious about anything, serious about enjoyment, serious about good feelings, serious about the pleasures of treating others well and having them treat us well in return.

In many respects, teaching students to live by the golden rule is one of the most valuable things we can do. We all lament the growing rates of crime and vandalism. We are distressed by a pervasive unwillingness to get involved with other people's problems. We wonder what happened to old-fashioned courtesy. We see school students exhibiting disgusting behavior, some of it downright criminal. We wring our hands in despair, or else we submissively resign ourselves to a what-can-you-do attitude.

Serious teachers know they can do a great deal. True, some groups of students seem beyond hope. While plentiful, such students are still far from being the rule. Most students want to be treated well. When they are, they become better able to treat others well. Most students want to know about manners and etiquette, even though older ones may be publicly derisive of them.

Serious teachers do two things: (1) they always model in their own classroom demeanor the behaviors they want their students to acquire. They are always polite and helpful; and (2) they talk with students about golden-rule behavior, insist that they follow its precepts, arrange practice sessions as necessary, and reinforce students when they exhibit desired behavior. If they are wise they do a third thing as well: they inform the students' parents about what they are attempting to achieve, and they ask for support from home.

Adequate Preparation

All teachers know that students can acquire quite a bit of school learning more or less on their own, without much instruction. This phenomenon is known variously as spontaneous learning, learning on their own, and learning despite the teacher. Teachers also know that students will learn faster, easier, more correctly, and in greater quantities when given good instruction, instruction that guides, explains, urges, reinforces, and holds students accountable. Coincidentally, that kind of instruction cuts down markedly on the amount of disruptive behavior in the classroom.

Therefore, serious teachers routinely prepare thoroughly for each day's teaching even though they could get by without it. Better teachers are able to teach off the cuff when necessary. They can ad lib and improvise. They can teach from the basis of personality rather than organization. However, they know that when they do so they are short-changing their students, failing to provide them the best instruction possible under the circumstances.

Serious teachers know the facts of teaching—that every single thing cannot be planned in advance, even the best devised plans sometimes fall short of the mark, and unexpected happenings call for spur-of-the-moment revisions. But they also know that day in and day out better planning leads to better learning and better classroom control.

Giving the Best Effort

Serious teachers make a more determined effort to teach well than do average teachers. They plan, communicate, motivate, encourage, insist, follow through. They do these things thoroughly and consistently, even when they feel like saying, "What's the use?"

No one teaches hour after hour to their full capacity. Everyone, including the very best in any profession you could name, has ups and downs, highs and lows, peaks and valleys. Serious teachers recognize that fact. When they are much below par they often admit it to the students and ask for their special help. They also plan against the lows, going farther than usual to motivate students and enliven instruction. The good days take care of themselves.

Serious teachers are seldom completely satisfied with their performance. Despite diligent work they often feel they could have done better. When outside observers compare serious teachers' efforts to those of other teachers, however, it becomes clear that serious teachers come close to giving their best effort consistently. Observers can also see that students are aware of the efforts teachers make. They tend to pick up on those efforts, responding positively in classroom work and behavior.

Keeping Students On Task

In the late 1970s the California Commission on Teacher Preparation and Licensing began a study that continued for several years. The commission wished to identify teaching traits and behaviors that contributed to success in teaching. The study, called the Beginning Teacher Evaluation Study (BTES), identified several teacher behaviors that correlated with student learning. Most of those behaviors had very low correlations with learning, suggesting that they had relatively little influence on whether students learned or not.

One of the behaviors, however, showed significant (though still relatively small) effect. That was behavior that kept students on task in learning. It was found that the more time students remained actively engaged in learning the material at hand, the more they learned. This finding corresponds with common sense, with what everyone would have expected. It's worth noting, however, because many common-sense expectations fail to prove themselves under close scrutiny.

Serious teachers make a determined effort to keep their students engaged actively with the tasks at hand. They use a variety of means to do so. They select worthwhile, interesting learning activities. They make sure the ideas are within students' reach, and that the work is challenging but accomplished fairly easily. They pace the work to match students' attention spans, vary it to prevent monotony, provide assistance to overcome frustration. They enliven the activities with humor and surprise. They provide interesting applications of material being learned. They try to keep students active physically, mentally, and emotionally. All these devices help students stay on task. The students in turn learn more and, of course, have less time and inclination to misbehave.

Follow-up

All of us have had teachers who began like a storm but ended in the doldrums. They promised so much, yet delivered so little. Maybe they made dire threats but didn't carry them out even when they should have. Or they made assignments but never checked to see how well they were done, or if they were completed at all. Such teachers fail to follow up on what they start.

Serious teachers finish what they start. At times, of course, they offer suggestions or begin activities that don't pan out. Naturally they don't stick doggedly to a bad idea. They discuss its drawbacks with students, then change plans. Everyone knows what's going on. Except when ideas go sour, however, you can find them as involved at the end as they were at the beginning.

To be more specific, serious teachers give students tasks that are worthwhile—valuable assignments worthy of being completed. They check student work at two points during progress. They check for errors or stumbling blocks, which they correct or remove. At completion they check again, to be sure the work is correct and understood.

Serious teachers establish, in consultation with students, rules that govern behavior in the classroom. They monitor compliance with the rules. Students who break rules suffer reasonable consequences, which have been discussed in advance. For the students' sake, the rules must be enforced.

Serious teachers do what they say they will do, when they say they will do it. You can count on them. If they promise to have materials ready on Tuesday, that is what they will do. If they promise a reward for good behavior, they will certainly come through with the reward. If they threaten to call your mother when you misbehave, you know they will surely do so. These are examples of following-up in teaching. Serious teachers give students important work and they expect proper behavior. They give all possible help along the way. And they will be there at the finish, to approve, acknowledge, redirect, or otherwise see each thing through to a proper end.

Taking the Extra Step

Two traits clearly set a serious teacher apart from others. Those are taking the extra step, discussed here, and its close ally, perseverance, discussed in the next section. Both show willingness and determination to help students learn and behave acceptably.

Most of us can recall teachers who took that extra step for us, who went above and beyond the call of duty because they cared about our learning. We remember those teachers as excellent in their work. Maybe they didn't tell the best jokes; maybe they weren't the prettiest to look at; maybe we didn't have a barrel of fun in their classrooms. But we learned. We grew. We progressed because they were always willing to do more than was asked, more than was expected.

What are examples of taking the extra step? Get a group of people together and they can think of them all day:

- Making a good-will visit to a student's home.
- Staying after school to help on a project.
- Arriving early to give special help or make-up work.
- Sending post cards to students while away on vacation.
- Meeting with parents to iron out difficulties.
- Arranging for field trips, special guests, exhibitions, performances, and celebrations.
- Making time to talk privately with each student once in a while.
- Finding ways to draw attention to fine work done by the class.

We could go on and on. The point is obvious: serious teachers are always looking for ways to help their students. They do those things, even when inconvenient. That's taking the extra step.

Perseverance

The Hoosier Schoolmaster (Eggleston, 1871) is a classic book in American education. Set in the 1850's, it describes the life of a young male teacher in a one-room school in Indiana. His students were of all ages, some much larger, stronger, and tougher than himself. The rough older boys prided themselves in running off the previous three schoolmasters. They intended to do the same thing again. But the Hoosier schoolmaster wouldn't be defeated, even though the bullies did their worst. He said to himself, "I'll be a bulldog. I'll set my teeth into this job. I'll hang on. I'll never let go. I'll never give up."

Most teachers don't get beaten up these days (some still do), but they all encounter recalcitrant students. Those ornery rascals may be stubborn, they may be resistant, they may be slow, or they may be doing any and everything to get attention. Whatever the case, they are slow to learn and fast to disrupt. That deadly combination often makes teachers throw up their hands in resignation. But serious teachers don't resign. Like the Hoosier schoolmaster, they are bulldogs. They set their jaws and never give up. If Sally has to have long division explained twenty times, that's what she gets. If George thinks his atrocious playground behavior will outlast the teacher's resolve to correct it, he has another thought coming. If Alex fails to complete his assignment the first twelve times, he can be sure his serious teacher will be expecting him to complete it on the thirteenth try.

Serious teachers just don't give up. They stay in there pitching, even when average teachers say "enough, already." Their magic is that they often make the slow faster, the stubborn more willing, and the ruffian more gentle. Sometimes they don't succeed. Even then, they, their students, and the students' parents all know they have given their best.

Communication with Parents

Later in this book you will read chapter 13 entitled "Parents as Teachers' Best Friends." Experienced teachers pass along these nuggets, worth more than their weight in pure gold:

- For routines to go smoothly at school, be on best terms with the school secretary.

- For your classroom to stay in tip-top shape, be on best terms with the custodian.
- For help with your students' learning, be on best terms with their parents.

Parents want their children to learn and behave in school. You can't find one in a hundred who doesn't. They are sincere about that. You can count on it. The trouble is, they don't know how to help. They don't know what's expected; they don't know how school is conducted; they don't know how to tutor at home; they don't know how to arrange good homework settings. They don't even know for sure that teachers care about their kids.

It is not hard to inform parents about all these things. Once you do say clearly what you hope to do for the students and how parents can help, you will find a cadre of staunch supporters. Serious teachers make the effort to communicate with parents. They know that the small amount of work involved will pay huge dividends. They invariably have systems for communicating. They get the details worked out, and information flows smoothly. Often you will see them use telephone calls, notes, newsletters, and personal conferences. They send many messages verbally through the students that describe (1) what they intend to accomplish with each student, (2) how parents can help at home, and (3) how and when they can be contacted in return. They make sure to follow up on the items communicated to parents.

When the parents see evidence of this interest in their child, they will do much to help and support the teacher. This push from home increases student learning and it cuts down markedly on student misbehavior. One caution: good communication doesn't imply being buddies with parents. To be most effective, teachers should always be professional. They should be friendly and kind, but they should be businesslike. Otherwise some parents will see them as wishy-washy, and will eagerly tell them how to teach the class.

Class Rules

Every class needs a set of rules that governs two things—work habits and personal behavior. To be most effective those rules must be jointly formulated, reasonable, positive, succinct, observable, public, enforceable, and enforced. Penalties for breaking the rules should be understood in advance. When the rules are broken, those penalties must be applied immediately, consistently, and impartially, without malice. Obsolete or unnecessary rules should be dropped. All rules should be seen as law. They are to be obeyed. If unreasonable they can be changed, but so long as they are in effect they apply to everyone, students and teacher alike. Let us examine those elements of good class rules.

Jointly Formulated

Students should take part with the teacher in establishing class rules. When people help make rules they are more likely to see them as reasonable and they are more likely to follow them. This is true for adults and for most school students. The teacher has responsibility for initiating rules discussions, for keeping them short and positive, and for ensuring that penalties for breaking them are reasonable. Students should make suggestions about desired behaviors, enforcement, and penalties. If they are very young, in kindergarten or first grade, they cannot give significant input. Still, they should be consulted. Each rule should be explained carefully so that students understand clearly what it means, why it is needed, and what will happen if it is broken. Young children should receive guided practice in doing what the rules require. They should see examples of behavior that breaks the rules, but they should not practice the rule-breaking behavior.

Reasonable

Curiously, when groups of people make rules for themselves they often go overboard and make too many rules. They make rules that don't affect significant behavior and rules relating to character instead of behavior. It is the teacher's responsibility to make sure the rules are reasonable—that they focus on important behavior, are understandable, can be remembered, and can be practiced.

Positive

Authorities urge teachers to formulate rules in positive, rather than negative terms. That means saying what students should do, rather than what they should not do. Remember Ginott's dictum, correcting is directing? He meant that the best way to correct misbehavior is to show students how to do it right. Good rules do the same thing. They tell students how to behave correctly. Examples:
1. Raise hands and take turns in talking. (Instead of "No talking out.")
2. Be polite to others. (Instead of "Don't interrupt;" "Don't hit;" "Don't take cuts in line.")
3. Plan ahead to get all work done on time. (Instead of "Don't turn work in late.")

Attention should be drawn to negative behaviors, too, so students will know what to avoid. This should be done in discussions about the rules, and before concluding the discussion, attention should be redirected to the positive.

Succinct

Haim Ginott advised teachers to use laconic language when dealing with student misbehavior. Laconic language is very brief and to the point. It focuses attention on the matter at hand and lets the student know what to do, without haranguing, preaching, or moralizing.

Class rules should be similarly succinct—brief and to the point. That makes them more effective and easier to remember. Examples:
1. Raise hands before speaking. (Instead of "We always raise our hands and wait to be called on before speaking, because we don't want to be rude to others by interrupting them.")
2. Take turns. (Instead of "We will take turns in everything we do, so that everyone will get an equal chance.")

Longer explanations can be made during rules discussions so that students will understand the reasons *behind the rules*. But they will be better able to remember the rules in their succinct form.

Observable

Rules should be addressed to behaviors that can be observed. It is not useful to make rules about being good, polite, considerate, or respectful, unless students know plainly what one does when showing those fine qualities. It is better to name specific acts, times, and conditions when possible. That was done in previous examples dealing with raising hands and getting work in on time. Other examples might be:
- Sit down and begin work promptly.
- Always say please and thank you.
- Stay in our seats.

The obvious difficulty with stating specific behaviors in rules is that you wind up with too many rules. Each behavior you aim for could be stated as its own rule. You might wind up with fifty or one hundred of them. That would never do. Students do well to remember as many as three rules in kindergarten, up to six or seven in upper grades. Therefore, a compromise is called for, which is to compose only enough rules to cover areas of main concern. These rules will have to be rather general. Within each of the rules will be a few specific behaviors that students can discuss, practice, and remember. Here are examples:

1. A rule for work in the classroom—
   Written: Always Do Your Best Work.
   Discussed: Start on Time.
               Finish on time.
               Be neat.
               Do work you would be proud to show to your parents.
2. A rule for classroom behavior—
   Written: Be Kind To Others.
   Discussed: Be friendly.
               Speak politely—say please, excuse me, thank you.
               Help someone every day.
               Take turns.
3. A rule on how to treat classroom visitors—
   Written: Treat Visitors As Special.
   Discussion: Greet them.
               Offer them a chair.
               Show them some of our work.
               Be especially kind and helpful to substitute teachers.
4. A rule about behavior outside the classroom—
   Written: Obey the School Rules.
   Discussion: Walk, don't run, in corridors.
               Be a good example for others.

These examples show how to make a few written rules that cover important areas of behavior while still giving attention to several discrete kinds of behavior that fit within the rules.

Public

The main rules, three to six in number, should be made public. They should be written in large letters and displayed in a conspicuous place. There they can be seen by students, teacher, and visitors. Attention can be drawn to them regularly as a form of review. When violations occur the rule can be pointed to. Discussions, if needed, can refresh memories on specific behaviors that the rule calls for. Many teachers like to post slogans about the room that draw attention to the rules and specific behaviors. Examples of such slogans are:

- The only way to have friends is to be one.
- Manners are happy ways of doing things.
- Be kind, for everyone is fighting a hard battle.
- Courtesy is making others feel good.

- Your tongue weighs practically nothing. Are you strong enough to hold it?
- We get what we earn.
- Try to listen more than you talk.

These slogans can be added one at a time on display in the room. They offer focal points for discussions with the students, and they are a good vehicle for review of class expectations. One caution, however: if the slogans and rules remain posted in the same place all year and attention is not drawn back to them regularly, the students stop seeing them. Their mere presence is not enough.

Enforceable

Rules that cannot be enforced are worse than useless. They are counter-productive because they tell students that rules don't mean a thing. For that reason, teachers must be sure that rules, jointly formulated and publicly displayed, can be adhered to.

Some rules that sound fine simply cannot be enforced. Reasons for that condition include limited teacher power, limited ability to observe, customs of the community, and individual traits of the students. The following cases show examples of rules that cannot be enforced.

1. Finish All Work On Time. If you have students who are handicapped, immature, or very slow workers this rule is unreasonable. It might be changed to "Do our best to finish work on time."
2. No Swearing. If your students come from a neighborhood where swear words fly like flakes in a snowstorm, you will not be able to enforce this rule. It would be better to compose one that says We Will Improve Our Language Every Week. You can then discuss specific language usage and keep a graph of class opinion about improvements.
3. Eat Three Balanced Meals a Day. Forget this one. It's a good idea, but as a rule it's a dead end street.

Enforced

Once rules have been established, they must be enforced. But before they can be enforced, they must meet the criteria discussed in previous paragraphs. In particular, rules are more enforceable when they are reasonable and when they have been composed cooperatively by teacher and students. Moreover, there should be few surprises in rule enforcement. Students should know the penalties in advance. When they break a rule, the appropriate penalty is assessed, dispassionately and matter-of-factly.

This dispassionate and matter-of-fact penalty assessment is embodied in a concept called *logical consequences*. Such logical consequences are reasonable penalties. Students know about them in advance. If their behavior violates class rules the penalties come as a logical consequence of the behavior they have chosen.

Choice of behavior and logical consequences are cornerstones of Glasser's view of discipline, which was discussed in chapter 7. Glasser feels that we all choose to behave the way we do. Good behavior is simply good choices. Bad behavior is bad choices. When students choose bad behavior for themselves they are simultaneously choosing the consequences (penalties or punishments) that inevitably accompany that bad behavior.

This approach allows teachers to enforce rules with a minimum of anger, distress, or ill feelings. Students probably won't like the consequences, but they have in effect chosen them. The teacher can even show sympathy for their unfortunate choice (but not back away from enforcement: that would render the entire system ineffective). The teacher can also follow up as Glasser suggests by helping the student make a new commitment and a new plan of action for making better choices of behavior.

Threats and warnings deserve brief consideration at this point. Most teachers use them far too much, with the result that students are confused. They continue to push to see how far the rules will bend. This in turn causes teachers anxiety, and when they finally decide to lower the boom, hostility and ill feelings are likely to result for everyone.

It is better never to make threats. It is enough for students to know the rules and the penalties that automatically arise when the rules are broken. That makes threats unnecessary. When angered, teachers are prone to say things that are difficult or impossible to carry out. The problem then becomes compounded.

An occasional warning can be used in place of threats. The warning should be given only once. If students don't know that, teachers should make it plain. The warning can be mention of the rule that is being violated. It can be given in the manner suggested by Ginott with the teacher using an I-message—"It is so noisy I can't do my work." Or the warning can be directed more pointedly: "The next time I have to mention the talking, I must enforce the penalty that you seem to be choosing." Then the teacher must follow through if necessary. Thus it is acceptable to give warnings once, matter of factly. They should never be given a second time, because that only keeps students guessing. Instead of second warnings logical consequences should be invoked.

Penalties

We hear so often that the punishment should fit the crime, and so it should. But we must remember that breaking class rules is not a crime, in any legal sense of the word. Still, punishment can be administered for breaking class rules if it is reasonable and administered dispassionately. Basically that means you can make students stay after school, do extra work, and relinquish privileges. You can even administer corporal punishment. With corporal punishment, however, you'd better be sure you are not angry at the time, and that you have a witness. Never, never strike a student (or pinch, pull hair, or shove) while you are angry. Few teachers use corporal punishment. It is considered inhumane and degrading and produces unwanted side effects. Parents seem eager to sue over corporal punishment, so even when teachers are legally correct they have reason to fear the headaches of legal suits, lawyers, court appearances, and emotional upset.

What, then, are suitable kinds of penalties for breaking class rules? The underlying requisites of interventions and penalties are:
1. It stops the misbehavior.
2. It shows the student how to behave correctly.
3. It makes right what was done wrong, if possible.
4. It does not degrade the student.
5. It allows good personal relations to continue.
6. It serves to improve behavior.

The models of classroom discipline presented in earlier chapters made many suggestions for good interventions and penalties. Those suggestions fit nicely into a scheme of preventive control, supportive control, and corrective control.

Preventive control consists of measures taken to reduce the incidence of misbehavior before it occurs and could include such steps as:
1. Providing interesting activities.
2. Arranging schedules that allow frequent changes of pace.
3. Making class rules and discussing them.
4. Establishing on-going, behavior-modification programs.
5. Notifying parents when having contests and finding other means for establishing student desire for good behavior.

Supportive control refers to steps taken to nip misbehavior in the bud, to catch it at its earliest and redirect it. Examples of such steps would be:
1. Implementing on-going behavior modification.
2. Watching students, moving among them, and helping with difficulties.

3. Changing pace or interjecting humor when frustration or boredom begins to build.
4. Holding regular class discussions about both positive and negative feelings to iron out problems before they become serious.

Corrective control refers to the steps taken after misbehavior has occurred. Nonpunitive measures often used include:

1. Taking time out—sitting apart from the class (but within view!) for a time.
2. Making right what was done wrong, or making it up through good deeds.
3. Asking the misbehaving student in a friendly tone of voice what he is doing. Have him make a value judgment about it.
4. Conferencing privately with the offending student, addressing the situation and the behavior rather than the student's character.
5. Calling parents if the misbehavior continues.
6. Having an administrator remove the student if nothing else works.

Great Expectations

Perhaps you remember the musical play *My Fair Lady* in which an English gentleman succeeds, after varied trials and tribulations, in transforming a cockney girl into a lady of fine speech and manners. That theme came from an ancient Greek drama entitled *Pygmalion*, about the king of Cyprus who fell in love with an ivory statue that he had made. When Pygmalion was at his prayer, Aphrodite gave life to the statue.

In 1968 Robert Rosenthal and Lenore Jacobson published a book entitled *Pygmalion in the Classroom* (New York: Harper and Row). That book reported studies that purported to show that students tend to live up to what is expected of them. If they are led to believe firmly that they will do well, students tend to do so. If they really believe they will do poorly, they follow suit. Rosenthal and Jacobson introduced the term self-fulfilling prophecy. They used it as a label for the phenomenon of people's behavior reflecting what is genuinely expected of them. The term is now used widely.

The conclusions reported in *Pygmalion in the Classroom* have been roundly criticized, mainly because of the methods of research and data interpretation that were used. Nevertheless, most authorities agree that student behavior is influenced by expectations that teachers hold. Teachers who are good at classroom control corroborate that view. They will tell you that you get pretty much from kids what you expect to get. That's over the long haul, of course. Daily problems arise, which have to be solved. Students have to be talked with regularly. But through those talks, the set standards, and the procedures used for correcting misbehavior, teachers can make essential points known—that they expect humane behavior from students, that they themselves will behave in humane ways, that their students can be the best, and that being the best one can be is eternally worth striving for. Truly believing in students, truly expecting the best from them: those are the great expectations that influence behavior so powerfully.

Summary

Many different ideas have been presented in this chapter, so many in fact that it seems desirable to summarize them. These ideas have to do with the roles that teacher seriousness, class rules, and great expectations play in student behavior and discipline.

Serious teachers were defined as those who truly value education, learning, and the golden rule. They prepare adequately for teaching, give their best effort, keep students on task, follow up with students, take the extra step, never give up, and communicate well with parents. Each of these traits influences how students behave and learn.

Rules tell students what is permitted in the classroom and what is not. They should be formulated by teacher and students together. They should be reasonable, positive, succinct, observable, public, enforceable, enforced, and call for appropriate penalties when broken. Rules remove much guesswork and game-playing. Punishments should be constructive, and they should be applied consistently and without malice, as the natural consequence of misbehavior.

Great expectations mean truly expecting the best of students and continually letting them know that. Students are rarely angelic. They misbehave under the best of circumstances. Still, they tend to behave in ways genuinely expected by the teacher. Expect the best, and students will lean in that direction.

Chapter 11

Models for Gentlemen and Gentlewomen

Modeling is a process of teaching through example that produces learning through imitation. It is not very well known. Only in the past decade has it received detailed attention. But the evidence coming from that attention makes one thing plain: for most social, behavioral, cognitive, and affective learning, modeling is the most effective of all methods of teaching.

Perhaps the greatest strength of modeling is that it describes a learning process, and in the very same terms it suggests teaching procedures. That unity of terms and processes lets teaching and learning be considered joint aspects of the same effort, instead of depicting teaching as a set of acts that causes students to go through a separate set of acts. This parallel of teaching to learning makes modeling uniquely useful to teachers.

Along with its practicality in teaching, modeling brings a host of added benefits. It is efficient, it provides remarkable guidance while reducing learner labor and error, and it greatly speeds the learning of complex behaviors. Most of all, it is the best way to teach students how to behave acceptably in the classroom. It is discipline's best friend.

In this chapter we shall see how teachers use modeling to help students learn both subject matter and good behavior. First, however, let's see what is required in teaching through modeling. Effective modeling requires the following three conditions. Each is essential:

1. *A clear, concise, accurate, attractive example (model) for learners to observe.* This model can depict concepts, relationships, processes, or behaviors. The model can be a live or recorded person, a verbal

description, a graphic or pictorial representation, or a tangible three-dimensional object. Models can be used singly or in combination.

2. *Careful attention by observers to the modeled event.* The crucial elements, features, aspects, relationships, and so forth must be noted in the modeled event. Attention can be directed by telling learners in advance what to look for. It can be redirected during the event as necessary. It will be increased by attractive models showing useful, interesting behavior or information.

3. *Retention (remembering) by observers of what is shown by the model.* This retention allows students to reenact at a later time what they observed during modeling. Coding, directed attention, emotional involvement, practice, and reinforcement are among established means of improving retention.

Learning through modeling is further enhanced by the following, which are helpful though not essential to the process:

4. *Practice in reenacting the observed concept, process, or behavior.* The learners practice the new learning in order to refine and strengthen it.

5. *Corrective feedback and reinforcement.* Corrective feedback, furnished during practice, helps learners reenact the modeled behavior more accurately. Reinforcement also increases accuracy. In addition, it can increase the likelihood that the learner will use the new learning in appropriate situations.

What Research Says about Modeling

Well over one hundred studies dealing with modeling have been conducted since 1960 that provide a solid research base to support its elements, procedures, and effectiveness. Albert Bandura, of Stanford University, deserves major credit for developing modeling as a teaching process. He recognized and documented the powerful influence that modeling exerts on behavior. The more he looked into it the more he saw that modeling's component parts could be molded, filed, and gold plated in the laboratory. That meant experimentation, which puts a gleam in scientists' eyes and stirs up much activity.

Special education was the first branch of public education to recognize the power of Bandura's work. People who work with the mentally retarded or educationally handicapped are ever watchful for procedures that speed and strengthen learning. They had earlier received a great boon with principles of reinforcement and behavior modification. Now modeling appeared. When used in conjunction with behavior modification, it produced results that brought smiles of satisfaction to special education's face.

Modeling's effectiveness is not limited to special education. Its powers are even more notable in the regular classroom. We have a growing body of evidence that suggests it is our most effective method for reaching many of the objectives within the three great domains of learning: psychomotor (physical behavior), cognitive (knowledge and its use), and affective (emotions, attitudes, and values).

The many research studies carried out in modeling provide a body of generalizations that can be considered principles of modeling, some of which are presented in the following lists.

Effectiveness of Modeling

1. Modeling effectively teaches behavior, concepts, cognitive skills and processes, language, creativity, values, attitudes, and interests.
2. Modeling teaches effectively not only through individual example but also through group example, simulations, psychodrama, behavior rehearsal, and role play.
3. Learnings acquired through modeling are generalizable. They are not limited just to replication within identical settings, but spread to numerous other situations and contexts.

Traits of Models

4. Traits of the model provide the main motivators for observational learning. They attract and hold attention, and they can increase observers' desire to emulate the observed behavior or process.
5. Model traits known to be effective in enhancing observational learning include familiarity, meaningfulness, clarity, prestige, social status, creativity, skill, brightness, known success, warmth, nurturance, and obvious desire to help.

Teacher as Model

6. Teachers are prime models for classroom instruction. They, more than any other models, possess the variety of traits known to be effective in observational learning.

Filmed Models

7. While live models tend to be more effective, models presented via television and film can be powerful.

Peers as Models

8. Evidence points to peer modeling for both children and adults as one of the most powerful influences in the acquisition of social behavior, interests, values, morals, sex roles, language, and cognitive skills.

Verbal Models

9. Verbal models alone or in combination with other models are highly effective. They assist learning by clarifying, organizing, focusing attention, providing cues for retention and reenactment, and increasing the likelihood of generalization.

Graphic and Three-Dimensional Models

10. Both graphic and three-dimensional models effectively transmit behavioral, cognitive, attitudinal, and emotional learnings.

The Self as Model

11. It has been shown that clearly visualizing oneself behaving in a desirable fashion can lead to improved performance.

Motivation in Modeling

12. Motivation is useful in attracting, focusing, and maintaining observer attention. This motivation is affected by personal traits of the models, teacher guidance, peer pressure, and reinforcement from the teacher.

Verbalization in Modeling

13. Verbalization refers to labeling of observations and to "talking through" acts and processes. It greatly improves the speed of learning and the ability to recall and reenact the modeled events.

Feedback in Modeling

14. Corrective feedback, given when learners are reenacting the modeled event, improves accuracy, especially for complex behaviors, processes, and concepts.

Retention in Modeling

15. Retention—what one remembers after observing a modeled event—is improved through attention to intent to remember, usefulness of the learning, verbalization, concise labeling, continued practice, and continued application.

Reinforcement in Modeling

16. Reinforcement used in conjunction with modeling usually speeds and strengthens learning.
17. Vicarious reinforcement—seeing the model being rewarded—increases imitative behavior.

Danger in Modeling

18. Modeling can effectively produce *undesirable* behaviors, just as it does desirable behaviors. Caution is required.

Modeling Applied to Discipline

Modeling is a process that occurs continually in life, where it accounts for the natural development of social behavior, customs, attitudes, values, and interests. Under laboratory conditions it has been used effectively for building, strengthening, and weakening many different kinds of behaviors including moral orientations, aggression, and general styles of individual and group behavior. Evidence shows that the process can be applied easily and effectively to modify all types of behavior that receive attention in classroom discipline.

Of particular interest in discipline are the behaviors associated with personal relations, self-concept, and classroom demeanor. Personal relations include such things as courtesy, manners, mutual support, and consideration for others. Self-concept has to do with an individual feeling of acceptability, competence, and belongingness. Classroom demeanor includes the numerous student acts that have bearing on classroom stability, calm, purposefulness, and order. It includes such things as moving about the room, asking permission, talking out, treatment of visitors to the room, and support of substitute teachers.

The remainder of this chapter addresses the role that modeling can play in classroom discipline. To help you understand what that role can be, how it functions, and how it is applied, discussions are presented within the following topics: modeling and principles of learning, effective models, steps in teaching through modeling, specific plans for teaching good behavior, specific plans for teaching manners and attitudes, and a review of modeling.

Modeling and Principles of Learning

If you reflect for a moment on the established principles of learning, you will see that modeling flows naturally into them. Over the decades, researchers and practitioners have formulated generalizations about learning that hold true for most learners, under most conditions, most of the time. Having passed the tests of time and practice, these statements have earned the distinction of being called principles. Among principles of learning, the following are preeminent. Students learn better when:

1. They are informed in advance as precisely as possible what they are expected to do and to learn.
2. They have a motivation level sufficient to help them pay close attention and proceed diligently through the learning activities.
3. They are able to practice the new learnings immediately and often in appropriately meaningful situations.
4. They receive suitable feedback as to the accuracy of their efforts and mistakes they are making, plus reinforcement for suitable efforts and improvements.
5. They are able to apply their learnings to the solution of realistic problems within realistic situations.

It follows that teachers teach better when they provide the conditions under which students learn better. This is not to imply that teaching is a simple task. It is not. But when skillful teachers adept at setting good learning environments and establishing good personal relations put modeling to use, they naturally provide the conditions named in the five principles listed. Here is how modeling meets these conditions:

1. *Knowledge of expectations* is provided very clearly, through the modeled event. Students are to replicate the model. Since they see or hear it, often in conjunction with verbal descriptions, they know precisely what is expected. Before the 1960s, students usually knew only vaguely what they were supposed to learn. Behavioral objectives then considerably sharpened their view (and that of their teachers). Modeling now provides another step forward for student knowledge of expectations.

2. *Motivation* in modeling comes from various sources. It can be established quickly at a high level by using live models that are attractive, prestigious, expert, and enthusiastic. Graphic and tangible models motivate highly when they are novel, colorful, and clear. Motivation is maintained through advance organization, vicarious and direct reinforcement, student enjoyment, and obvious worth of what is being learned.

3. *Practice* has clear direction in modeling. The students attempt to reenact the modeled behavior precisely. Practice is provided in various forms—covertly when students attempt to see themselves in their minds' eye performing correctly, and overtly when they physically reenact the behavior. Ideal practice conditions allow all students to reenact the behavior so errors can be noted and corrected.

4. *Corrective feedback and reinforcement* enhance the effectiveness of modeling. They are easier to apply with modeling than with many other methods because both students and teachers know that the replicated behavior should match the modeled behavior. When errors are made the teacher can specify exactly what needs to be done differently. This specification can be made humanely and constructively simply by remodeling and guiding student reenactment. Similarly, reinforcement specifies exactly what the student is doing right. This makes reinforcement more effective that when it is given in statements that are positive but vague.

5. *Application* of new learnings does not naturally occur better with modeling than it does with other methods of teaching. However, learnings acquired through modeling have excellent application potential. They are quite precise, allowing students to use them purposefully and competently.

These five points make up the heart of the modeling method of teaching. You will find them stressed and restressed in the prototype lessons that appear later in the chapter.

Effective Models

Effective modeling can be done behaviorally (live or filmed demonstrations), verbally (oral or written descriptions), and graphically (photographs, cartoons, drawings). Evidence suggests that a combination of two or more models used together is more effective than one alone. That is, while models are demonstrating a behavior, for example, they may also describe orally what they are doing and why.

For teaching acceptable classroom behavior live models are most effective. Teachers are very effective in this role as are other adults. Peer models, used correctly, are very effective also.

Models are effective to the degree in which they capture attention, hold attention, and tend to be imitated. Traits of live models that contribute to their effectiveness include:

1. Level of competence shown by the model.
2. Purported expertness of the model.
3. Celebrity status of the model.
4. Social power of the model.
5. Model ability to reward imitators.
6. Age of the model.
7. Sex of the model.
8. Ethnic status of the model.
9. Physical attractiveness of the model.
10. Personality attractiveness of the model.

When systematic reinforcement is applied to observers during modeling, the effects of model traits become less powerful. For example, an unattractive model can be more effective than an attractive model if observers are rewarded when they imitate the model's behavior.

Effective traits of verbal and graphic models have not been explored systematically but desirable qualities of such models would probably include (1) clarity, (2) succinctness, (3) apparent correctness, and (4) attractive format, style, and language.

Steps in Teaching Through Modeling

Bandura's experimental work in modeling did not deal with teaching. It dealt with spontaneous imitation learning, especially in areas of fears, phobias, and interpersonal relations. The experimental work done by others following Bandura's footsteps has delved into many other aspects of imitation learning, including traits of models, generalization of learning acquired through imitation, the theoretical components of imitation learning, and the effects of reinforcement on imitation learning.

Thus, modeling as a teaching process has grown out of attempts to apply its principles to the classroom. This happened first in special education and is only now occurring in regular classroom instruction. You realize, of course, that the process of modeling has always been crucial in learning and teaching since time immemorial, and that it is essential to the socialization of numerous species of animals besides man. But it is only now that its principles are being refined and applied in a systematic, organized, technical way.

In the mid 1970s the special-education department of Cajon Valley, California schools devised and implemented a five-step sequence for teaching handicapped students through modeling. The author of this book collaborated with them in applying and refining the process in regular classrooms. The sequence proved easy to learn, easy to apply, and very effective in promoting various kinds of learning. Following are the five steps of the process. Later you will see them applied to actual teaching plans.

Step 1. Provide a good model for the students.

The model should incorporate as many desirable traits as possible.

Step 2. Call for group verbal reenactment in unison of what was modeled.

Repeat two or three times. Be sure all students participate.

Step 3. Ask for volunteers to reenact the modeled event individually.

Usually two volunteers suffice. This step serves three purposes. First, it allows the teacher to assess correctness of the replication. Second, it serves to remodel the behavior for other class members. Third, it provides opportunity for the teacher to reinforce the correct behavior. The reinforcement occurs vicariously for the other members of the class.

Step 4. Draft two nonvolunteers to replicate the modeled behavior.

This step serves the same three purposes as Step 3.

Step 5. Have students apply the new learnings immediately in a realistic situation.

This application provides additional practice and it further establishes the value of the learning. These conditions aid retention and transfer of learning.

In applying the steps you realize that the model is not presented cold, out of the blue. As with any other lesson you set the stage for student involvement. Some people use an air of exuberance, mystery, or surprise. Others preview what is to come, what should be learned, and what the learning is good for. The beginning leads into the model, which in turn guides the remainder of the lesson.

The five-step sequence is designed to cut student errors to a minimum. Still, students will make some errors. When they do the teacher does not point to the guilty individuals. Instead the behavior is remodeled, as it first was. Then students are called on again for reenactment. This recycling procedure provides two benefits. One is that it avoids student embarrassment or hurt. Another is that group attention is diverted from the error and directed back immediately to an appropriate response.

During the entire process, teachers remember to provide feedback and reinforcement. The two are most effective when combined. They should specify in positive terms what the student is doing right. Negative comments are not used. Comments that are positive but vague are kept to a minimum. Instead of saying, "Good. That's fine. Nice work." the teacher might say, "Good. You are remembering to raise your hand before talking." Most of us do not use enough reinforcement and encouragement with our students. It takes practice to remember to reinforce students by telling them what they are doing right.

Specific Plans for Teaching through Modeling

This section presents six specific plans for teaching desired behavior. The first three deal with aspects of classroom demeanor, and the second three with manners and attitudes. Each plan is divided into two parts, background and application. The background tells about the plan and preparations that should be made for its use. The application details its actual use with a group of students. As reminders, the five steps in teaching through modeling are shown in the left margins.

Plan 1. How to Read in a Group

Background: This two-part lesson teaches students five important behaviors for reading in groups. Those behaviors are:
1. How to sit.
2. How to hold the books.
3. How to follow along with the reader.
4. How to read loudly.
5. How to read with expression.

The teacher first models for a group of five students. They are told that they will teach the rest of the class. The five students then model the behaviors in the form of a demonstration for the class. The lesson effectively improves group reading behavior for students from first through sixth grade. With modifications it can be used to teach desired behaviors in group activities at all grade levels.

Objective: Upon completion of this lesson students in reading groups will be able to sit correctly, hold their books properly, follow the reader accurately, and read aloud with suitable volume and proper expression.

Application:

Part 1

Initiate   Bring five students to the reading circle. Give them reading books opened to the same page. Tell them there are good ways and poor ways to read in the reading group. We are going to learn the good ways—how to sit, hold the book, keep up with the reader, read loudly, and read with expression.

Teacher models
Group
reenactment   Model each behavior for the students: sitting, holding the book, keeping up with the reader, reading loudly, and reading for expression. After modeling each behavior call on the group to reenact it together.

Volunteer
reenactment   Call on volunteers to reenact each behavior.

Draftee
reenactment   Call on nonvolunteers to reenact each behavior.

Part 2

Have this group of five students model how to read in a group for the remainder of the class. They can do it as a skit, with a different student modeling each behavior. The teacher directs the modeling sequence to obtain group, volunteer, and draftee reenactment.

Immediate
application   Follow with group reading lessons. Tell the students you will be looking for those who remember all five parts about reading in the group.

Continued
application   Ask students to recall the five important behaviors at the beginning of subsequent group reading sessions.

Plan 2. How to Behave in the Math Center (Lab, Shop, Kitchen, etc.)

Background: This lesson teaches students how to conduct themselves when using the math learning center. It applies equally to any other part of the curriculum where specific duties, behaviors, and manners are desired.

Older students from another class model the behaviors. Arrangements are made with them and their teacher in advance, and they practice before or after school the behaviors they are going to model. The lesson is effective for learners at any grade level.

Objective: As a result of the lesson the students will demonstrate these modeled behaviors when using the math center: (1) how to go to the center, (2) how to select an activity and begin work, and (3) how to ask for help when needed.

Application:

Initiate   "Class, we have a special surprise today. I have invited some students from Mrs. Simmons' class to show us how they work in the math center. They will use our center, and they will show you how they do these things I have written on the board."
1. How to go to the center.
2. How to select an activity.
3. How to ask for help.

Students model   "Let's watch how they do these three things." The models, who are seated, get up, go to the center, select an activity, and begin work. After a moment, one raises a hand. The aide or teacher responds.

Volunteer verbal reenactment   Call on volunteer students to:
1. Recall the three things being modeled.
2. Describe how students went to the center, selected an activity, and asked for help.

Draftee reenactment   Call on nonvolunteers to do the same.

Immediate application   Thank the models and allow them to return to their class. "Now let's see if we can do as well as the older students did. I will call on four people to show us what they have learned." Call four names. Those people go to the center and begin work. Repeat with others, if desired. (Give feedback and reinforcement with specific mention of what was done correctly.)

Continued application   Periodically review desired behaviors. When students violate them, correct individually and/or follow with group discussions.

Plan 3. Ignoring Inappropriate Behavior

Background: This lesson teaches students how to ignore inappropriate behavior they see in the classroom. Their ignoring of such behavior removes the reinforcement that misbehaving students get from peer attention. The lesson is conducted by means of group discussion and role playing. Peers model the ignoring behavior. They also model the reinforcing responses made to students who ignore the inappropriate behaviors.

The lesson can be used effectively in grades one through six. In fifth and sixth grades, however, the point must be stressed that this is a serious activity, even though it may be fun. Otherwise students may decide to mimic the inappropriate behaviors rather than ignore them. Be sure to discuss the effects of inappropriate behaviors, how they disrupt lessons, and how they can hurt others' feelings.

Objective: As a result of this lesson, students will be able to:
1. Name at least three acts that are inappropriate in the classroom.
2. Tell and demonstrate the meaning of ignore.
3. Improve in their tendency to ignore inappropriate behavior when it occurs.

Application:

Initiate "Class, sometimes we see students in our group do things we know are not right, things that show bad manners. Have you ever noticed people doing those things? What are some of them?" (List on board as students mention them. Elicit mention of name calling, loud laughing, making noises, talking out, etc.)

"Sometimes when we hear or see someone do these things, we think it would be funny to do them, too. Soon, everyone is doing them. The result is that we can't get our work done. We annoy other people, and sometimes hurt their feelings. Because these acts disturb our work and hurt peoples' feelings, they are inappropriate. Inappropriate means they are not the right thing to do in the class. When you see inappropriate behavior, what you should do is ignore it. Ignore means you don't pay any attention to it.

"Today we are going to practice ignoring inappropriate behavior. Let's take some of the behaviors listed on the board. We will role play how to ignore them. Role play means to pretend we are really doing the things. I would like four of you to help me, please.

Peers model "Fine. Sit in these four chairs. Tom, choose one of the behaviors listed on the board. When we begin, you can do the inappropriate behavior. Sarah and John will be students.

"They will ignore Tom—pay no attention at all to him. Lupe, you be the teacher. When you see Sarah and John ignoring Tom's behavior, thank them for ignoring it. You can let them help you collect the papers since they did what they knew was right. The rest of you are the audience. Be very quiet. You will get a chance to role play, too, if you are quiet and pay attention. All right, Tom, begin."

Group reenactment   Repeat with other students role playing ignoring inappropriate behavior.

Application   "I will be looking to see who can ignore behaviors in the class. I will find a way to thank you when you do." (Be sure that students who play the teacher's role do not say hurtful things about the offender.)

Plan 4. I am Likeable and Capable (IALAC)

Background: This lesson helps students become aware of the damaging effects of criticism, sarcasm, and ridicule, and it teaches students how to speak to others in ways that bolster their self-esteem. It is adaptable to all grade levels.

Three kinds of models are used: graphic, teacher, and peer. The teacher describes the graphic model and demonstrates good and poor ways of speaking to others. A peer model demonstrates some damaging kinds of remarks. The teacher then models positive remarks that help repair damage done to self-esteem. The graphic model can be made to look like this:

Each letter is then used to describe what it stands for. For example, "I—me, myself, separate person, different from everyone else; I look different, I act different, my feelings are different, etc." Continue with "likeable" and "capable."

Objective: As a result of this lesson, students will increase the number of positive comments they make to each other.

Application:

Initiate — Show model of letters IALAC on chart. Tell students each letter will help them feel better about themselves, more likeable and capable, and teach them how to make others feel better, too. Discuss meanings of likeable and capable. Discuss the importance of feeling good about ourselves. Give each student an IALAC tag, a 3" x 5" card with IALAC written on it.

Teacher models, group reenacts — Say, "I am likeable and capable. Maureen, are you likeable and capable? Let's hear you say after me—I am likeable and capable." Continue. Have all students say it together.

Peer negative model — Awareness: Peer leader models behaviors that cause people not to feel likeable and capable. When student model makes remarks that criticize others the students tear a small piece off their IALAC tags.

Teacher positive model — Model behaviors that repair damaged IALAC—e.g. offering help, showing consideration, going out of the way to be kind, helping one see the positive side. This is done in role-playing pairs—first teacher and student, then

Paired reenactment — Student-student pairs practice saying IALAC corrective remarks.

Volunteer reenactment — Teacher describes a situation in which a student's work has been criticized harshly by the teacher. Ask for volunteers to reenact positive responses.

Draftee reenactment — Call on two nonvolunteers to make some positive comments, either to the same or to a new hypothetical situation.

Immediate application — Each student makes a new IALAC tag and wears it the remainder of the period. Teacher and students consciously make positive remarks to each other.

Continued application — Periodically review IALAC, concern, compassion, etc., in group discussions. Call for continued and renewed efforts from students to make positive, supportive comments to each other.

Note: Remember to reinforce all desired student responses. Use verbal praise that specifies what was done right. Be sure that the negative-model aspect of the lesson is kept in perspective. The tearing of the IALAC tags could become reinforcing to undesired behaviors.

Plan 5. Active Listening to Others

Background: This lesson, appropriate for third grade through high school, provides the rationale for the active-listening theory. It is useful for improving communication and enhancing self-concept. Students are taught to use several door-opener statements, such as "I see," "Go on," "I'm listening," "Tell me more," and "Uh huh." They also receive practice in decoding the hidden, emotional messages in conversation, and in supplying the feedback called for by those messages.

Two graphic chart models are needed, one that shows door-opener statements and another that shows decoded messages. They are shown in the illustrations that follow. Puppets may be used to assist in the role-playing situations. It is helpful to have on hand several index cards written with various problems around which role-playing situations can be built.

Objective: After completing this lesson, the student will be able to (1) explain why active listening techniques are valid and useful, and (2) use both door openers and active-listening feedback statements in their conversations, when appropriate.

"I hate Mr. ..."
(I wish he liked me.)

"This work is stupid!"
(I don't understand it.)

"I don't want to play."
(They don't want me.)

"Uh huh."
"Tell me more about that."
"I see."
"You feel that..."
"I think I understand..."

Application:

Initiate Discuss with students the importance of effective communication. Demonstrate what can happen when people cannot communicate. Try using a teacher-puppet skit of a deaf person who always misunderstands, or better yet, of Abbott and Costello's "Who's on First" routine. Have students identify what the communication problem is.

Introduce model Show "Listening Tips" chart. Have students read door-opener statements with teacher. Explain that with these phrases, you will show how they can help people talk about their problems.

Teacher models Using the puppet or a volunteer as the "problem owner," the teacher models a short conversation, using the door openers.

Group reenactment Teacher has the puppet or volunteer talk to the entire group as they respond with the door openers from the chart.

Volunteer reenactment Ask for two student volunteers to talk, using door-opener statements.

Draftee reenactment Call on two nonvolunteers to talk, using door openers.

Introduce model Using the "What Feelings Do We Hear" chart, discuss with the students how different feelings can be heard in voices and expressions.

Teacher models Teacher demonstrates some problem situations where feedback statements from the chart would be appropriate.

Group reenactment Repeating the same situations modeled by the teacher, have the entire group use feedback statements from the chart in reply to the problems.

Volunteer reenactment Call on two volunteers to discuss problems, using both door-opener statements and feedback responses. Have the rest of the class count how many times each type of statement is used, and if any other comments (advice, judgement, etc.) are used.

Draftee reenactment Call on two nonvolunteers to discuss problems following the same procedure used with volunteer reenactment.

Immediate application At the close of the lesson ask students to summarize and evaluate how active-listening techniques would be helpful to them in talking with their friends and classmates. Be sure to reinforce any active-listening techniques used by students during the day.

Periodically review the "Listening Tips" chart and elicit
from children actual experiences when these tips helped
or could have helped them. Continue reinforcement of
active listening done by students during the day.

Plan 6. How to Behave with a Substitute Teacher

Models and activities used in this lesson teach students the vulnerability of substitute teachers, the feelings they have in attempting to perform their jobs, how students can help substitute teachers, and the information about the classroom that the substitute would need in order to work effectively.

Two charts are needed for models. They can be copied from the illustrations tht follow. Colored pens can be used for emphasis.

Objective: After completing this lesson the students will be able to:
1. Identify and recognize the feelings of insecurity and newness that substitute teachers have.
2. Identify and perform behaviors helpful to a substitute in the classroom.
3. Identify and prepare an orientation plan for substitutes.

Figure 11.1. Charts for Graphic Models.

Application:

Initiate Discuss with students what types of feelings they have when they are in new situations, or when they must perform a job under harsh criticism. (insecurity, helplessness, frustration, anger, etc.) Select a peer leader. Send him from the room while an object is hidden somewhere in the classroom. Tell the students that their role in the situation will have three parts:

1. When the student first reenters the room is silent; no encouragement or discouragement is offered in the search for the hidden object.

2. At a signal from the teacher, students will criticize and offer misleading hints.

3. At a second signal from the teacher, students will encourage and offer hints to the student.

Have the student relate feelings that were experienced during each condition. Write comments on the board. Ask students to recall statements and behaviors that were most helpful to the student under stress. Write these on the board.

Peer models Call on prestigious students to model helpful statements that are written on the board.

Volunteer reenactment Call on two volunteers to reenact helpful comments and behaviors.

Draftee reenactment Call on two nonvolunteers to reenact helpful comments and behaviors.

Application Ask students to reiterate how this experience can help the substitute teacher in the performance of the job. Have them suggest how they might apply the helpful behaviors and statements.

Introduce second model Tell the students you are going to set up role-playing situations in which they will use these helpful behaviors. Show the chart that contains hints on helpful ideas. Review notes on the board.

Teacher models Select a student to play the role of substitute. Teacher models providing helpful behavior to the "substitute." Use suggestions from teacher-made chart or from student comments written on the board. For example, the student explains the opening activities procedure to the substitute.

Paired reenactment Divide the class into pairs. One person is the substitute and the other is a student. Example: Substitute has just entered the room and is looking over teacher's notes.

Volunteer and draftee reenactment

Immediate application

Continued application

Student approaches respectfully and explains normal class routine.

Call on two volunteers, then two nonvolunteers (in pairs) to reenact their role performance.

Conduct a group discussion on (1) what an individual can do when an entire group is misbehaving with a substitute; and (2) what an individual can do when a substitute doesn't know where important items are located.

Assign groups, individual students, or the entire class to work on putting together an "Orientation Plan Book for Substitutes," using the class chart as a guide. Assign individuals to act as substitute guides for days when the teacher is not present.

Review of Discipline through Modeling

What is Modeling?

Modeling is a process of teaching through example and learning through imitation. The process accounts for the learning of most social behavior. It is instrumental in the acquisition of knowledge, values, interests, attitudes, and accepted modes of behavior.

How Does Modeling Work?

Research into modeling indicates that the process involves the following components and functions:
1. Demonstration—an act is demonstrated, depicted, or explained.
2. Attention—observers focus their attentional processes on the demonstration, depiction, or explanation.
3. Memory—observers code and store the observed information, so they can recall and reproduce it when appropriate.

It has been further established that the process is usually enhanced when the following conditions are added:
4. Practice—observers reenact what they have observed.
5. Feedback—reinforcement, suppressors, and corrective feedback can be used to shape students' reenactments.

Who or What Can Serve as Models?

Effective models include teacher, peers, other adults, films, photographs, cartoons, diagrams, three-dimensional objects, puppets, and oral and written descriptions. Verbalization about the model or process usually increases its effectiveness.

What Do Teachers Do in Modeling?

The teacher's role in modeling is as follows:
1. Selects behavior to be learned.
2. Selects most appropriate models.
3. Sees that the behavior is modeled clearly, accurately, and succinctly.
4. Assists in helping observers focus attention on what is being modeled.
5. Assists observers in remembering what they saw.
6. Provides for suitable practice in reenacting the observed behavior.
7. Provides corrective feedback during student reenactment.
8. Provides reinforcement following desired behaviors.

These role functions can be carried out efficiently using the five-step process of modeling, group reenactment, volunteer reenactment, draftee reenactment, and application.

What Do Students Do during Modeling?

The students' role in modeling is as follows:
1. Focus attention.
2. Remember what is observed.
3. Reenact the observed behavior when appropriate.

References

Bandura, A. "Modeling and Vicarious Processes, ch. 3" in A. Bandura. *Principles of Behavior Modification*. New York: Holt, Rinehart and Winston, 1969.

Bandura, A. *Social Learning Theory*. New York: General Learning Press, 1971.

———. "Analysis of Modeling Processes," *School Psychology Digest* 4(1):4–10, 1975.

Belcher, T. "Modeling Original Divergent Responses: An Initial Investigation," *Journal of Educational Psychology* 67(3):351–358, 1975.

Botvin, G. and Murray, F. "The Efficacy of Peer Modeling and Social Conflict in the Acquisition of Conservation," *Child Development* 46(3):796–799, 1975.

Lepper, M. et al. "Generalization and Persistence of Effects of Exposure to Self-Reinforcement Models," *Child Development* 46(3):618–630, 1975.

Melamed, B. and Siegel, L. "Reduction of Anxiety in Children Facing Hospitalization and Surgery by Use of Filmed Modeling," *Journal of Consulting and Clinical Psychology* 43(4):511–520, 1975.

Santiesteban, A. "Effects of Video and Audio Models on the Acquisition of a Teaching Skill and Concomitant Student Learning," abstracted in *Research in Education* ERIC document #ED 104808, 1975.

Yates, G. "Influence of Televised Modeling and Verbalization on Children's Delay of Gratification," *Journal of Experimental Child Psychology* 18(2):333–339, 1974.

Chapter 12

The Sweet Smell of Success

Success and Failure

Over a hundred years ago Emerson wrote "success in your work...is hat and coat, is food and wine, is fire and horse and health and holiday." Success is also very motivating, else why would people always say "nothing succeeds like success?" You have heard that expression a few times before. But what does success mean? The answer seems simple enough, yet the word is trite and its meaning, therefore, merits examination. To get a grasp on the meaning of success we can look at intent, accomplishment, self-judgment, feedback, and recognition.

Intent refers to what we hope to accomplish, to what, how much, and how quickly. In teaching and learning intents are called objectives. There they are spelled out. We try to state them in behavioral terms, that is, in terms of actions that can be observed. That way, we know what we are trying to achieve and we have an observable, objective standard that tells us whether we have accomplished what was intended. Sometimes we state objectives in terms of experiences. We refer to experience objectives when we believe that an experience is eminently worthwhile, but we cannot say what the observable outcomes should be. An example of an experience objective is holding and petting a rabbit. We can't specify the outcomes. Yet, most teachers agree that holding and petting a rabbit is a most worthwhile experience for young children.

Accomplishment refers to whether and to what extent we have reached the stated objectives, and it is necessary for recognizing success. If we don't reach our goals we cannot consider ourselves successful. At best we can compliment ourselves on making a good effort.

Self-judgment is a check on ourselves. We look to see whether we have made a strong effort, performed at our best, or slid by with the least effort. Often only within ourselves do we know the truth and that, in the long run, determines whether we see ourselves as successful or unsuccessful.

Feedback from others is also important in our view of success. What others say about our efforts and how they say it tell us whether they consider us successful.

Recognition, the final element in determining success, is essential too. When we know we have made our best effort and have come close to reaching our goals, even if we have received helpful feedback, the feeling of success may yet never occur unless our efforts are recognized by others. Recognition means that people who are important to us know our efforts and seem to appreciate them. The importance of recognition illustrates the key role that others play in our perceptions of ourselves.

Failure means we did not accomplish our intents, that we know we performed half-heartedly, or that we received no recognition at all, leaving us with the feeling that what we did was unimportant.

Is failure good for us? We often hear that it is. People say, "We learn by our mistakes;" "Experience is the best teacher;" "The reach must exceed the grasp;" "It is better to have tried and failed than never to have tried at all." There is no doubt that we *can* learn from our failures. There is no doubt that we ought to do so, when possible. Of course we learn from trial and error, and we learn from the school of hard knocks. But that does not mean that failure is the best-paved path to learning. Evidence points to the contrary. Failure is bad for students. It hurts self-image, decreases motivation, and leaves a residual feeling of incapability. Therefore, we should not include failure as an important part of teaching. It does little to help students. And can do much to harm them. When failure does occur, as it surely will even when we are making our best efforts, it should occur in a fail-safe environment. There students know it is acceptable to make mistakes, that they can fail when giving their best. They know, however, that failure is unacceptable if it results from lack of effort.

Here it is important for us to distinguish between two senses of the word failure. The first sense relates to those conditions just mentioned—trying hard but not quite reaching the objectives, making errors, missing the mark a bit. Those kinds of failures are really just errors. They are benign. They are not hurtful unless made so by teacher or peers. The second sense of the word failure has to do with a pervasive feeling of imcompetence, inferiority, and incapability that can develop in every person. That sense of failure comes from many sources: consistent, repeated errors; derisive, sarcastic feedback; continued lack of acceptance from others important to us. Those things produce a lasting sense of failure that affects individuals in all aspects of school. That sort of failure cannot be considered good. Its effects are too damaging and too lasting to be considered valuable in any way.

What Experts Have Said

Many experts in counseling, therapy, and teaching have explored the effects of success and failure. They are unanimous in extolling the virtues of success, and in deploring the detriments of failure. The following paragraphs give attention to the ideas of a few of those writers. You have seen some of their names before.

Self-Concept

Many people have investigated self-concept, that is, the opinions that each of us holds about ourself. Their investigations have made it increasingly evident that what we believe about ourselves directly affects the ways we learn, relate to others, and function in life.

Self-concept is built on experience. A strong self-concept grows out of successful functioning in different aspects of life. A poor self-concept grows out of lack of success, out of failure—failure to achieve, failure to gain acceptance, failure to find warm relationships with other people.

If we sum the findings and opinions about self-concept, we must conclude that for strong self-concept, nothing is so important as success. Nothing is so damaging to self-concept as failure.

Freud

Sigmund Freud explored the growth of human personality. He found that in the earlier stages of life, success with major life tasks resulted in adequate personality development, while failure with those life tasks resulted in fixations and defense mechanisms that hindered normal functioning.

Freud gave special attention to the libido as the driving life force. The libido was sexual in nature, though diverse. Its locus was not confined to the genitals, but was spread through many parts of the body. Freud believed that human personality depended in large part on what happened to the libido-energized individual during two stages of early life, the oral stage and the anal stage.

In the oral stage of early infancy the libido exerted its influence mainly in the mouth, and was responsible for the pleasures associated with sucking. When babies were allowed sufficient sucking combined with simultaneous gentleness and kindness, their personalities pushed ahead in healthy ways. If they did not receive sufficient sucking, if they did not feel warm and loved and cared for, they developed oral fixations, that remained with them thereafter.

In the anal stage of early childhood the libido influenced the process of toilet training. When the child was treated gently, with care and appreciation, and not made to feel dirty, naughty, or unloved, healthy personality development continued. If scolded and viewed with distaste or contempt, the child developed anal fixations that remained throughout life, and caused the individual to function in less than optimal ways.

Freud also described other stages, other fixations, and many defense mechanisms that grew out of people's inability to cope successfully with primary life functions. Some of those defense mechanisms were described in chapter 1.

Erikson

Erik Erikson, you might recall, described eight stages of man. Those stages spread across the normal life span. Each stage was centered around one primary goal. Successful resolution of that goal brought adequate personality development. Unsuccessful resolution brought a damaged personality, resulting in the individual's being unable to function to the fullest.

Three of Erikson's stages overlap the typical school years. Each of these three stages begins with the letter "I." Teachers can think of them as Erikson's three I's: initiative, industry, and identity.

Initiative is the major goal of the stage that occurs between the ages of three and six. It is the time when children's powers are growing rapidly. They have a great desire to explore, move outward, and try things on their own. If accepted and supported in this desire the individual becomes self-assured. Adequate feelings about the self ensue. If hindered through too many restrictions and scoldings, the child will develop a sense of guilt, rather than initiative. That basic feeling of guilt about one's own actions is difficult to erase later.

Industry is the major goal of the stage that occurs between the ages of six and twelve. It develops as individuals find success in productive, task-oriented activities. Success comes as a result of adult approval, as the child explores newer abilities that form an emerging sense of power for dealing with life. Failure in this stage produces a sense of inferiority. Failure comes when individuals are reprimanded, when they receive reproof, when they are frowned on for what they do. This feeling of inferiority is one of the most painful and lasting complexes that individuals can develop. Once established, it is almost impossible to eradicate, even though great successes may come later.

Identity is the third of Erikson's three I's. It is the major task for individuals between the ages of twelve and eighteen. This is the time when the individual is moving into adolescence and later into adulthood. The major task is to find a sense of self-identity. Success in this task comes from the opportunity to explore role models, from having suitable and adequate models available, and from adult support as individuals try out the traits and characteristics of models they admire. Failure produces a sense of identity confusion. The individual is belittled, even scorned. Conflict occurs between the individual and parents and other adults. This conflict should be seen as natural and necessary. While it is anything but pleasurable, it constitutes an essential step in normal personality development.

Maslow

Perhaps you recall Maslow's hierarchy of needs. Maslow believed that six levels of needs, some higher and some lower, described the prime motives that direct our lives. He believed that the lower-level needs had to be met before the higher levels could be considered. For Maslow, meeting those needs was equated with life success. Inability to meet them produced failure. Ultimate success meant reaching the highest need levels.

For higher-level needs to come into play one has to be successful in meeting the needs for belonging, love, and esteem. Meeting those needs releases the need for self-actualization, which for Maslow was the highest level of human functioning. In terms of general success and failure, success can be seen as meeting one's needs for belonging, love, and esteem. They permit one to function to the fullest, allowing as they do a general sense of comfort and acceptance. Failure can be seen as an inability to achieve belonging, love, and esteem. Without them, one cannot give attention to self-actualization.

Dreikurs

Rudolf Dreikurs believed that every person has a single, prime need in life. That prime need is for acceptance, by family, friends, colleagues, and social groups. Children in school, like everyone else, strive for acceptance. They want to belong more than they want to learn, more than they want to be best in the class, even more than they want to be naughty.

Dreikurs sees people as successful when they meet their need for acceptance. When they are unable to meet this need they see themselves as failures. The sense of failure then causes them to turn toward mistaken goals—attention, power, revenge, and isolation.

Dreikurs, then, believed that students become successful as they are accepted by their classmates and teachers. This acceptance, this success, sets the stage for all other achievement.

Glasser

William Glasser says that schools offer youth their best opportunity for success and recognition. Schools are, he says, the only places where genuine success and recognition are available to many. This success is essential if students are to reach fundamental life goals, which include genuine esteem from others. Such esteem is essential before students can have a feeling of self-worth and take positive control of their lives.

Glasser emphasizes success and stresses that failure is the worst thing that can happen to people. By this, of course, he means not merely making errors, but acquiring a general sense of failure, incompetence, inability to deal with life. The worst failure of all is the failure to find acceptance from others. The desire for acceptance is the greatest motivating force in life.

Schools and teachers have great power to supply success. They can also supply a sense of failure. Glasser deplores factors such as grading that foster a sense of failure. He suggests many activities for helping students control their own behavior, in order that they can come to see themselves as successful.

In the final analysis, Glasser says, success is within the grasp of every student. Success comes from making good choices, from choosing behaviors that bring acceptance, recognition, and esteem. Failure comes from making bad choices, from choosing behaviors that bring hostile reactions and prevent acceptance. What teachers should do is help students make good choices. They do this by continually calling upon students to make choices, showing the results of those choices, and seeing that the natural consequences follow student choice, good or bad.

Gordon

Thomas Gordon is the author of best-selling books entitled *Parent Effectiveness Training* (1970) and *Teacher Effectiveness Training* (1974). These books explain Gordon's ideas about how to communicate effectively with school-age students. Among the tactics included is one that is especially related to school success: the *no-lose approach.*

The no-lose approach is especially helpful in resolving conflicts that occur among students. When disputes occur, as they inevitably do in the classroom, they must be resolved. Typically, that resolution casts one side as the winner and the other as the loser. This division is fine for the winner, but it is not so good for the loser, who ends up hurt and debilitated.

Gordon describes his no-lose approach in which both sides are seen as winners in the following way. The disputants first clarify the nature of their differences. Next each suggests a few procedures that might resolve the dispute. They then look for common grounds, selecting one of the solutions that is acceptable to both parties. They implement the solution on a trial basis. If it doesn't work they go back to the drawing board, suggesting other solutions and selecting another to try. This procedure allows everyone to experience success, all are winners, none losers.

Skinner

The work spearheaded by B. F. Skinner has shown the power of reinforcement in shaping behavior. We can think of reinforcement as reward. When individuals behave in desirable ways, we reward them for it. This reward, this reinforcement, provides a sense of success. Skinner and the many researchers who have followed in his steps have shown that reinforcement is most effective when student responses are almost always correct. That is, students should be directed in ways that cause them to behave correctly almost all the time. When correct, they are reinforced. This procedure shapes desired behavior quickly and strongly. If too many errors occur resulting in too little reinforcement, learning is slowed. It may even proceed in erroneous, undesired directions.

For Skinner, and indeed his mass of research evidence supports this position, learning must bring continued success. Failure should be eliminated to the extent possible. Unlike other authorities whose views we have examined, Skinner did not deplore failure as damaging to the personality. He simply saw it as inefficient, as obstructive to rapid, strong learning.

Rosenthal and Jacobson

Rosenthal and Jacobson emphasized the importance of expectations as facilitators of success. They showed that students tended to be more successful when teachers expected them to be successful. Their view once again illustrates the importance of self-concept. When students truly believe they are capable and competent they tend to behave in those ways, ways that bring more success. When they see themselves as incompetents and failures they tend to behave in ways that reflect incompetence and bring added failure. Teachers should expect all students to achieve. This expectation should be genuine, and it should be communicated in genuine, assertive ways to the students.

Block

James Block is one of the foremost proponents of mastery learning. Mastery learning holds at its core the notion that all students can achieve high levels of school learning, levels that we would call mastery. This view contrasts with the prevailing view in education which holds that within any group of students some will achieve mastery, others will achieve acceptable levels, but a large percentage will be below average, dipping into levels of failure.

Block and others of similar persuasion feel it is morally wrong to allow large numbers of students to gain very little from their instruction, expecially when it is technically feasible to promote high levels of learning in most students. This feasibility undergirds the viewpoint of mastery learning.

Block says that contrary to popular opinion, degree of learning is not related to intelligence. Rather, intelligence indicates speed of learning. People who have higher IQs learn faster than people who have lower IQs. That does not mean they learn with greater depth or permanence. They simply learn faster. That relationship between intelligence and speed of learning points to the factor of time in the classroom, time devoted to student learning. Block believes that all students can reach mastery levels in learning provided they are given sufficient time together with adequate instruction and support. This means that time should be made flexible in learning rather than being fixed into periods as is now done in school.

By making accommodations in time allotments, all students can achieve success, all students can reach high levels of learning. Mastery learning can reduce the incidence of failure, reduce the number of students who see themselves as incompetent, and increase success for students who have been barely wetting their toes in the seas of information that comprise the school curriculum.

Success and Discipline

When people think of discipline they rarely see it as the avenue to student success. Instead they think of controls as being necessary for stifling outbursts, shutting down misbehavior, keeping students orderly, and teaching respect for adults.

In reality, however, discipline is the prime road to ensuring student success in school. As elaborated in chapter 2, discipline brings sanity to the classroom, promotes learning, and brings a sense of accomplishment and joy. Therefore, we should view discipline as the factor that contributes most toward student success.

This view has been reiterated time after time in the models of discipline examined earlier. The Redl and Wattenberg model showed how to support and correct student self-control, always with the intent to help students achieve, to find success. The Kounin model showed how to use withitness, overlapping, and the ripple effect to help students keep on task, to help them be successful. The neo-Skinnerian model, emphasizing behavior modification, showed how rewards help students learn behavior that brings success. The Ginott model showed how teachers can protect students' egos, while building a strong sense of success. The Glasser model showed that good choices result in good behavior, and that good behavior is the only path to success in the classroom. The Dreikurs model showed how students continually aim at acceptance in the classroom, and how acceptance frees students to be successful, as opposed to the mistaken goals that bring failure.

The Canter and Canter model showed how teachers can be assertively in charge of classrooms, thus keeping down distractions, helping students stay on task, and insisting on adequate behavior, all of which contribute to success.

Many teachers fear that forceful discipline produces bad results. They feel that if they set strong standards, stick by their guns, and do not take into account the moods and external forces affecting students, the students will be stifled, thwarted, manipulated. They fear that students will not like them. Exactly the opposite is true. No one advocates harsh, abusive discipline. Firm, humane, consistent standards help students learn and experience success. They cause students to like teachers better, like the school better, and think better about themselves. These desired effects do not occur in the absence of controls. Teachers needn't fear that good systems of discipline will damage students or student-teacher relationships. If teachers want to be admired, respected, and ultimately liked, they must be fair, firm, consistent, and insistent in helping students make good choices.

How to Provide Genuine Success

We have considered many opinions about the importance of success in school, about how it affects self-concept, and how it affects achievement. These opinions unanimously placed highest importance on the value of success. Given this importance, the task for teachers becomes one of providing genuine success for students. They need to know how to maximize student success efficiently and effectively.

Student success can be ensured by giving attention to the following: objectives as targets; curriculum that progresses; materials that help; teacher direction and urging; group esprit de corps; competition that improves; and parental help. We will examine each of the factors to see how it contributes toward genuine success for all students.

Objectives as Targets

Objectives describe what we want to accomplish. They are the targets or goals toward which instruction is aimed. They are specific. They tell us what we hope students will be able to do as a result of instruction.

To be effective, these objectives must be clear. They must be public. They must be attainable. They must specify actions that are recognizable. To be clear means to be understandable. Teachers and students alike understand what the objectives say and mean. Vague terms, therefore, are not used. Simple, straightforward words are used to specify the observable actions.

The objectives must be public; that is, they should not be secrets kept by the teacher. They should be shared with students, sometimes with parents to let everyone know what is being aimed at, what is expected. Ample evidence shows that clear knowledge of objectives is helpful in motivating and guiding student learning.

Objectives should be attainable, meaning that they should describe ends that students can reasonably expect to reach. They should not be too difficult. Neither, of course, should they be too easy.

Objectives should name behavior that is recognizable. Such behavior includes things we can see or hear people do, things such as talking, writing, demonstrating, explaining, drawing, computing, and so forth. We should avoid objectives that use vague, unobservable terms such as "know," "understand," and "appreciate," not because they are worthless ends, but because we cannot recognize those acts when students perform them. If we want to use an objective such as understand, we are obliged to specify the behavior that tells us that students are understanding. Such behaviors might include explain, list, put into own words, or demonstrate.

Once objectives are made clear, public, attainable, and recognizable, we have a set of goals that will guide the efforts of teachers and students alike. They can be used as check points to indicate progress, as guidelines to direct further work, and as criteria for judging whether students have reached the intended instructional goals.

Curriculum That Progresses

Much of the curriculum that fills the school day comes from curriculum guides, textbooks, and other materials provided to the teacher.

Besides that part of the curriculum there are numerous other activities that teachers provide for students. Teachers need to be sure that those activities always lead students forward. They do so when they are worthwhile, at the right level of difficulty, interesting, and in proper sequence.

Curriculum that leads students forward and provides new learnings, new attitudes, and new abilities, enables students to make the progress that shows success. Time-fillers, regardless of how enjoyable they may be, do little toward providing student success. On occasion teachers need to fill awkward bits of time. They usually have fun activities to keep students occupied. Reliance on such activities may allow students to have a good time in class, but they provide little worthwhile learning.

Activities must be at the right level of difficulty. The tasks we give students must be suited to their levels of functional ability. They must be neither too hard nor too easy. When too difficult, they frustrate. When too easy, they do not pull students forward.

The curriculum should be as interesting as possible. Interest holds attention, and attention is necessary for learning. All curriculum is not exciting. It is difficult to find ways of making interesting the study of grammar, parts of speech, or punctuation. But even those activities can be enlivened through competition, humor, and application to real writing for display or publication.

Finally, the curriculum must be put into a sequence that allows students to build new learnings on top of prior learnings, to move from the familiar to the unknown, to progress from the concrete to the abstract, to move, in spiral fashion, to ever higher levels of knowledge and understanding. Such sequencing lets students see how knowledge is tied together. It lets them see they are making steady progress. It provides a means for achieving and for receiving recognition of that achievement.

Good curriculum, then, consists of worthwhile learnings, organized in such a way that they lead students forward. Curriculum leads students forward when it is at the proper level of difficulty, when it is interesting, and when it is ordered into a sequence that allows learnings to build in incremental fashion.

Materials That Help

Instructional materials enliven learning by making the subject more interesting, clearer, more understandable. They provide extensions, examples, illustrations, problems, and entertainment. They allow students to explore further afield, and they permit easier application of new learnings into realistic situations. These attributes of materials greatly extend and enhance the teacher's capabilities.

Materials are interesting when they deal with topics familiar to students, the mysterious, the unknown; when they are colorful, show movement, and include humor and novelty. Materials must be interesting if they are to hold students' attention. Otherwise, teachers will have to force students to use them.

Materials are useful when they clarify, when they provide explanations, examples, illustrations, and anecdotes. Clarity is necessary for helping students obtain meaning.

Good materials also allow students to practice what they have learned through repetition, drill, review, paraphrasing, rewording, and translating from one medium to another. These methods of practicing cause students to go over the material again and again, beyond the point of full learning.

Materials allow students to explore. There is no way most of us can visit the Amazon jungle, the Pyramids, Antarctica, or the Laplanders in Finland. There is no way we can see molecules, solar systems, or the inner workings of nuclear reactors. Materials help provide those experiences, allowing students to range far beyond the confines of the classroom.

Finally, helpful materials allow students to apply their new learnings going beyond practice and overlearning. Application involves use of the new knowledge. Materials help by providing problems for students to solve through application of knowledge.

Teacher Direction and Urging

The teacher is the prime motivator in every classroom. Remember that point. It is the key. Like it or not, many students do not work well on their own for long periods of time. They are not self-directed when it comes to academic learning. They are not self-controlled. These things depend on the teacher. This fact places the teacher continually on stage, guiding, exhorting, entertaining, monitoring, providing feedback, providing if nothing else simple physical presence that keeps students on task.

The importance of this function cannot be overemphasized. It is more important to student success than any other factor, more important, perhaps, than all other factors combined. We see an occasional person who learns without a teacher. Such people constitute a small minority. Most of us do not have sufficient motivation. Neither do we have proper help and guidance. Too much learning must occur through trial and error, even when motivation is present. Most students require urging, direction, enthusiasm, spark, feedback, and someone to crack the whip, gently of course. These things enliven learning and greatly increase the likelihood that students will be successful in school activities.

Esprit de Corps

Success depends in large measure on morale. Morale is closely related to the phenomenon of esprit de corps, group spirit. Esprit de corps enlivens an entire group. It provides stimulation, direction, sense of purpose, sense of value. Every teacher hopes for good esprit de corps. It can be provided by getting across to students that they are special, that they are the best potential, that excellence is within their grasp. Perhaps they will be the best learners, the best behaved students, the best models for others. Perhaps they will be the best representatives of the school. Once a reputation has been established for a group or teacher, the reputation feeds into esprit de corps. The group has something to uphold. Every student strives to perpetuate the reputation, be it for excellence, innovation, creativity, good behavior, responsibility, or whatever.

Esprit de corps provides a strong feeling of group success. Even in situations without it, where poor morale exists, some students will find success. But many will not. Many will feel defeated. That's why a sense of group spirit is so important. Individuals identify with the group, are proud of the group, are motivated to do the best possible for the group.

Esprit de corps provides a sense of joy, of societal pleasure, that is important to most individuals. Teachers should use all devices at hand for establishing and maintaining strong esprit de corps.

Competition That Improves

Competition is known to bring success and recognition. It carries a certain joy of combat. For these reasons it is motivating to students, and it can be helpful in making learning more exciting. Competition has its drawbacks, however. If there are winners there must be losers, and losing is not motivating. No one likes it. Unfortunately, the people in greatest need of success are those who seldom win. That fact has caused teachers to have second thoughts about using competition in learning. They judge that its bad effects, including failure, frustration, and sometimes overinflated egos, outweighs its good effects. They have tended to replace it with cooperation, where students are caused to relate in ways considered more positive. Cooperation, unfortunately, is not nearly so exciting and motivating as competition.

Competition doesn't always have to be hurtful. It can be quite helpful. It is stimulating and exhilirating. When people compete against their own past performance, rather than against other individuals, competition is useful. When they compete as part of a group against past group performance, or against other groups, competition is good for all concerned.

Teachers can thus make competition helpful by allowing students to strive against independent goals and past performances. This sort of competition can be used for both individuals and groups. It allows individuals to remain rather anonymous, insulated within the group or kept private, as when competing against past performance. They do not show themselves in bad light, and they do not have a sense of failure when they don't do as well as the best in the group.

Competition against standards and against past performance is useful and highly motivating. Its value comes from the ability to see genuine progress. Teachers can help students keep graphs that show their individual performances against lists of objectives or against past performance. These graphs must be kept private so that students cannot be compared publicly against other students. Group efforts, however, can be displayed. Group averages on math or spelling tests, for example, can be charted. This can show comparative performance, and it provides motivation for the entire group to try to exceed former marks.

Parental Help

Parents can make exceptional contributions to the feelings of success for students and teachers alike. They can be so helpful that chapter 14 is devoted entirely to the contributions they can make and to how teachers can acquire their cooperation. For our purposes here it is sufficient to say that parents can make a great contribution toward genuine success for students. The burden is on teachers to initiate the understanding and cooperation that make parental contributions possible. The teacher must find ways to communicate extensively with parents allowing explanation of programs, information about goals, and information about activities and materials. Teachers should ask for parent support, both psychological and for direct instructional support at home. Oftentimes parents cannot provide instruction. They can help, however, by providing a time and place for students to do homework, seeing that students complete the work, and communicating back to teachers any questions or difficulties encountered.

All parents want their children to learn. They want them to behave acceptably in school. Almost all are willing to help in the instructional process because they have such a stake in the education of their children. Since most do not know how to help, teachers must take the first steps in establishing working relationships with parents. They do this by informing, explaining, and asking for help. A small amount of effort pays large dividends.

How to Recognize and Publicize Success

At the beginning of the chapter we saw that a major factor in acquiring a feeling of success is receiving attention and acknowledgement for one's efforts. That feeling of success is incredibly important. It behooves teachers to establish and maintain procedures that allow all students to be recognized for their efforts and accomplishments. The remainder of this chapter explains several ways for bringing such recognition to students.

Chart Group Gains

It was mentioned previously that competition can be motivating and can provide direction and interest for students. The kinds of competition provided must be in the form of group performance or in the form of personal gains against past performance. Group gains can best be shown by means of graphs, time lines, class diaries, and sometimes by class murals. Students can make these graphs and charts easily and quickly. They can be colorful, attractive, and informative. They can be posted and used as constant reminders.

Time lines can be placed high around the walls of the classroom, using either paper or cord. Paper can have events and dates written or drawn on it. The cord can be knotted, with tags or objects tied to it in chronological sequence. Examples of entries might be such things as finishing unit 2 in the Spanish book, completing the fives in the multiplication tables, having put on a science fair, and so forth. The advantage of a time line is that it shows class performance, progress, and a record of achievement.

Class diaries do much the same thing as time lines, except the records are kept in written form. Students can take turns making entries in the diary. The group can contribute. A good time is at the end of day or during the period when a rapid review is conducted. The diary provides documented history of class activities and accomplishments. Students will enjoy reading in it later.

Some groups, particularly art classes and upper-elementary classrooms, can prepare murals that illustrate activities and accomplishments. The mural can be added to at regular intervals depicting significant events and accomplishments. Making the mural is enjoyable, it helps fix events in students' memories, and it provides a sense of accomplishment and success.

Chart Personal Gains

Individual student performance must not be shown publicly in the classroom, if it compares unfavorably with that of other students. Individual efforts and accomplishments can be compared against stated objectives or past performances. They can be graphed to provide records that are instructive, rewarding, and motivating. They must be kept private, however. They can be kept in individual folders accessible only to the teacher, who uses them in conferencing with students and their parents.

Charting personal gains can be even more motivating than charting group gains. One is anonymous within the group, but at the very center of attention as an individual. Where individuals might show poorly when compared to the best students in the class they can show significant progress against their past accomplishments. This progress is reinforcing and motivating to further efforts.

Records of personal gain also serve well in conferencing with parents. Parents want to know as specifically as possible how their child is doing, how well he is reading, how well he is understanding American history, how well he is performing in public speaking. They are pleased to see charts that show the child reaching objectives, improving in efficiency, in amount of work attempted, or in number of correct responses. These charts help present the teacher in a good light because they show that the teacher has a specific plan for the student and that results are being obtained.

Review Progress

One of the most helpful ways to publicize success is to review on a frequent basis the achievements and learnings that have occurred in the class. This may be done at the end of each period or day. Two to five minutes is all it takes. Review may also be done at the end of each week, at the end of each unit of instruction, or at other selected intervals.

Such review reminds students what they have done, it gives them a sense of accomplishment, and it instructs them on how to report to their parents, who will want to know what they have been learning at school.

Review should remind students about the initial objectives and show the progress made toward those objectives. This clear marking of progress provides a genuine sense of success. Review can end with a brief notation of what is to come next.

Informing Parents

Parents should be informed regularly about experiences, activities, achievements, and future plans for their children. This information can be provided in three ways: (1) through student reports to parents, (2) through teacher communication with parents, and (3) through materials that show parents what their children are doing in class and for homework.

Student reports to parents are excellent. Students can be instructed on how to tell parents, in a few minutes' time, what they have done and what they have learned during the day. Parents can set a time for such reports, perhaps at dinner. A few sentences are enough to tell what the major activities of the day have been. Students become able to do this through the process of systematic review. This review prevents students' being speechless when parents ask them what they learned that day. They will be able to think of something more to say than "I don't know" or "nothing."

Systematic communication from the teacher is also an excellent way to inform parents. This procedure requires effort and time, but pays good dividends. Teachers can send notes, make telephone calls, and send newsletters. These things can tell parents what the teacher is attempting to accomplish, and about ways they can help at home. Parents usually hear from teachers only when something is going wrong, which causes them to be defensive and makes them dread to hear from school. When teachers take the time to inform parents about what is going right, about what their children are doing that is good, they create a bond of cooperation.

Samples of work sent to parents can be useful, too. Worksheets, reading assignments, sample questions, and an occasional test can be sent home as illustrative. Parents may want to do a few of the activities themselves. Such materials can present a clear idea of what is going on at school, especially when accompanied by brief explanatory notes from the teacher.

Sharing in the Classroom

Students need to receive attention from their peers, to have their classmates recognize their efforts and their accomplishments. They can get this attention through oral presentations, displays of work, and bringing into the classroom some of their own handiwork. Individuals can do demonstrations. Small groups can put on skits. Displays of art, musical presentations, and reading stories and poems are good ways for individuals to share their accomplishments.

Some students are shy and reluctant. Some will not have much to share. Teachers should encourage all to share, if they can. Students should not be forced, if they are terrified. Shy students can often share better if they use puppets, hold an animal, or wear masks or costumes.

In classes where large group activities are possible, such as project work in science, social studies, art, drama, and so on, provisions can be made for students to put on public exhibitions as culminating activities for their work. Aiming toward exhibitions provides motivation for completing work of high quality. If you know your parents and relatives are going to see what you have done, you put a little extra into it. Science fairs are popular. So are class plays, musical performances, readers theatre, choric verse, and displays of arts and crafts. People who are invited to come to the exhibitions and performances can talk with the students, who explain their work or performance. This is certain to bring attention and positive comments.

Class Newsletter

Many classes can produce a class newsletter on a monthly or quarterly basis. This newsletter can explain what is going on in the class, contain samples of student work, present announcements of displays and performances, and include anything else the class desires. To be most effective its tone should be businesslike, and it should leave an impression of good learning.

The newsletters can be delivered to parents, administrators, other teachers, and other students. Local newspapers are usually interested. Few avenues publicize so well the efforts and achievements of the class. Public relations are not the least of the benefits. Schools and teachers are targets for considerable criticism. Much of this criticism occurs because we do a poor job of informing about the good things we do. People simply don't hear about the significant learning we provide. Newsletters can fill that void. They inform and they bring a sense of respect.

Genuine Compliments

As students inform parents, as they share with classmates, as they put on performances, as they contribute to class newsletters, they put themselves in positions to receive recognition and genuine compliments. These compliments do much for self-esteem. They provide a sense of appreciation, competence, and success.

Other activities deserve equal attention but cannot be so easily shown outside the classroom. Examples are good manners, helping others, making the best effort, being friendly, and showing good sportsmanship. Students who exhibit these things deserve attention, too. To provide this attention, some teachers set up systems that encourage students to compliment each other. These compliments must be genuine and sincere. They should specify what it is that draws the compliment. To be sure that all students receive deserved compliments teachers may instruct students to look for someone who has been very helpful, been a good sport, worked hard, someone who is improving. They encourage students to spread the compliments around. They discuss how it makes them feel to receive compliments and how they feel when they give them.

The teacher will need to keep track, too. Some students will receive few compliments. The teacher should fill that lack by being alert to who needs compliments. Something good can be found about every student, even the laziest, most disruptive, most unlikeable. Those people, especially, can profit from genuine compliments given for small improvements.

Students should also be taught how to compliment themselves, how to recognize their own desirable behavior and reward themselves for it. They can be encouraged to state to themselves what it is they have done, and tell themselves they are proud of it. This may sound silly, but it helps students focus on desirable behavior and self-control. Teachers can ask students to share from time to time what they have complimented themselves on. That draws attention to their efforts and gives other students a chance to compliment them, too.

Continual Teacher Reinforcement

Earlier we saw that the teacher is the prime motivator in the classroom, always on stage, always directing, always encouraging, always helping. The teacher is also the main source of reinforcement, providing rewards to students who behave in desirable ways, who try harder, who progress, who relate well with others. Because the teacher is such a significant figure to students, rewards coming from the teacher have special power. They cannot be matched by rewards from any other source. Recognizing the power of teacher rewards, we should be sure to provide them. These rewards should come mainly in the form of recognition, acknowledgement, compliments, and occasional praise. These statements should stipulate what the student has done right or well. They should thank the student for showing that behavior. Teachers need not use tangible rewards except in rare occasions when student behavior presents a problem so severe that verbal rewards do not improve it.

We must remember that teachers are among the two or three most important people in almost every student's life. While students may act as though they don't appreciate teachers, while they may even act disrespectfully toward them, they still see them as gigantic figures in their lives. Most students eagerly seek teachers' approval, dote on their recognition, and want their attention and acceptance. This fact reemphasizes the power that teachers have for providing feelings of belonging and success for students under their guidance.

References

Block, J. *Mastery Learning: Theory and Practice*. New York: Holt, Rinehart and Winston, 1971.

Dreikurs, R. *Psychology in the Classroom*. New York: Harper and Row, 1968.

Erikson, E. *Childhood and Society*. New York: W. W. Norton, 1950.

Freud, S. *The Ego and Mechanisms of Defense*. London: Hogarth Press, 1937.

Glasser, W. *Schools Without Failure*. New York: Harper and Row, 1969.

Gordon, T. *Teacher Effectiveness Training*. New York: Peter H. Wyden, 1974.

Maslow, A. *Toward a Psychology of Being*. New York: D. Van Nostrand, 1962.

Rosenthal, R. and Jacobson, L. *Pygmalion in the Classroom*. New York: Holt, Rinehart and Winston, 1968.

Skinner, B. F. *Science and Human Behavior*. New York: Macmillan, 1953.

Chapter 13

Parents as Teachers' Best Friends

Since its inception, American education has had a noticeable difference from education provided elsewhere. The founding fathers realized that education should be controlled by the people, not by a national government. They did not mention education in the Constitution. They wrote in the Constitution that matters not included therein should be left to the individual states. That put education into the hands of state governments, which made general laws to regulate it. Those laws, in turn, put matters of educational policy under the jurisdiction of local communities. The communities elect representatives to sit on boards of education, which control what happens in American schools within the broad guidelines set down by state legislatures.

The tradition of local control was established long before the Declaration of Independence. Laws made in the colonies provided for the establishment of elementary and secondary schools, first intended to teach children how to read and write. Later, the schools were seen as agents for democraticizing society, for maintaining an educated citizenry that could govern itself. As immigrants began to pour into the country, the schools took on the added duty of forging a common bond among the multitudes of ethnic groups that became American citizens.

These forces for democratization, literacy, citizenship, and social unity supported keeping educational control in the hands of the populace. Such matters, especially in an age of great diversity, isolation, and slow communication could not be managed effectively from a single location in Washington. A factor even more powerful in maintaining local control of education was the great, pervasive spirit of individuality that characterized early America. People wanted to do things for themselves. They didn't want unknown people hundreds or thousands of miles away telling them how they should educate their children.

This tradition of local involvement in education remains strong in the United States. It has eroded somewhat, because of federal regulations aimed at equality, the availability of funds from the federal level, and a burgeoning willingness in society to let someone else do things for us. Still, all citizens, parents of school age children or not, pay attention to education in this country. Everyone feels a direct stake in education of the young. We have kept at full blaze the belief that we have a right to be involved in public education, whether we choose to exercise that right or not.

That feeling of legal and moral right to participate in education has kept parents closely involved. They maintain their right to criticize policy, curricula, teaching, and everything else. While criticism is vexing to educators who seldom see it as justified, it is needed to keep education effective as a democratizing agent. Active parental involvement is equally important. It ensures a balance, a stability, a compromise between lofty educational goals and social, political, and economic reality.

This involvement unnerves many teachers. They wish parents would leave education to them. They know they are the professionals. They know what should be taught, and how they should teach it. They see parental involvement as a hinderance to their efforts, a nuisance that cuts deeply into their time and energy. Other teachers see parental involvement differently. They know it takes up their time. It interferes with their schedules and diminishes their efficiency. But they have learned that small investments of time can pay huge dividends. They know they can rally parents to their side, count on them for support, and count on them for help. They know that simply having parents support their efforts will forestall two-thirds of the battles they would normally expect to encounter with students. Those teachers will tell you it is worth the effort to cultivate parents. They will tell you that in these times of educational adversity, parents can be teachers' best friends.

Parents and School Discipline

All parents want their children to learn and behave acceptably in school. Some of them may not act as though they do, but you can't find one in a thousand who will say, "Nah, I don't care if my kid learns or not." or, "Behave? Heck no. I hope he misbehaves." Of course there is a difference between saying you care and really caring.

But if we assume that parents really do care even when they don't seem to, we will be correct most of the time.

It is easy for teachers to get a one-sided view of parents' concern about schooling. There are occasional students whose parents cause difficulty, either because they will not support the teacher or because they continually interfere in negative ways. A few such cases can camouflage the value of the vast majority who really do care. It is that large majority of caring parents that teachers can count on. They will support and they will help, teachers have only to say the word.

The Gallup Poll on attitudes toward education points out, year after year, that parents of school children give good marks to education, schools, and teachers. They think education is doing a good job. They point out some things they think need shaping up such as discipline, use of drugs, and citizenship training. But they are very supportive of what teachers and schools are doing.

What Parents Expect from Teachers

Parents don't expect teachers to promise the moon. They don't expect them to turn every dull Jack into a budding Einstein. But they do have a few clear expectations that teachers should heed including the following:

1. They expect teachers to *care* about their child, to give attention to interests, joys, fears, and the child as a person.
2. They expect them to *teach* the child. They want their child to learn the basics, become literate, and know and appreciate something of art and music.
3. They expect teachers to *excite* their child about learning, make them want to learn and help them enjoy school.
4. They expect teachers to *encourage and support* their child's efforts; to urge, prod, and nurture the process of growth.
5. They expect teachers to *discipline* their child. They know that order and self-control are necessary not only in school but in life outside school.
6. They expect teachers to *inform* them about their child's educational program and progress. They want to know about successes, difficulties, failures, and problems that require attention.
7. They expect teachers to make a *strong effort* in teaching, to be serious and dedicated, to do the best they can.

What Parents Need to Know

When it comes to schooling and discipline, parents need to know four things: (1) what, exactly, is expected of the students; (2) how those expectations are going to be enforced; (3) how their child is doing, generally and specifically; and (4) what they can do to help.

Expectations in discipline come from two sources. First, they come from the school code. Most schools have established such codes, or are in the process of doing so. Those codes tell generally how students must behave and how they will be treated if they violate provisions of the code. Second, they come from individual teachers who have their own standards, expectations, and enforcement procedures. Teachers seldom communicate their discipline programs to parents. They should do so, because their programs are much more specific in terms of standards and enforcement than is a school code.

These expectations should be as few in number as necessary to cover the territory. They should be stated briefly, in simple language. They should be clear and easily understood. Both the school code and the individual teacher expectations should be distributed to all parents. At conferences and open house, they should be repeated. Parents need and want to know these expectations.

Enforcement must be coupled with the expectations. Parents need to know what the enforcement procedures will be. The school code will probably explain enforcement from the school level. Teacher enforcement should not run contrary to the school code. It may augment it, and it will be formulated to match the age of students, and the personality and philosophy of the teacher. An outline of enforcement procedures should be composed by every teacher and sent to the parents. It should tell what will happen for the first offense, the second, and the third. There should be no surprises for parents when it comes to enforcing the proper behavior of their children in school.

Knowledge of how their child is behaving is information that every parent wants and has a right to expect. This information should be both general and specific, and it should be communicated regularly. General information comes in statements such as "a good citizen," "needs to get along better with others," "usually works up to capacity," "not making best effort." Specific information comes in statements such as "engaged in name-calling three times last week," "did not disrupt class at all this week," "shows courtesy and manners to adults and other students."

This knowledge can be sent via notes and telephone calls. The notes can be written personally or entered on forms made for the purpose. Two telephone calls made each afternoon after school reaches parents of an entire elementary class in only three weeks. Secondary teachers have to make selective calls. There are too many students to reach personally on a regular basis. When students require special attention, the information communicated to parents should be quite specific.

Help from parents is always appreciated by teachers. Most parents are more than willing to support the teacher's efforts with their child at home. They will seldom ask to help, especially as their children progress beyond the primary grades, but that does not mean they have lost interest. Parents can support teachers by backing their policies, reinforcing procedures at home, providing special places and times for students to do homework, insisting that homework be done as assigned, reporting back to teachers on problems and successes, and continually emphasizing that school is a place for serious learning.

Parents usually collaborate with teachers if teachers ask for their help. They have a stake in the education of their child. They will do what they can. They need, however, to be asked, and they need to be instructed about how they can help.

Why Parents Don't Participate

Parents are vitally interested in their children's education, yet most of them take a hands-off approach to what goes on at school. That seems paradoxical, but the reasons they are reluctant to participate are easily understood.

One reason that parents don't come forward to participate in their children's education is their unwillingness to interfere. They feel that education is the job of the school. Parents shouldn't meddle. They should only back what the school is trying to do. Trust can be put in teachers to do what is best. There is a clear division of effort: teaching is for schools and upbringing is for parents. Neither should short circuit the other.

Another reason why parents don't participate is because they feel insecure about what to do and how to do it. It takes some nerve to make overtures to a teacher and parents feel uneasy, embarrassed, out of their medium when they do so. They want to be involved, maybe just a little bit, maybe a great deal. But they are timid. They would eagerly come forth if teachers would encourage them.

A third reason why parents don't participate is simple ignorance. Ignorance doesn't mean stupidity, it means not knowing. They don't know how to help. They don't know what to do at home, how to reinforce what the teacher is doing, how to arrange study places and times, or how to instruct their children when difficulties in school work arise. Parents want to help, but they need some instruction from teachers. This instruction can be communicated by way of notes and newsletters that ask for parents' help, tell them in simple terms how to provide it, and indicate how parents can follow through on a routine basis.

What Parents Will Give

Teachers are amazed at how much parents will give, how much they will put into the education of their child, and how much they will contribute to the education and enjoyment of the entire class. Most kindergarten teachers rely on parent collaboration. It comes naturally there. Mothers are torn by their child's entering school. It is difficult, indeed, to sever the bonds. So parents hover around eagerly, hoping to be involved somehow in the kindergarten program. This involvement continues in declining fashion through the first grade, then fades away. Still, parents rally to classroom needs through the upper grades and into secondary levels when they are needed and called on.

Help from parents comes in varied forms. The most important of these forms is backing. If parents support teachers and schools, if they convey that idea to their children in no uncertain terms, if teachers know they have support and backing, the entire educational enterprise moves forward with vigor. Parents back school programs almost without exception if they believe that the teacher has a specific plan for their child and is truly trying to help the child learn. Teachers who reassure parents of these facts draw strong support.

Parents can help with home study. They will, when asked and informed, set aside a time and place for students to do uninterrupted home work, without distractions. This time can be sandwiched in, through, and around favorite television programs. Seldom must there be a family fight over missed programs. Rarely does the child need to do more than an hour's homework which can be fit around TV without undue trauma.

Parents can provide simple instruction at home. To make this feasible, teachers can send brief, direct instruction sheets home with the child. Those sheets tell what is being taught and how. They tell how the parents can help the child. They should make it plain that parents should only help when students encounter obstacles to progress. Parents should not do the work for the child.

Teachers at all levels can count on parents for donations of time, services, goods, transportation, and even money. Many teachers hesitate to ask parents to make contributions to school outings, projects, and performances. Many parents, however, are more than happy to become involved. They enjoy feeling themselves a part of the educational process. They like to be around schools again and will usually come through bountifully, when help is needed.

Many parents are eager to volunteer to help in the classroom. They may be hesitant to do so, because they feel presumptive. They are afraid they might not be wanted. If teachers open the door they can almost always secure volunteer parent help. This help can be used for in-class work with students; for producing plays and other performances, including costuming, sets, musical assistance, and transportation; for going on class outings where drivers, supervisors, and chaperones are needed; and for helping by preparing and working in class carnivals and festivities surrounding athletic events.

Communication is the Key

There is a vast deposit of parental support and help available to teachers. That deposit is locked by apathy, insecurity, ignorance, timidity, and a hands-off view of education. The key that unlocks that lock is communication, and that communication must first come from the teacher.

A masters degree study conducted by Janet Mulder at San Diego State University in 1978 investigated the effects of teacher communication on parental attitude toward teachers at the elementary and junior high level. Now a teacher, Mulder had previously worked for several years in business, as a buyer for a chain of department stores. She knew from that experience how important good communication was in establishing ties between merchants and consumers. She suspected that the same thing was true for teachers and parents. Mulder went to several different public schools and asked the principal of each school to identify a teacher that the public considered especially outstanding. She interviewed each of those teachers to determine whether communication had anything to do with their perceived excellence.

She found that outstanding teachers without exception maintained elaborate systems of communication with parents. They used a variety of techniques and devices, but they were consistent in advising parents of their educational intents and how they were attempting to accomplish them; and how the parents' child was doing and what they could do to help. Mulder did not seek any objective data to indicate whether the teachers were, in fact, superior when it came to student learning. She did not even presume that they were. But parents fully believed that the teachers were exceptional. That belief rallied parents strongly behind the teachers' efforts.

A more elaborate research project has been ongoing in the college of education at San Diego State University. Entitled "Education for Dignity and Rapid Achievement" and called EDRA, it has involved many teachers and hundreds of school students. EDRA has three thrusts: academic achievement, self-concept, and exemplary personal relations. Teachers in EDRA use a small number of strategies to keep students on task, progressing, feeling good about themselves, and seeing that learning is serious, though enjoyable, business.

One of the strategies that all EDRA teachers use is an organized system of communicating with parents. This communication is intended to show that the teachers are serious about teaching and learning. They intend to do the very best for every student. EDRA teachers inform parents, tell them how they can help, and ask for their support. This has resulted in an extremely positive attitude from parents and excellent support for their children's learning.

The Mulder and EDRA studies merely illustrate a fact that is known to many teachers. A small but significant number of teachers capitalize on the fact which bears repeating: parental support and help have immense value in the educational process. The key to securing that help is good communication from the teacher.

How to Communicate with Parents

Granted that communication is essential, how does one go about arranging an effective communication system? Experience has shown that two elements are important in communication with parents. They are style of communicating and content of the communication. In other words, they are how you say it and what you say. Let's examine these two elements. Then, in the next section, we will explore suitable vehicles through which the content can be disseminated.

Style

Parents expect teachers to be professional. They expect them to be knowledgeable, communicative, and friendly. They expect them to have the best interests of their child in mind. They do not expect teachers to be their pals or buddies. They do not want them to be silly, wishy-washy, or disorganized. The first consideration in style is to be professional. That means to know what you are doing, to say what you mean in simple terms, to maintain your poise, and to be willing to listen.

Along with being professional, teachers should be disarming. Remember that most parents are very sensitive about hearing from a teacher, at least at first. Tradition has it that parents hear from teachers only when their kid has upset the apple cart. That means they are going to get blamed, scolded, and made to feel bad. Teachers disarm these fears by being friendly (but not silly) and straightforward, indicating they are pleased to have the opportunity to work with the child and parents for the year. They disarm by showing they are optimistic, have high expectations, and feel sure that by working together they can help the child make good progress.

Teachers should be frank. They should tell it like it is, no shading facts, no hemming and hawing. But this frankness must be combined with a positive attitude about further growth. This principle applies for both positive and negative comments. If students have been excellent, emphasis should be put on their potentials for continued advancement. If they have been below par, a positive plan should be stated for improvement.

Frankness must also be linked to a feeling of support. Remember that parents' egos and feelings are on the line. A supportive attitude from the teacher engenders a supportive attitude from the parent. Support is shown through genuine interest in providing quality education for the student, through describing the plan for providing that education, through soliciting parental feedback regarding the plan, and through stressing the positive advantages accruing to the student when teacher and parents work together.

Within the aura of frankness and support, teachers should do their best to be brief, plain, and businesslike. Whether in written communiques sent home or verbal messages delivered personally, short, concise messages are always preferable to long, wordy messages. They should always be written in plain English. Jargon and special terminology are familiar and comfortable to teachers, but indecipherable to parents. To be businesslike is to state the information in a brief and plain way, matter of factly, showing that the teacher's professional judgement has been brought to bear and this is the result. Brevity must be maintained. Teachers tend to be overly wordy. Parents do, too. They often need someone to talk to. Communication with parents cannot serve a therapeutic function—that takes too much time. It should serve nothing more than the basic function of exchanging information that bears directly on the education, progress, and well being of the student.

Content

The content of communication with parents, to the extent possible, must be confined to educational matters. Those matters fit into five categories: learning, discipline, self-concept, how parents can help, and class news.

Learning as content of communication directs attention to objectives, activities, and homework. Objectives are the specific goals toward which education is directed. Parents and students should be informed of those objectives. That way everyone knows exactly what is being aimed at. For parental information, the specific objectives may be grouped into larger goals, such as mastering the multiplication tables, learning the classification of animal and plant kingdoms, or being able to describe the interrelations of the legislative, executive, and judicial systems in American government.

Activities describe the means that will enable students to achieve the goals and objectives. They tell what should go on inside and outside of class. When described to parents, the activities should be summarized. One can say that the textbook will be used in combination with lectures, tests, and student reports. Or that twenty minutes of instruction will be provided each day, followed by twenty minutes of practice, requiring about fifteen minutes of homework three times a week. Or that group-project work will occur in class, culminating with a fair in which student work will be displayed for viewing by parents, visitors, other teachers, and students.

Homework should be described fairly explicitly: five problems each night, outline a part of the chapter, write five paragraphs, correct errors made in work done during class. It should also indicate what the parents can do to help. Examples might include providing a quiet place at a regular time, so that the student develops the habit of doing homework at a set time and place, free from distractions; reading a nursery rhyme to the child each evening; discussing with the child the day's learnings by having the child report verbally, explain what the information means, and discuss its importance and applications; providing needed instructional help in simpler processes of mathematics, phonics, outlining, finding the main idea, and so forth.

Discipline describes the methods of control that will be used. Communication should spell out rules, enforcement procedures, and necessary backing from home. The tone should be entirely positive. Parents should see clearly that discipline helps their child to make good choices, behave responsibly, and remain open to learning. They should see that good discipline promotes good learning.

Communication about discipline should solicit parental support. Parents should be asked to support the system in the following ways: (1) impress on their child the importance of proper behavior; (2) show their agreement with the discipline approach being used; (3) indicate that they will back up the teachers efforts at positive control; and (4) attempt to practice some of the same disciplinary techniques being used at school.

The fourth point requires understanding of the control system being used. If it is behavior modification, parents should be informed in simple terms that the procedure involves supplying rewards after the child behaves appropriately. If it is informed choice followed by natural consequences, parents should understand that rules must be laid down, together with consequences that will invariably follow student compliance or noncompliance. The consequences must be within reason, but they must be enforced. Parents learn that they no longer need to use threats or bullying, but they must have the fortitude to enforce the choices that their child makes. They need not feel guilty about it. The child, after being fully informed, has chosen the consequences that follow.

Self-concept is closely related to discipline. It grows out of behavior that produces learning, followed by attention given to the progress that the student has made. Disruptive behavior hinders learning. For students to progress in ways that bring success and recognition they must attend to the educational tasks at hand.

Students must have regular attention drawn to their successes. That attention comes from teacher, parents, and other students. Teachers and students can provide recognition in a systematic way within the classroom. Parents need information about their child's progress and about how to acknowledge it. Progress can be reported through notes, samples of work, graphs that show attainment of objectives, graphs that show improvement over past performance, and oral reports given by the student to parents every evening. Parents can respond with shows of pleasure, moderate praise, and moderate rewards. Praise should be limited to statements such as, "You should be really proud of yourself;" "this speaks awfully well for you;" "good going—it makes me feel good to see you trying so hard."

Rewards should be moderate, too. They should be given in the form of desired activities rather than in money or gifts. Those activities can be discussed in advance. Good progress can be rewarded by such activities as going to a motion picture, getting to stay up late on Friday or Saturday night, getting to go to the park or to lunch with Dad, or getting to spend the night with a friend. Praise and rewards of the types mentioned draw attention to accomplishment. They are directed at the student: *"You* should feel proud of yourself." *"You* get to go with Dad because you have done so well." They should not be directed at other people or things. They should not say *"I* am really proud of your work." "Here is five dollars. Keep it up and there will be another five next month." These things make other people and other things the focus of attention. For self-concept, the focus must be on the student who is achieving.

How parents can help is an indispensable ingredient in communication. Parents give increased support when they feel a part of things, when they feel they are contributing directly to the child's learning and behavior. We have already seen that parents can help through backing, support, donations, volunteering, providing simple instruction, and practicing some of the same control techniques that are used in school. But we have to realize that parents do not automatically know how they can help. Nor are they sure that help is wanted. Teachers have to solicit their help and they have to inform them how help can be provided. The solicitation must be genuine, and the information must be explicit. In discipline, for example, the teacher can say, "We have a plan that will help all the students learn more and behave better. These benefits will be seen at home as well as school. I must have your help in order to make the plan work, and I am sincerely asking you for that help." After describing the plan briefly and plainly, the communication indicates what the parents can do. "Together, we can help your child greatly. For your part, I hope you will support what I am doing at school by discussing it with your child. Ask your child regularly how class behavior has been. Please use as much of this plan as you can in disciplining your child. Try to set up two or three rules about home work, chores, and polite talk at home. Decide on positive consequences (mild rewards) that will come to the child for compliance with the rules. Decide on negative consequences (mild punishments such as missing a favorite television program or going to bed a half hour early) that will come if the child breaks the rules. Help your children see that they are *choosing* the consequences that follow, good or bad. Then be sure that the consequences are applied. Do not worry that this will harm the child or the relations between you. This plan builds responsibility and it helps children understand that learning and good behavior are important. Together we can help your child learn in a way that will make all of us proud."

When asking for other kinds of help the explanations, while explicit, need not be so lengthy. An example might be, "We have decided to have a class bake sale on Saturday, November 24 to help raise money for our trip to the zoo. We need cakes, cookies, pies, and brownies. May I count on you to contribute something for the sale? If so, please check the blanks below and have your child return the form to me. Thank you very much for your continued support."

Class news items serve a very valuable function. They keep parents apprised of what is going on in school and remind them that significant learning is occurring through interesting activities. These news items, best conveyed through a class newsletter, should report on activities associated with school curriculum. They should never be gossip items. They should describe specific activities in the class, name students who received best citizen and other awards, report on favorite class books, tell how many students got perfect spelling, math, or grammar papers, describe individual and class projects in science, social science, and creative writing, report on class productions in drama and music, report on special visitors to the class, and report interviews, opinion polls, and aspirations of various class members, being sure that each student is included once in a while.

These items have special interest for parents. They furnish topics for discussions with children about what is going on in school. They show that activities of academic importance are occurring in abundance. They keep parents' attention attuned to the important life that their child is leading in school. And they show that the teacher cares about students and parents.

Vehicles for Communication

Style and content of communication have to be transmitted in some coherent form. Some vehicle, some avenue, some technique must be employed to convey messages to the parents. Many such vehicles have been mentioned already. They will be repeated and elaborated, along with vehicles not previously mentioned, in the sections that follow.

Open house is a time when parents and other interested people in the community are invited to visit the school and the various classrooms. Most elementary and junior high schools have open houses. Many high schools have them, too. They are usually held in the fall of the year, after teachers have had a chance to get their programs established, but before the school year has progressed too far.

Open house gives teachers an opportunity to explain their programs directly to parents. Usually they outline what they are attempting to accomplish, the course of study, homework, grading procedures, typical activities, and discipline requirements.

Parents have the opportunity to see the facilities, ask questions of the teachers, and examine samples of work done by students. Often there is a general meeting, too, where the school principal gives an overview of school programs and policies. Open house provides one of the best vehicles for communicating with parents because parents and teachers can see each other in a friendly, nonthreatening atmosphere. The main difficulty with open house is that not all of the parents attend.

Newsletters get to all parents. They, too, can outline goals, programs, procedures, activities, and discipline methods. They can include many other things of interest to parents. They indicate that the teacher has a strong interest in the students, and that parents are seen as important parts of the educational process.

Newsletters for primary grades should be written by the teacher. Students can give input. Content should be limited to aspects of the educational program plus notes about field trips, parent conferences, performances, feast days, holidays, and special events.

The primary-grade newsletter should be limited to one page. It should be sent home at least once a month. Each issue should remind parents of how much their help is needed and appreciated. Upper-elementary and secondary newsletters can be larger. Students can do much of the work in writing and producing it. Production of the newsletter can be done as part of the language arts program. Illustrations can be added by students skilled in graphic arts.

The contents of the upper-grade newsletters should also revolve around the educational program. They should not be gossip columns. Activities, special events, and outstanding student work can be featured. Book, motion picture, television, and music critiques can be included. The teacher should write a teacher's column. This newsletter, too, should communicate directly to parents, showing interest in their involvement in school and appreciation for their contributions.

Teachers should send notes home to parents on a regular basis. Canter's model of assertive discipline calls on teachers to send notes home with two students every day. These notes inform the parents about something good that the student has done. The intention is that each student will be motivated to do something laudable. These notes should be quite personal. They should be handwritten. They may be written on duplicated forms which saves time, but the personal touch given by the teacher's own handwriting has strong effect.

Notes can be used to remind parents of performances, trips, special snacks, money for lunches and admissions, and so forth. They should always mention the teacher's appreciation for the parents' cooperation.

When students get into serious trouble at school, parents get a call from the teacher or principal. This makes calls from school an unnerving event for parents. Wise teachers work early to forestall the unpleasantness associated with telephone calls from school. Some elementary teachers try to call the home of each child early in the year. They set aside time to make five or six calls each evening. Within a week they make contact with the parents of most of the children. They speak in a friendly tone, saying they just wanted to call and let the parent know how pleased they are to have the opportunity to work with their child. They name the two or three things they intend to work hardest on, and they say that with "both of us working together, we can make this a very good learning year for Sally." They indicate that notes and other information will be sent home occasionally and end by thanking the parents for their attention.

Homework assignments serve better than anything else to inform parents of the objectives and activities stressed at school. Some of the homework is self-explanatory. The student has to read a chapter or complete a worksheet. Parents can easily tell what it is about. Other assignments are not so easily understood. Perhaps the student is to prepare an outline of a chapter, correct mistakes on work done at school, or do a summary and analysis of national news presented on television. Parents may not understand exactly what is expected, and will not know how to help.

When assignments are not quite clear, teachers can prepare brief notes that explain the assignment. The notes can be used by students and parents to keep the work on target. For instance, they can remind that outlining is done by finding the main idea in each paragraph, together with smaller ideas that support the main idea. The main ideas are numbered with Roman numerals. The smaller ideas are numbered with capital letters beneath the Roman numeral. These reminders help parents know what students are supposed to do, enabling them to help the student when necessary.

To remain informed of daily activities, parents should be encouraged to ask their child to tell briefly what happened in classes that day. Teachers should prime students with brief reviews, to help them know what to tell parents. These reports require little effort and they have large advantages. They help the student remain aware of learning and progress. They help parents understand and support the instructional activities at school. They provide an entry for better academic communication between parents and child.

Most elementary schools schedule conferences between the teacher and the parents of each child individually, usually during January or February. Some schools have them twice a year, once in the fall and again in the spring. Junior high and high schools seldom have regularly scheduled conferences. Those teachers have so many students it would not be feasible to conference with the parents of each. They call parents for conferences when difficulties arise with the student.

Conferences between teacher and parents can be very productive and enlightening. But they are delicate and require tact. Parents are on unfamiliar turf at school. They are nervous, apprehensive, wondering what is going to happen. It is the teacher's responsibility to put parents at ease, to set a positive, friendly, businesslike tone for the conference. Teachers are nervous, too, but they have to be poised and take the lead. Because these conferences are delicate yet so important in establishing positive relationships, teachers must put a good deal of thought and preparation into them. Here is advice provided by an elementary teacher who has been widely recognized for her ability to conference profitably with parents (*Courtesy of Ruth Charles*):

1. Responsibility for the success or failure of the conference rests with the teacher. Plan each conference well.
2. Greet the parent in a friendly, relaxed manner.
3. Don't sit behind a desk. Set side-by-side with the parent at a table. This helps establish a cooperative relationship.
4. Begin by chatting about the student as a worthwhile person. Mention good traits. This reassures the parent.
5. Guide the parent through the student's file, commenting on samples of work included there.
6. Encourage the parent to talk. Listen carefully. Be accepting. Do not argue or criticize. Parents cannot be objective about their own child. Arguing and criticizing cause resentment.

7. Keep in mind at all times that PARENTS ARE YOUR BEST AL-
   LIES. Let the parent know you feel this way. Show that you both
   want the best possible education for their child.
8. End the conference by describing your plans for the student's future progress. Earnestly request the parent's help in supporting
   your efforts. Thank the parent for talking with you about the
   child.
9. When preparing for conferences, keep these things in mind:
   a. Have a folder for each child, with the child's name written on
      it in an attractive, impressive manner.
   b. Include a profile of skills covered, skills mastered, and skills to
      be introduced later.
   c. Include samples of the student's work, with tests that back up
      your evaluation.
   d. Make notes that remind you of anecdotes that provide insight
      into the child's behavior and progress.
   e. Think of yourself in the parent's place. Always be tactful and
      polite.

Most schools have an organization of teachers and parents.
These organizations are active in some schools, but relatively inactive
in most. Schools that have good participation provide excellent opportunities to communicate goals, activities, efforts, and progress. They
offer a good place to present skits and other performances that show
what the students are learning. Such performances are fruitful for
drawing attention and providing a forum for students to show something of their accomplishments.

Some teachers are very active in having their classes put on performances and displays for the public. These activities draw favorable
attention to the teacher, the class, and the school.

Typical examples of these activities include musical productions,
plays, choric verse, readers theatre, science fairs, art exhibitions, and
athletic events. Parents eagerly turn out to see their child perform and
to see work displayed. The whole affair presents a most positive picture. Parents are enthusiastic; students are proud and excited. Teachers are shown as truly wanting to help students and give them a
chance to shine. This attitude rallies parents to strong support of
school and the teacher's entire program.

Building Classroom Discipline

Chapter 14

Flour and Spice: The Ingredients of Discipline

So far this book has been a tasting party for discipline. We have sampled the piéce de résistance of various great chefs, set tooth to a few traditional recipes, and nibbled occasional hors d'ouevres. Sampling teaches us a great deal about the taste of discipline. But it doesn't necessarily teach us how to concoct it for ourselves.

Making a personal system of discipline is the task that remains. That will be the topic of the final chapter, but first we need to prepare ourselves for that task. We can best do that by reviewing and coordinating the key ideas presented in the preceding chapters.

Behavior, Misbehavior, and Discipline

Human behavior is the totality of what humans do, and they are capable of an incredible variety of acts. What is called misbehavior consists of particular acts that someone does not approve of. The term has no precise limits. What is misbehavior for one person, group, or context might be entirely acceptable, even laudable, when done elsewhere.

Teachers, however, show general agreement as to what constitutes misbehavior in the classroom, pointing to such things as unruliness, disruption, disrespect, defiance, cruelty, sarcasm, lying, cheating, fighting, name calling, surliness, and refusal to work. Such misbehavior is the reason for classroom discipline. Misbehavior has negative effects on classroom atmosphere, student learning, and teacher effectiveness. Thus, teachers wish to do everything reasonably possible to forestall misbehavior and to correct it quickly and effectively when it does occur.

Discipline is teacher influence that does three things: (1) keeps students on task, (2) helps them establish responsible behavior, and (3) insists on their exhibiting good human relations. It is necessary in school learning for several reasons:

1. Society demands it.
2. It facilitates learning.
3. It enhances socialization.
4. It is necessary for democratic participation.
5. It fills a psychological need.
6. It brings a sense of joy to learning.

Discipline is not an easy task for teachers. It is fairly difficult to implement and maintain at an optimal level. The reasons for this difficulty lie in the facts of human nature, which include our drive to explore, our eagerness to imitate others, our continuing search for acceptance, our desire to protect our self-concept, and our natural resentment toward other people's telling us what to do. Fortunately, teachers know a good deal about students' traits, interests, and abilities, which are more or less consistent from community to community. This knowledge helps teachers control and channel student behavior. Teachers also have on their side the fact that parents and students alike want good discipline and consider it necessary for learning. They admire teachers who hold high standards and enforce them humanely, fairly, and consistently. Teachers should never be reluctant to discipline. It is the key to learning, sanity, and joy in the classroom.

Styles and Strategies of Discipline

The state of the art in discipline is reflected in the writings of various authorities who have gained wide respect for their practical suggestions for dealing with student misbehavior in humane, effective ways. Previous chapters described their ideas and suggestions in detail. Included were:

1. Redl and Wattenberg's system of setting limits, assisting students with difficulties, supporting their self-control, talking with them about misbehavior in straight forward ways, and following through consistently when misbehavior occurs.
2. Kounin's system for dealing with the class as a whole, where the teacher is ever attentive to class and individual behavior, deals with issues simultaneously, maintains a group focus, and manages lessons and transitions efficiently.
3. The Neo-Skinnerian method of using systematic reinforcement to motivate and shape desired behavior, through rewarding students who are behaving acceptably.

4. Ginott's suggestions for talking effectively with students, using sane messages that address the situation rather than the students' character, correcting through redirecting, showing genuine emotions of pleasure and anger, and avoiding the labeling of students.
5. Glasser's system for causing students to choose good behavior and its consequences, rather than bad behavior and its consequences, through forcing students to make value judgments about their classroom actions and consistently invoking the logical consequences of their behavior.
6. Dreikurs' suggestions for helping students find their genuine goal of acceptance, which brings good behavior, instead of turning to the mistaken goals of attention, power, revenge, and seclusion, which bring attendant misbehavior.
7. The Canters' suggestions and system for assertively taking charge, allowing no one to interfere with teaching or learning by using a systematic process of setting clear limits and following through with logical consequences, positive and negative, for the behavior that students choose.

Also given prominence were three factors that have powerful influence on student behavior:
1. Modeling, which depicts acceptable behavior through clear example, and which students imitate.
2. Success, which is motivating toward good behavior and builds strong self-concept.
3. Parents' roles in discipline, providing support and backing for the teacher in a joint effort to provide the best learning environments and establish habits of good personal relations.

Twenty Recurring Themes

The material presented in the chapters just reviewed reveals several recurring themes. These themes communicate the basis, the rationale, and the general procedures for good classroom discipline. Twenty such themes are clearly evident. They are listed here, with brief commentary.

Theme 1. Many students will misbehave, despite good teaching.

Students are very active. Some of their behavior is desirable in the classroom; some is not. Even the best preparation, the best activities, and the most interesting materials will not eliminate all student misbehavior.

Theme 2. All students can behave acceptably.

There is no excuse for bad behavior. All students, except for some with known brain dysfunction, can behave acceptably. Behavior is a matter of choice. Students choose to behave the way they do.

Theme 3. All students seek acceptance, belongingness, and success.

Most social behavior in the classroom is related to the student's desire to attain acceptance, to gain a feeling of belonging, and to enjoy a measure of success. Students tend to behave in socially acceptable ways when avenues to those three goals remain open. When the avenues are closed off they turn to unsuitable means for reaching their goals. Those unsuitable means compound the problem of discipline. For that reason, teachers should help students attain their prime goals in acceptable ways.

Theme 4. Discipline is necessary in the classroom.

Without discipline students cannot reach their goals. Too many destructive behaviors occur from other students and from the individual student himself. Students have a psychological need for limits, humanely and consistently enforced, which show that the teacher prizes the student, expects the best effort and behavior, and is willing to do whatever is necessary to help.

Theme 5. Success is a powerful motivator, with a snowballing effect.

When students grow in learning and behavior, and when they are recognized for that growth, they experience a feeling of genuine success. That feeling spurs them on toward greater growth. Their self-concept becomes strong and positive. When they encounter continued failure, the opposite results occur. They lose incentive, they feel incapable, and they develop a self-defeating attitude about themselves.

Theme 6. Discipline helps bring success.

Some students can achieve success in classrooms with poor discipline, but they are few in number. The majority cannot transcend or remove themselves from the destructiveness of poor classroom behavior. They cannot channel their own behavior in productive ways. Discipline guides behavior and suppresses destructiveness. That, in turn, allows students to make progress and gain recognition that produces success.

Theme 7. Discipline is not stifling; it is liberating.

Many teachers are hesitant to impose structured systems of discipline in the classroom for fear of stifling student initiative. This fear is groundless. Discipline liberates students by removing counterproductive behavior. It allows them to work toward their goals instead of being pushed hither and yon beneath a false banner of freedom. Great achievements are made rarely, if ever, without strong discipline. That discipline ultimately comes from within, but highly productive people usually point to a teacher who expected the best of them and would accept nothing less.

Theme 8. Good discipline is a combination of several factors.

Effective classroom discipline is not a single approach, a single way of talking with students, a single way of rewarding or punishing. It is a combination of factors. Teacher personalities are different. So are class personalities. Teachers must build their own systems of discipline out of factors that match their personalities and the traits and needs of their students.

Theme 9. The teacher is the most important figure in class discipline.

Wise teachers involve students and parents in the process of establishing rules of discipline. But it is the individual teacher that sets the tone, establishes the expectations, enforces those expectations, and never rests until all students begin to escape from self-destructive behavior.

Theme 10. Effective school discipline requires the collaboration of many different people.

The individual teacher is certainly the most powerful figure in classroom discipline. But even the most competent teacher requires the collaboration of others. Parents play essential roles in good discipline. So do school administrators and the entire instructional and support staff. Everyone should be involved and support each other.

Theme 11. Teacher persistence and genuine caring are essential.

You can't love all your students, but you can care genuinely about their behavior, for their sake as well as your own. Teachers who care never give up. They are never satisfied so long as a single student is behaving in ways that interfere with teaching and learning.

Theme 12. Teachers show persistence and caring in the way they communicate with students.

They do not attack students. They comment only on behavior. They call on students to make value judgments about their own behavior. They invoke consequences in calm, forceful, matter-of-fact ways.

Theme 13. Discipline depends on consistency and follow-up.

As nearly as possible, teachers must react the same way every time to student misbehavior. They must not appear exasperated or angry when invoking consequences, although it is fine to show anger at other times. They must always follow up on student behavior. Disruptive behavior cannot be ignored.

Theme 14. Seriousness, rules, and high expectations underlie effective systems of discipline.

Three things are essential in any program of discipline: seriousness about teaching and learning, a good set of rules, and the genuine expectation that students will abide by those rules.

Theme 15. Students choose to behave the way they do.

Behavior is a matter of choice. No one is forced against his will to behave in a certain way. Good behavior is a matter of making good choices. Bad behavior is making bad choices. Teachers have the obligation to help students choose behavior that leads to success and belonging.

Theme 16. Students who choose to break rules must endure the consequences that accompany the rules.

Consequences are not arbitrary punishments. They are results that students choose just as they choose their behavior. Teachers must explain in detail the consequences and their linkage to the rules. When students choose to break the rules teachers invoke the consequences. The entire process is depicted as students' choosing the consequences.

Theme 17. Misbehavior should be corrected through redirecting the student.

Correcting is directing, Ginott said. Students don't automatically know how to behave correctly. They need to be shown proper behavior, reminded of it, and reinforced when they do what is expected.

Theme 18. Behavior is shaped in desired directions by rewarding students when they behave acceptably.

Behavior is shaped by its consequences. Both rewards and punishments shape behavior, but rewards are the more effective under most circumstances. Students work harder to earn rewards than they do to escape punishment.

Theme 19. One of the best ways to teach good behavior is through example.

Students imitate teachers. If teachers are kind and respectful, students tend to be kind and respectful. Because imitation learning is so powerful, teachers should endeavor to provide the best possible examples.

Theme 20. Parents are teachers' best allies in discipline.

All parents want their children to behave acceptably in school. They will, if informed, support reasonable systems of discipline. They need only see that the system is just and that it serves the best interests of their child. Given that, they provide psychological support and follow up at home.

Twenty Major Strategies and Techniques

Embedded within the twenty major themes we have just examined are a number of specific strategies and techniques that teachers have found useful in controlling student behavior. Twenty of those strategies and techniques are clearly identifiable.

Strategy 1. Take charge in the classroom.

Every authority on discipline agrees: teachers must take charge firmly in their classes. They are boss. There should be no doubt about it. They can be pleasant, but they must be forceful. Student input is valued, but the teacher calls the shots.

Strategy 2. Make good rules for class conduct.

Rules should be short and clear, five or six in number. Students should be involved in establishing them. The rules should be stated positively, if possible, and posted in the room. They should be explained so that all students understand. Consequences for abiding by the rules and for breaking them should be explained. Rules should be reviewed periodically.

Strategy 3. Expect the best of students; say it and show it.

Rules are made and posted to inform students and remind them of expectations. Every student can abide by them and every student is expected to do so, voluntarily, because they are in students' best interests. Nothing but the best behavior will suffice.

Strategy 4. Enforce the rules consistently.

Rules are worthless if not enforced. Students understand them plainly and they understand the consequences plainly. When they choose to break the rules, they choose the consequences. Teachers should, without hesitation, invoke the consequences that are chosen.

Strategy 5. Allow no destructive behavior.

Never allow students to behave in ways that disrupt teaching or learning. Such behavior is destructive. Good discipline assists constructive behavior, permitting good instruction and promoting good learning.

Strategy 6. Manage groups and lessons efficiently.

Pace lessons so that boredom doesn't become a problem. Move from one lesson to another smoothly, without waste time. Boredom and rough transitions provide fertile grounds in which undesired behavior can grow.

Strategy 7. Teach students how to choose good behavior.

Show students that they can choose between good and bad behavior. Show them that good choices lead to success, to acceptance, to esteem. Help them to decide whether their choices are good or bad. Reinforce them when they make good choices.

Strategy 8. Use effective styles of talk with students.

Ginott stressed effective communication that addressed the situation rather than attacking the student. Glasser described how to confront misbehaving students in productive ways as did Canter and Dreikurs. Hostile talk and wishy-washy talk are both ineffective. Speak plainly and matter of factly. Be calm, but be forceful and insistent.

Strategy 9. Provide an abundance of genuine success.

Every student longs for success and recognition. Provide genuine success through progress and recognition. Reinforce students in ways most effective for the group and individual. Help students keep charts that show graphic evidence of progress. Call their progress to the attention of their parents.

Strategy 10. Reduce failure to the lowest possible level.

Failure and errors are not synonymous. One can make errors and still be successful. Failure results from lack of growth. Even with growth, lack of recognition can cause the feeling of failure. Failure should be kept to a minimum because it is self-perpetuating. When people see themselves as failures, they tend to behave as failures.

Strategy 11. Shape behavior through systematic reinforcement.

Implement a system of behavior modification. Be sure it is in keeping with the maturity level of the students. Systematic reinforcement motivates and shapes behavior for all types of students at all age levels. It is the single most effective technique for building the kind of behavior you want to see in your students.

Strategy 12. Confront misbehavior forcefully but positively.

Some misbehavior can be ignored, but when it becomes disruptive to teaching and learning it must be dealt with. Teachers must have the fortitude to confront students who are disruptive. Skills of confrontation were described by several authorities, including Ginott, Glasser, Canter, Dreikurs, and Redl and Wattenberg.

Strategy 13. Invoke the natural consequences of good and bad behavior.

When students comply with rules they should be rewarded. When they break rules they should be punished. In either case they are aware of the consequences beforehand. They choose to behave or misbehave; at the same time they are choosing rewards or punishments. This principle must be made absolutely clear to the students. The teacher, in turn, must apply it consistently and dispassionately.

Strategy 14. Do all you can to support good behavior.

Discipline tends to focus on misbehavior. That is the source of problems for teaching and learning. However, good behavior should continually be supported. That is the ounce of prevention. How to support good behavior was explained in the works of several authorities, including Skinner, Canter, and Redl and Wattenberg.

Strategy 15. Teach good behavior through good example.

Be the best model you can be for your students. Show concern, manners, courtesy. Be polite and helpful. Have students practice the behaviors modeled for them. Reinforce them when they repeat desired behaviors that you have modeled.

Strategy 16. Stress good manners and living by the golden rule.

Make it plain from the outset that you have high standards of student conduct. You expect students to use good manners. You expect them to live by the golden rule. Forbid them, right out, to use sarcasm or cruelty. Reward them when they comply. Invoke natural punitive consequences when they violate established limits.

Strategy 17. Establish a good support system for your program of discipline.

It is very difficult to go it alone. There will be times when students refuse to obey your directions. For those occasions you must be able to count on immediate, positive support from principal, parents, and other teachers. Means of establishing such a system were described in the Canter model.

Strategy 18. Set up a productive communication system with parents.

Parental support is very important. You can secure it if you inform parents of your program, activities, and expectations regarding student behavior. Rules, consequences, and enforcement procedures should be described to parents. Stress that your control system is necessary for maximum learning, and that it teaches students to relate to each other in positive ways.

Strategy 19. Communicate regularly and clearly with students.

By talking with students formally and informally you show that you are concerned about them, that you care about their learning and behavior. One way to maintain good communication is through the use of classroom meetings conducted in circles as suggested by Glasser. Students feel involved when kept informed about their learning, behavior, problems, and future. They support the teacher and class, causing fewer behavior problems.

Strategy 20. Be persistent; never give up.

Don't quit, don't excuse misbehavior, don't cave in before student hostility. Keep your poise. Keep trying. The essence of discipline is caring enough that you will let nothing interfere with teaching and learning. That is the best contribution you can make to the welfare of your students.

Chapter 15

20/20 Foresight: Building Total Discipline

You hear a lot about hindsight. It's perfect, people say, 20/20. The trouble with hindsight is it comes too late, after the horse is out of the barn. It is easy then to see that the gate should have been closed. You don't hear so much about foresight. People do mention it. "With a little foresight," they say, "such and such could have been avoided." A little foresight isn't sufficient for good discipline. That requires a great deal of foresight, thoughtful and accurate.

This chapter culminates our odyssey into discipline. Here is where words stop and action begins, where we use good foresight, where we begin to apply what we have learned. That foresight allows us to build before the fact a complete system of good discipline.

Facts of Life

Five facts of classroom life underlie all systems of good discipline. These facts are no will-o'-the-wisps. We can count on them, and we must deal with them.

Fact 1. Students are going to misbehave in school.

Students are not always angels. They will act up, misbehave, and disrupt. Some do it a little, others do it a lot. But even the best of 'em have their bad moments. That's why we need discipline.

Fact 2. All students can behave.

Every single student can behave acceptably in school. Students choose their behavior. Teachers need make no excuses for them. They can just as easily choose to behave well.

Fact 3. Students need discipline.

They need it to protect against self-destructive behavior. They need it to protect against disruptions from others. They may act as though they don't want it, even when they do. But they all need it.

Fact 4. Teachers can't teach well without discipline.

Research has shown that some teachers spend 80 percent of class time trying to control students. Even good classes can wipe out 30 percent of the teaching time. Without discipline teachers cannot fill their prime function, which is to teach.

Fact 5. Teachers can learn to discipline well.

Teachers used to say you either had it or you didn't. They meant that discipline was instinctive; you couldn't learn it. We know now that discipline is a skill, a procedure, and a set of techniques that all teachers can develop.

Rights in the Classroom

In the Canter model we examined rights of teachers and students. Teachers have a right to teach, and students have a right to learn. Effective teachers must recognize their teaching rights and insist that those rights be met. They form the infrastructure upon which discipline is built. Without that structure discipline is so much facade that falls away at the slightest tremor. The following six rights are essential in teaching:

Right 1. The Right to Teach.

Teachers exist to teach students. All their other duties, however necessary, are a distant second. They must have the right to teach, to organize and present material, to manage activities, to concentrate on making learning exciting and valuable. Nothing must interfere with that right.

Right 2. The Right to Meet Learning Needs.

Teachers must be allowed to aim instruction at specific needs of students. Of course they can't meet all needs, social, emotional, and physical. They can meet needs in academic learning, however, and self-concept, and good human relations. In those areas they must be allowed to direct their efforts toward maximum student growth.

Right 3. The Right to Be Free from Disruption.

If teachers are to teach toward specific student needs they must be permitted freedom from disruption. Students must not disrupt this teaching and learning process. Routine disruptions from lunch counts, visitors, special programs, and so forth, should be kept to a minimum.

Right 4. The Right to Discipline.

Teachers must realize that they have a right and a duty to discipline students. Discipline is necessary for the well-being of all. It must be applied firmly, consistently, and humanely.

Right 5. The Right to Have Support.

Teachers cannot go it alone in discipline. If they do not have the support of their principal they are lost. If they do not have the support of parents they are weakened. Teachers must have strong support they can count on.

Right 6. The Right to Do it Your Way.

Teachers are obliged to be humane. Inhumane treatment of students is immoral, unethical, and often illegal. Within the constraint of humaneness teachers have the right to use a system of discipline that best meets their teaching needs and the learning needs of students. They are responsible for planning a coherent system of discipline and communicating it to students, administrator, and parents.

These six rights are basic. They must be understood by teachers, administrators, students, and parents. They must be accepted and prized. They should be communicated and reiterated in class, in staff meetings, and in meetings with the public. When everyone understands that these rights are fundamental to the educational process the structure exists upon which to build a sound system of positive discipline.

Three Faces of Discipline

When we say discipline, we automatically think of correcting bad behavior. Misbehavior is the bane of teaching. Discipline is supposed to reduce it. We think first of the misbehavior, then of the teacher powerfully turning the misbehavior into energetic, productive scholarship and good manners. There is more to discipline than correcting bad behavior. Correction is the iceberg that is seen above the water. Its mass lies below the surface, unseen. Most of discipline goes unnoticed.

Discipline has three facets, all large and powerful. Correction is one of them. The other two are prevention and support. The following paragraphs explain these three facets.

Preventive discipline is the face that has to do with forestalling misbehavior, with preventing it from occurring in the first place.

Teachers have been told that good curriculum prevents discipline problems. Or that good management does the trick, or scowling, or getting your bluff in the first day. These tricks don't work too well. If they did we would have no behavior problems. Each, however, contains a nugget of truth. Good curriculum and good management are positive, productive steps. They will be emphasized later. Scowling and bluffing may work at first, but they turn students against teacher. Good prevention rallies students to you, not against you.

Supportive discipline consists of a number of gentle though very effective techniques that nip misbehavior in the bud. You see it just beginning. Effortlessly you turn the student back on track. You don't lose your temper, get nervous, or traumatize anyone. Feelings remain positive. Specific supportive techniques will be discussed in the section on total discipline.

Corrective discipline consists of the moves teachers make to suppress, correct, and rechannel misbehavior. It is what teachers do to get the horse back into the barn after the gate has been left open, or after the horse has kicked its way out. (The horse is usually as much to blame as the gate keeper.) We have noted many excellent techniques of corrective discipline in earlier chapters. Those techniques will be repeated in the section on total discipline.

You can see that classroom control involves much besides correcting mistakes. The adage about an ounce of prevention wouldn't have lasted if it weren't true. But we would be foolish if we pretended that prevention can be 100 percent effective.

Total Discipline

When we attend to all three faces of discipline we begin building total discipline. This term does not imply that we will be able to eliminate all discipline problems. It indicates that we are attending to all aspects of discipline, to its totality. That total approach provides a much more effective system for dealing with misbehavior than does any combination of bluffing, scowling, yelling, threatening, correcting, smiling, reinforcing, whimpering, or sweating. In total discipline you attend to the entire picture. You don't delude yourself into believing that you will eliminate all problems. But you know you are doing your best in utilizing what is known about controlling student behavior in the classroom.

In this section we will return to the three faces of discipline, preventive, supportive, and corrective. We will examine what teachers can do within each of the faces that will be of most value in building a system of discipline suited to the needs of teachers and students alike.

1. Preventive Discipline: Power-Packed Ounces

You can't prevent all behavior problems, but you can prevent many of them. The steps to take in prevention are not difficult and they have high payoff. Here we examine ten things teachers should do in preventive discipline. Six of them occur during preparation and four of them occur in performance.

Preparation. Before teaching ever starts there are six things teachers can do to prevent misbehavior. They have to do with the physical setting, the curriculum, the teacher's attitude, expectations and limits, support systems, and planning for the unexpected.

The *setting* refers to the physical aspects of the classroom. The classroom should provide physical comfort, advantageous seating, and efficient traffic patterns. Physical comfort depends on adequate ventilation, heat, lighting, and furniture. Ventilation is important to keep a supply of fresh air to students. Stuffiness produces lethargy and inattentiveness. Adequate heat, around 70°, is necessary for concentration. If students get too cold they get tense; they can't sit still or concentrate. Lighting should be such that work space is clearly illuminated. Light sources should be overhead or to the backs of students. Never seat students so they must look into direct light from windows. Eye distress produces nervousness, tension, anxiety, and frustration. Furniture should match the physical sizes of students and should encourage postures that reduce fatigue. Be sure that feet reach the floor and knees go comfortably under tables. If furniture makes students stretch, slump, or crouch, they will soon seek relief.

Don't seat students too closely together. Physical closeness is a hotbed for misbehavior. It encourages talk, laughter, and inattention. Students in pairs reinforce each other's misbehavior. Allow students to sit close together only after they have proven they can and will control themselves.

Traffic patterns should be efficient. They should not produce congestion. Movement about the room allows opportunity and encouragement for misbehavior. Routines for movement should be established and modified to support student self-control.

The *curriculum* has to do with objectives, activities, and materials for learning. If improper, it can produce student apathy, boredom, fatigue, and frustration, all of which erupt into misbehavior. Teachers should provide activities that are as interesting and enjoyable as possible. Those activities should allow students to make genuine progress toward objectives. They should provide challenge but still remain attainable. Novelty and variety should be added. When we hold student interest we remove many of the conditions that encourage misbehavior.

The *attitude* of the teacher should be established before teaching begins. Teachers must determine that they will be in charge, that they will be at the helm making the decisions. They do well to consult students and ask their opinions, but teachers have the final say. They must be in charge, no question about it.

Expectations and limits can be decided on before teaching begins. Every person needs to do a realistic self-appraisal. This establishes what can and cannot be accepted. It identifies thresholds of tolerance for noise, movement, and talk. It links expectations, in the form of rules, to good learning and good behavior. It remembers that teachers have needs and rights just as students do.

Out of these limits and expectations grows a specific set of rules. Teachers should decide in advance on five or six rules they want students to live by. Those rules are nonnegotiable. They must be explained to students clearly, in terms of real behavior. Reasons must be explained showing how rules contribute to learning and enjoyment. They can be written out on a chart, then used as a basis for discussion. The chart is posted in the room for periodic reference.

Connected to the set of rules is a system of positive and negative consequences. The positive consequences tell pleasant things that happen to students when they comply with the rules, and should be stressed first. The negative consequences describe undesirable things that happen to students who break the rules. These negative consequences must be humane, but they must be things that the students do not like or want.

It must be emphasized that students choose the consequences, good or bad, through their behavior. Good behavior means the student chooses good consequences. Bad behavior means the student chooses undesired consequences. The teacher doesn't reward or punish. Students reward or punish themselves by how they behave. The teacher simply administers what the students choose to have happen to them.

The teacher should also decide on the method to be used for enforcement of rules and invocation of consequences. Specific means of rewarding, confronting students, correcting misbehavior, and following through with consequences were discussed in several different models.

The *support systems* must be identified and established before the discipline program is put into effect. It is essential that the principal approve and support the program and be willing to follow through when the teacher needs help. It is highly desirable that parents understand and support the program, too. They have follow-through responsibilities when the student refuses to comply with demands of teacher and principal. It is desirable, as well, that at least one fellow teacher be brought into the plan. Two teachers working together can reinforce each other, and they can use each other's classrooms as isolation for students who misbehave in their rooms.

One final preparation must be made in preventive discipline. That is to prepare for *special and unexpected events*. You know such events will occur although you don't always know when or what they will be. Examples are visitors to the room, animals in the room, substitute teachers, injured students, fights, and emergencies such as fires, ill students, and sudden teacher illness. Decide in advance which of these things are likely to occur and how you want your students to deal with them. Prepare to discuss such events and to train students how to behave when they occur. Discussions should be held with students following the introduction to expectations, limits, and rules of behavior.

Performance. Many discipline problems can be prevented by what the teacher does routinely. The way of talking, sense of humor, ability to manage, charisma, attention to every student—all these things can forestall behavior problems. Four elements of performance merit attention: management of teaching, teacher on stage, the golden tongue, and acceptance for everyone.

Management of teaching refers to routines and the delivery of lessons. Routines are very important in management. They establish how students are to enter and leave the room, sharpen pencils, obtain materials, replace materials, ask to go to the restroom, and so forth.

The delivery of lessons should be done in ways that highlight suspense and interest, maintain flow, end at the right time, prevent flat spots, and provide smooth transitions. Materials associated with the lessons must be distributed and collected efficiently. Attending to these details eliminates the rough spots in lessons that allow misbehavior to occur.

Teacher on stage refers to the mannerisms and speech the teacher uses while directing lessons. Teachers cannot discount their roles as entertainers. They have unique power to attract and hold student attention. They should use gestures and voice control to further their entertainment value. From that basis they should concentrate on teaching through example using the techniques of modeling. Modeling is the best way to teach correct behavior, manners, courtesy, and living by the golden rule. Don't think of entertainment only as making students laugh and have a good time. Entertainment includes drama, mystery, and suspense. It includes excitement and helps students enter into a spirit of good learning. There is nothing wrong with cracking a joke now and then. Students appreciate it. But they don't need a stand-up comic for a teacher. They do better to have teachers skilled in dramatic techniques who can hold attention, instill a sense of mystery, and portray the best in human relations.

The golden tongue refers to language teachers use in talking with students, and to the way they speak sincerely and humanely. Much has been said about good communication. Authorities have stressed sane messages, congruent communication, and being a genuine person. You should decide how you want to speak with your students so as to remain genuine without using cutting tones, sarcasm, or attacking students' character. You may want to practice polite speech, saying thank you and please. You may want to practice a variety of comments that show mild praise, approval, and acceptance.

Acceptance for everyone is a technique that does much to prevent behavior problems. Various authorities stress that students' prime objective is to be accepted, to feel wanted, to feel that they belong in the class. One way to foster a sense of belonging is to give attention to every student every day. Canter says that elementary teachers should praise every single student every day, and that secondary teachers should praise each student as often as possible. Other authorities say to speak directly to every student individually sometime during the day. Some teachers set up systems where students acknowledge each other, through greetings, participation, and genuine compliments.

Teachers have the main responsibility for providing a sense of acceptance, but students have their responsibilities, too. These should be discussed with the students, who can give their input on how they want to be acknowledged and how they want to acknowledge each other.

2. Supportive Discipline: Power to the Superego

Teachers want to do what they can to prevent misbehavior. That is a priority item. But not all misbehavior can be prevented. Despite teachers' best efforts, there are times when students become restive, have difficulties, are seduced by attractive objects, fall under the spell of intriguing classmates, or for myriad untold reasons just feel like kicking up their heels.

At the first signs of incipient misbehavior, teachers should implement techniques of supportive discipline. This type of discipline simply helps students maintain self-control. The techniques are subtle. Unnoticed by others, they get students back on track.

Teachers can do many things to assist self-discipline. Some of those things are described in the following paragraphs, which give attention to supporting self-control, reinforcing good behavior, requesting behavior, making good choices, resolving conflicts, communicating and counseling, and providing success.

Supporting Self-Control. When teachers catch first glimpse of incipient misbehavior they can apply any of eight techniques that help the student get back on course without trouble. Following is a discussion of those techniques.

Signals can be sent in a private way to a student needing support. The teacher catches the student's eye, holds eye contact for a moment, frowns, shakes the head, or gives a hand signal.

If signals fail, the teacher can use proximity. This is simply moving closer to the student, showing awareness and willingness to help. Nearness is usually enough. Sometimes a light touch on head or shoulder helps.

Showing interest is an effective way to help students who are beginning to lose interest in their work. The teacher moves alongside, looks at the work, and comments favorably on it or on the student's efforts. Sometimes a light challenge helps, as when the teacher says, "You have gotten a lot of this done already. I bet you will get at least five more done before we have to stop. What do you think?"

Humor is an effective device when students begin to get restive. Students enjoy humor. It gives them a change from the routine and a brief respite from tension. A momentary break is all that is needed. You must be careful, though, that the humor doesn't excite joking and horseplay, which will put an end to the lesson at hand.

Hurdle help is assisting students who have come up against a problem that has them stumped. Most students stop work if they get stuck. They begin asking others for help, or they sit and do nothing. The teacher watches. When it is evident that a student is stuck they give a hint or correct an error that allows the student to move ahead.

Restructuring means changing an activity in midstream to add excitement or reduce difficulty. When students get bored or when the work is too hard for them they have a tendency to misbehave. A change in the activity can solve the problem. Changes in schedules are important, too, to add variety, provide reward, and accommodate instruction to special events.

Establishing routines reduces confusion. Students may be unsure about how to go to the reading area, get their laboratory equipment, or request special help. When confusion is evident, teachers can take a few moments to say "Here's how we do that," and proceed to demonstrate the routine.

Removing seductive objects assists student self-control. Toys, books, rubber bands, animals, notes—a great variety of such things appear regularly in the classroom. They intrigue students and draw attention away from the lesson. Teachers can remove the object without fuss and return it to its owner at the end of the period or day.

Reinforcing Good Behavior. One of the very best techniques for supportive discipline is providing ongoing reinforcement. This is done in an informal way with nods, smiles, and pats; and words such as thanks, good, and keep it up. This procedure shows students that the teacher is aware of them, their work, and their behavior. It shows that the teacher cares and appreciates. Often that is all it takes to keep students working hard.

Requesting Behavior. As students begin to drift away from the lesson teachers must draw them back. They may do this by demanding better behavior or by requesting it. For mild misbehavior requests are preferable because they produce no resentment or hostility. Teachers have three ways of requesting correct behavior: hints, I-messages, and questions.

Hints remind students of what they are supposed to be doing. Examples: "Remember, we are trying to finish early today." "All of you are supposed to be using your encyclopedias." "The award for best manners will be given at the end of this period."

I-messages inform students about the teacher's needs. "It is so noisy I can't talk with Jack." "I am feeling very nervous about the behavior I am seeing." "I'm afraid we are not getting as far as I hoped we would."

Questions are like hints, but they are put as interrogations. "Do you remember our two rules about talking?" "Are we getting our fifteen problems completed before lunch?" "Do you suppose I can count on your cleaning the work area quickly?" There is no intention that these questions be answered. They are simply reminders.

Making Good Choices. Much has been said in this book about behavior as student choice. Glasser, the Canters, and Dreikurs base their models on the premise that students choose to be good or bad. They also choose the consequences that naturally or logically accompany their behavior.

The Canters and Dreikurs say that all students can behave adequately. They choose to act in a good way or they choose to act in a bad way. At the same time they choose to receive positive consequences or negative consequences. Glasser puts greater emphasis yet on the matter of choice. He says that schools provide the best place in most students' lives for making the choices that bring success and belonging, effects that are necessary for adequate functioning in society. He advises teachers to force students to make value judgements about their choices. In so doing, they learn how to make better choices, choices that lead to success.

Teachers can help students make better choices by stressing behavior as choice, providing suitable alternatives to bad behavior, and having students make value judgements about their misbehavior.

Behavior as choice can be stressed continually. Students must see that they do, in truth, have the right to choose how they will behave. They must see at the same time that all behavior has its consequences, and that teachers will always invoke those consequences.

Alternatives to bad behavior must be clarified. This can be done in group discussions using anecdotes to describe student misbehavior and to show what they could have chosen to do differently. Suitable alternatives can be found for tattling, fighting, arguing, stealing, talking out, and speaking sarcastically and cruelly. Alternatives might include writing the messages out to hand to the teacher, writing out the arguments for teacher and class to consider, setting up a system for loaning books and materials rather than stealing them, and practicing statements that acknowledge and compliment.

Value judgments provide the avenue toward students' making responsible decisions on their own. Students can be caused to respond when they misbehave in the manner suggested by Glasser. They are asked to state what they are doing. They are then asked if their behavior is helping either themselves or the class. Finally, they are asked to name a behavior that would help themselves or the class. If unable to think of any, the teacher suggests two or more alternatives from which the student selects. The teacher insists that the student follow through on his commitment to the behavior he has chosen.

Resolving Conflicts. People disagree. They argue and they fight, especially during childhood and adolescence. Piaget says that arguing is good for kids. It builds their thought processes and their self-confidence. But conflict is not good for the classroom. It disrupts. It hinders teaching and learning. Conflicts can be resolved without producing disruptions. Hurt feelings can be avoided. Three techniques make this possible and they are described below.

Verbot is when the teacher says, "We don't do that. It is forbidden. Stop it now." If teachers see students move toward dispute, fight, or name-calling, they use the verbot. That stops the behavior at once. They do not discuss it. They do not call for value judgments. They say, "That's all," and they separate the disputants if necessary.

Write it out is a way of dealing with conflict that serves two purposes. First, it lets disputants cool off, since it takes a bit of time. As they write out their points of view the whole thing begins to look silly. They drop it. Second, it eliminates disruption.

If two students get into an argument or fight, the class grinds to an immediate halt. Everybody is caught in a turmoil of emotion. If the disputants are nabbed immediately and directed to write, nobody pays attention. Classwork goes on as usual.

The no-lose approach, popularized by Thomas Gordon, is used when disputants have strong differences even after a cooling-off period. With this approach each person names or writes two or three suggestions that would correct the situation. They consider their suggestions together, helped by the teacher or other intermediary. They look for a suggestion acceptable to both. When they agree on one, they implement it. If it works, fine. If it doesn't, they repeat the process. The result is that both parties are satisfied with the result.

There is no winner, no loser. Good feelings result, rather than hostility and hurt.

Communicating and Counseling. Communication and counseling
provide excellent assists to supportive discipline. They are furnished
in various ways, including the following: verbal reinforcement, active
listening, congruent communication, language of acceptance, positive
problem-solving, making value judgments, and telling it like it is.

Verbal reinforcement consists of words and tone of voice that students find rewarding. It includes words and expressions such as
good, wow, fine, thanks, good going, and keep up the fine work.
Verbal reinforcement becomes more powerful when it describes exactly what is being rewarded: "Thank you, Jimmy, for raising your hand
before speaking." "I surely appreciate the way everyone came into the
room and got to work immediately." "Since you all completed your
work without interruptions, there will be no homework tonight."

Active listening is a way of helping students express themselves,
without value responses to what they say. The teacher (active listener)
nods, says "Uh huh," "Go on," "I think I understand what you
mean." The teacher reflects back feelings and opinions expressed by
the student: "I can see that you are upset." "You feel that you haven't
been given a fair chance." This technique is used during group discussions or individual conferences. It is not used for dealing quickly
with misbehavior during class time because it requires too much time
and it interferes with the work of other students.

Congruent communication is a process of matching teacher talk
with the demands of the situation. It includes using sane messages,
in which the teacher addresses the situation rather than the character
of the student. It involves laconic language, short and succinct, when
student misbehavior must be suppressed immediately. It instructs
students on how to behave correctly. It is to the point and can be
used during class time.

Positive problem-solving is used during group discussions. It is
especially effective as a part of classroom meetings. A problem is
identified. Students contribute comments, always positive, for helping solve the problem. No blaming and backbiting are allowed. The
teacher contributes little, but does help direct the discussion. Positive
steps are taken to solve the problem.

Making value judgments causes students to decide whether their
behaviors are worthwhile or not. The intent is to cause the students to
make better choices that lead to success. Glasser advocates this technique for confronting student misbehavior during class time. Most
teachers find it too time consuming and too disruptive. They prefer
using it during discussions or private conferences.

Telling it like it is has a place in communication, but it should be
used infrequently. It consists of the teacher stating the reality of the

situation, in no uncertain terms. Distasteful and hurtful language are not used. Example: "We have something here that is forbidden in this room. Cruel language was used. James, I will not tolerate cruelty. Never, ever, do that again."

Providing Success. Time and again these pages have mentioned the value of success. It motivates, it builds self-concept, and it removes many of the causes of misbehavior. For those reasons it is a powerful factor in supportive discipline. Success does not correct misbehavior, but is does support good behavior. The student hopes for continued success and recognition from others. Self-assurance grows. The student realizes that good behavior has worthwhile payoffs.

3. Corrective Discipline: Pounds of Cure

We do our best to prevent misbehavior by organizing teaching well and establishing a tone of seriousness. We do our best to support self-control through attention, communication, and success. You wonder that misbehavior could ever get through those filters. In fact it does have a hard time if prevention and support receive close attention. Still it does occur. Students violate established rules. They choose bad behavior. When they do so, they must be corrected.

Corrective discipline is what most teachers, students, and parents think of when they hear the word discipline. It is the kid acting up and the teacher jumping on him. The teacher has a frightful look on her face. Blue blazes leap from her tongue. She brandishes a willow rod. Students quiver in puddles of sweat.

Corrective discipline falls well short of that fearful stereotype. In a relatively inconspicuous way it stops misbehavior, redirects it, and reteaches correct behavior. It is done through squelching grossly inappropriate behavior, confronting students who misbehave, redirecting their behavior, invoking natural or logical consequences, following through consistently, and assertively insisting that teaching and learning rights be met.

Squelching misbehavior must be done if the behavior is a gross violation of rules such as fighting, cruelty, and cursing. The teacher stops it immediately, either through emphatic verbot or through banishing the offenders to the principal's office. Misbehavior can be stifled more gently when it does not fall into the emergency category. A good example is the Canters' suggestion of putting students' names on the board as a warning. Later checks call for punishment.

Confronting students who misbehave received much attention in the models proposed by Glasser, Dreikurs, and Redl and Wattenberg. Students must be called to task. Confrontation during class time, however, leaves much to be desired. It disrupts and stops the normal teaching and learning process. It may pit teacher against student in a power struggle in which one or the other is bound to lose. It is hurtful for students to lose. It is disastrous for teachers to lose. Confrontation is best done in two steps: First, deal with misbehavior in a way similar to that suggested by Canter. Later, talk with the student in private to establish judgments and positive courses of future action.

Redirecting student behavior is a primary aim of corrective discipline. We want bad behavior changed to good behavior. Ginott tells us to correct students by directing them, by telling them how to do it right. Redl and Wattenberg suggest appraising reality with the students as a way of getting back on path. Canter and Glasser get at redirection through invoking consequences and insisting that students choose behavior that leads to success. Redirection is one point on which all experts in discipline agree. The purpose of discipline is first to stop the disruption and second to teach students how to behave correctly.

Invoking natural consequences lie at the heart of both the Glasser and Canter models. Consequences are linked to rules. Everyone knows in advance what they are. When students choose to misbehave, teachers invoke the consequences immediately. The understanding is that teachers do not punish. Students choose consequences through their behavior.

Consistent follow-through is absolutely essential in any system of discipline. Students must know that rule violations bring negative consequences, every time. No getting out of it. Teachers who don't follow through invite more serious misbehavior, and they will surely get it. Follow-through applies also to plans for positive behavior that teachers and students develop jointly. The teacher monitors student adherence to agreements, providing reinforcement or additional negative consequences when necessary.

Assertive insistence on teaching and learning rights is the great contribution made in the Canter model. Teachers have a right to teach. Students have a right to learn. No one has a right to interfere through disruption. Teachers have a right to apply firm, humane discipline. They have a right to support from administrators and parents. They must insist that students abide by the consequences of their behavior. They must not back down.

The Models and Total Discipline

Total discipline is an approach to classroom control that puts equal emphasis on preventive control, supportive control, and corrective control. It allows teachers to select and build their own systems of discipline so they match needs of students and teacher alike. It allows teachers to use the right amount of control while avoiding overkill.

The following diagrams show the contributions to total discipline from the seven models of discipline and the chapters that support them.

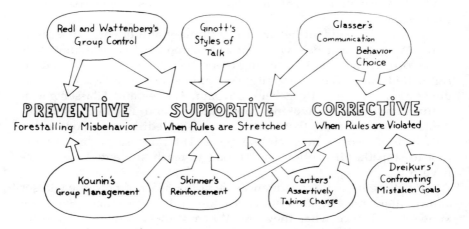

Figure 15.1. Faces of Discipline and Most Effective Model Applications.

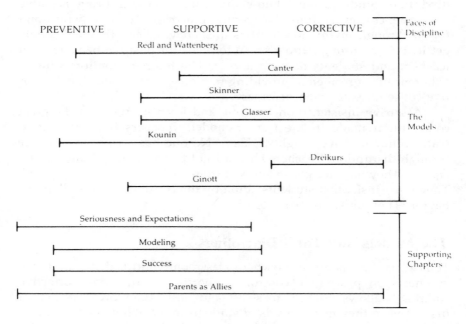

Figure 15.2. Influence and Overlap.

Total Discipline Your Way: Twenty Steps

Total discipline provides a balanced approach to classroom control. It attends equally to preventive, supportive, and corrective measures. It allows teachers to select just the right amount and style of discipline to meet learning and teaching needs in accord with ages of students and personalities of the class and teacher.

The following twenty steps show how to construct your own system of total discipline.

1. Determine that you will have discipline, and have it your way.
2. Set your limits. Think about what you will and will not allow students to do regarding talk, movement, noise, self-control, getting to work, finishing work, good manners, and so forth.
3. Write our your rules. State them positively. Keep the list to no more than five or six. Put them on a chart that can be displayed in the room.
4. Establish your support system. Explain your rules and system to the principal and as soon as possible to parents. Indicate that you need their approval and must have their support. Enlist the support of a fellow teacher, if possible.
5. Arrange your classroom environment to enhance discipline. Be sure students are comfortable, not distracted by the surroundings, and not seated too closely together.
6. Discuss rules and consequences with students on the very first day. Be sure they understand what the rules mean, in terms of overt behaviors, and what the consequences will be for both compliance and noncompliance.
7. Assert your rights to teach, to discipline, and to ensure student learning. Make sure students understand that you will let nothing interfere with your right to teach and their right to learn.
8. Work to enliven and smooth out your curriculum. Try to provide work that is worthwhile and interesting. Establish routines and procedures that contribute to efficient flow while eliminating dead spots and confusion.
9. Be the best example possible for your students. Always act in the very ways you want them to act. Speak in the ways you want them to speak. Think what those are. Practice them. Make a checklist and keep it in the room as a reminder.
10. Interact with your students on a personal level. Talk with them. Help with individual difficulties. Conference with them individually while the class is at work. Show personal attention to every single student as often as possible.
11. Help students choose good behavior. Be sure they understand that good behavior comes from making good choices. When they choose good behavior they choose pleasant consequences. Help

them identify alternatives to bad choice, bad behavior, and bad consequences.

12. Confront misbehavior. Do not let rule violations go unnoticed or unenforced. Try to confront misbehavior in a way that does not disrupt teaching and learning, but do not ignore it, excuse it, or accept it.

13. Follow through consistently. Always apply positive consequences. Always invoke negative consequences. Every time. Without fail. Show students that you never give up in trying to help them.

14. Reinforce good behavior. Set up a system so you will be sure to reward students for behaving acceptably. Positive reinforcement is the most powerful technique at your disposal for establishing good behavior.

15. Use sane messages when talking with students about misbehavior. Talk about a situation and about how to correct it. Do not tell students they are awful, inconsiderate, beastly, or moronic.

16. Develop a system for conflict resolution. Do not allow student fights or arguments to disrupt class. Do, however, help students resolve their conflict, if it is serious. Have them write out their complaints or use the no-lose approach.

17. Communicate regularly with students and parents. Use classroom meetings to talk with students about education, school problems, upcoming activities, and so forth. Use newsletters, notes, phone calls, and guided homework to keep parents informed and secure their support.

18. Provide acceptance and success for all students. Acknowledge every student every day. Ensure academic progress. Graph that progress. Be sure others recognize it, together with other contributions any student makes. Be sure parents know about it.

19. Stick by the principle of "least necessary discipline." This means avoiding overkill, using only the amount of discipline necessary to protect teaching and learning rights. For some classes the amount and type of discipline will be light. For others it will be heavy. Do not use too little, or too much.

20. Never give up. Never give up. Never give up.

Index